Women's Social Activism in the New Ukraine

T0341770

New Anthropologies of Europe
Daphne Berdahl, Matti Bunzl, and Michael Herzfeld, founding editors

SARAH D. PHILLIPS

Women's Social Activism in the New Ukraine

Development and the Politics of Differentiation

INDIANA UNIVERSITY PRESS
Bloomington and Indianapolis

This book is a publication of

Indiana University Press
601 North Morton Street
Bloomington, IN 47404-3797 USA

http://iupress.indiana.edu

Telephone orders   800-842-6796
Fax orders   812-855-7931
Orders by e-mail   iuporder@indiana.edu

The paper used in this publication meets the minimum requirements of American National Standard for Information Sciences—Permanence of Paper for Printed Library Materials, ANSI Z39.48-1984.

Manufactured in the United States of America

Library of Congress Cataloging-in-Publication Data

Phillips, Sarah D.
   Women's social activism in the new Ukraine : development and the politics of differentiation / Sarah D. Phillips.
       p.   cm. — (New anthropologies of Europe)
   Includes bibliographical references and index.
   ISBN 978-0-253-35164-7 (cloth : alk. paper) — ISBN 978-0-253-21992-3 (pbk. : alk. paper) 1. Women social reformers—Ukraine. 2. Non-governmental organizations—Ukraine. 3. Ukraine—Social conditions—1991–
I. Title.
   HQ1236.5.U38P45 2008
   303.48'409477—dc22

                                                                                    2007047359

1 2 3 4 5   13 12 11 10 09 08

In loving memory of my mother, June H. Phillips,

my grandmother, Erah Howell, and my friend, Faina Neiman.

"She hath done what she could."

Contents

Preface

Kyiv, Ukraine. January 1999. Svetlana and Vira, the director and assistant director of the charitable fund "Our House," which provides assistance to large families (those with three or more children), are working late. They have been in the cramped, one-room office all day, handing out food baskets to the seventy member families. It is freezing outside and not much warmer in the office, where the walls, zigzagged with ominous cracks, barely seem to support the sagging, leaky roof. We all have our coats on; Svetlana wears a denim jacket with an American flag stitched on the back, humanitarian aid from the United States. The office smells of instant coffee, cigarette smoke, and mothballs, the latter emanating from cardboard boxes of donated clothing from France and Germany that crowd the office, stacked up to the ceiling. Svetlana and Vira keep checking their watches—they both have three children to get home to. It is mostly mothers who have stopped by to pick up the "rations"—cooking oil, cereals, spaghetti, and condensed milk donated by a local businessman. They sign their names in a notebook, and Vira hands each of them two plastic bags full of food. Most pause to chat with Svetlana, Vira, and other mothers before venturing back out into the cold. One woman asks Svetlana about subsidies for housing payment—to what discounts are large families entitled? Which families qualify, those with five children, or do families with three children "count," too? Another relates how glad she is that she bought her son's school uniform a size too big last fall—he has almost grown out of it already.

Finally, all the bags are claimed and it is time to close up. Svetlana, exhausted, sinks into a rickety wooden chair, lights an unfiltered cigarette, and offers me more coffee. She lets out a deep sigh and rubs her temples. Having composed herself she looks at me with tired eyes and asks, "Do decent, hard-working people live like this in your country, too?"

Though I did not know it at the time, thus began my first interview for this project, an ethnographic investigation into the lives of women leaders of nongovernmental organizations (NGOs). By January 1999 I had already spent a year in Kyiv, the capital city of Ukraine, carrying out research on Ukrainians' utilization of alternative medicine after Chernobyl. As I elicited narratives from people about Chernobyl, illness, and the body, it became clear that the suffering caused by Chernobyl had been compounded by other sources of suffering during the twelve years since the nuclear accident in 1986. Although narratives on Chernobyl, its causes, and consequences abounded in my informants' unsolicited speech, they also spun out narratives of unemployment, marginalization, and abandonment by the state, usually with little or no prompting from me. Through these litanies, people linked health issues with social issues and

Figure 1. A young member of Our House association for large families picks up a food basket, 1999. Photo by author.

underscored their belief that the end of state socialism was accompanied by devastating losses in social welfare and safety. I met many people like Svetlana, a single mother of three, all struggling to survive the market "transition" that had left them vulnerable—economically, socially, and psychologically. The withdrawal of state subsidies for large families, changing state regulations governing "large family" status, growing unemployment, and the implementation of fees for medical care and education had led to the impoverishment of many large families in Ukraine. Other groups were similarly affected, especially the chronically ill and disabled, the elderly, and single-parent families. As I continued my research, interviewing practitioners and patients of nontraditional healing methods and trying to elicit Chernobyl narratives, I became increasingly aware that my project was not addressing the intense social suffering I encountered every day, suffering manifested not only in embodied illness but in quotidian practice and widespread disillusionment. As a privileged researcher from the United States, I found it ever more difficult to ignore the pervasive social and bodily suffering that I knew surrounded me.

During a brief respite from research during the fall of 1998, I returned to the United States and established a charitable foundation called the June Phillips Memorial Mission to Ukraine (JPMMU) in honor of my mother, who died of cancer in 1991. The foundation is affiliated with a small church in North Carolina and relies on private donations; I serve as the director of the foundation on a non-salaried basis, and the assistant director, Olha, lives in Kyiv. The focus of the JPMMU has evolved over the years, but we have retained our initial emphasis on two areas: the foundation assists individuals in health crisis such as the critically ill and the chronically disabled, and often works for marginalized categories of citizens through mutual aid associations such as Our House. Individualized projects allow the foundation to work closely with persons with acute needs; involving mutual aid associations and similar institutions enables us to reach large numbers of disadvantaged persons simultaneously and channel support through existing infrastructures. Examples of typical activities include paying for hospital and surgical bills; donating medical equipment (wheelchairs, mattresses) and medicines; offering food, school supplies, and clothing to needy families; and providing technical assistance such as computers to individuals and charitable groups.

It was under the auspices of the JPMMU that I first found myself in the office of Our House talking to Svetlana and Vira when I returned to Kyiv for an additional year of fieldwork in 1999. A friend had recommended their organization as a potential addressee of donations from the JPMMU. Our foundation did assist Our House until the group scaled back operations in 2001; members received food baskets, school supplies, and other necessities several times a year. That frigid night in January would be the first of many evenings and afternoons spent with these two activists, who shared my interests in social justice struggles and learning about the lives of women in different parts of the world. Their commitment to social change and their insights into the effects of socialist collapse on the lives of everyday people inspired me to pursue research on women NGO leaders in post-Soviet Ukraine. They captivated me with their stories of life in the Soviet Union, and related their tales of personal hardships and triumphs with amazing humor. Thankfully, they also forgave my nosiness and constant need to tape record their narratives. These two women opened my eyes to the processes of post-Soviet "differentiation" described in this book, and set me on the road to a project far more meaningful and timely than the one I had originally conceived.

Even though I had no plans to conduct an ethnographic study of mutual aid associations and other civic organizations when I founded the JPMMU in 1998, my foundation work and research were inevitably related and often intertwined. I therefore have been confronted with difficult ethical questions about my motivations for assisting NGO activists, on the one hand, and studying them, on the other. In many respects, the dilemmas I have faced in the field are no different from those experienced by most anthropologists: power differentials between the anthropologist and those studied, the fieldworker's multiple roles, and relationships requiring give and take (Silverman 2000:197).[1] Ironically, for me the JPMMU turned out to be a solution to some of these problems yet also a source of new fieldwork quandaries.

My work with the JPMMU meant, in many ways, that I had much in common with the women I began to study: we were all interested in the revival of communities and social change, and we had experienced profound life changes in getting to the places where we were interacting with one another. These parallel experiences often shifted our relationship of scholar and the observed to one of friendship, although our friendships required constant negotiation as I never left behind my role as scholar for long.[2] In the field I sought to heed Lila Abu-Lughod's (1991) calls for a tactical humanism by encountering people in human and not just cross-cultural terms (Silverman 2000:198). The desire to help the activists I had gotten to know had multiple roots: they were my friends but also my informants who sacrificed their time and energy to assist me with my research. When negotiating my multiple identities as researcher, sponsor, and friend, a question continually arose: "How involved is *too* involved?"

I approached this quandary case by case, constantly second-guessing my decisions about whether and when to offer organizations and individual women in my study assistance through the JPMMU. There were always compelling arguments both for and against such interventions, and the boundaries between scholarship, service, and friendship were always murky. If I carried out research and humanitarian assistance simultaneously, was I using my position as a potential source of sponsorship as leverage to extract information and time from informants? On the other hand, was it ethical to study the ins and outs of resource-deprived NGOs yet withhold assistance I was well placed to offer? Was it morally right to extract painful narratives of poverty and neglect by the state and do nothing, even when resources to help were at my disposal?

All anthropologists are likely to face these dilemmas during the fieldwork endeavor. If we take seriously the maxim (as stated in the American Anthropological Association's Code of Ethics) that anthropologists "should recognize their debt to the societies in which they work and their obligation to reciprocate with people studied in appropriate ways," we are compelled to work out how fair return is to be defined in our specific case, and what constitutes culturally and ethically appropriate forms of reciprocation. Anthropological advocacy can take many forms, such as using one's research to further the cause of oppressed populations, dispelling erroneous stereotypes about people suffering from stigmatized diseases, uncovering social injustice and structural violence, and engaging in community-centered praxis.[3] I suspect that more anthropologists than we might realize have established or worked with foundations and advocacy groups in the communities they study.[4] For me, responsible anthropology has come to mean using the resources at my disposal to assist my informants, friends, and their organizations in the ways they ask me to (if they ask at all, and many do not). Sometimes this has meant direct assistance from the JPMMU, but, more often than not, I have shared resources unrelated to the foundation (information, networking, letters of support, assistance with

English-language translations, documenting NGO events with video and photographs, and others). These are engagements I have tried to extend beyond the period of intense fieldwork during 1999, and I am still in touch with most of the groups described in this study.

I have no illusions about the privileged position I occupy in the research encounter, but there are moments when our roles as activists have put women such as Svetlana, Vira, and me on common ground, and their long-term involvement in the NGO sphere makes them the experts and me the initiate. Indeed, many of these activists have been constant sources of advice, contacts, and support as I carry out my own advocacy work with the JPMMU. I have also found that the challenges of negotiating my roles as researcher, donor, and friend have made me a better anthropologist, and for this I have Svetlana, Vira, and the nine other activists I worked with in Kyiv to thank. The blunders I have made in negotiating relationships with these women have revealed my weaknesses and exposed me as a well-intentioned person with many faults and insecurities. These activists seem to appreciate my earnest clumsiness in relationships, and the snafus we have muddled through together have engendered a real trust between us. The result, I believe, has been a richness of my ethnography that I cannot imagine would have been possible otherwise. Each anthropologist must weigh the benefits and risks of acting on the maxim that no anthropologist can dodge involvement, always with the goal of a responsible and meaningful anthropology.

Acknowledgments

This book was made possible only through the support and assistance of many people and institutions. For their role in this project I am grateful first and foremost to those individuals in Ukraine who participated in my research, especially the eleven social activists whose stories shape this book. I wish I could name them one by one and shout their praises from the rooftops, but to protect their privacy I must refrain from doing so. I hope I have represented these women's lives well and that they will recognize themselves in the stories I tell. In Ukraine I have also benefited from the friendship and support of many colleagues and friends, especially Yury Sayenko in Kyiv and Olga Filippova in Kharkiv. Through the years they both have opened countless doors for me, and I have cherished our friendship and collaboration. Olha Alekseeva, Olga Filippova, Sasha Savytskyy, and Natalka Yasko cheerfully helped me gather information on Ukrainian legislation for this project, and they all displayed great patience at my often odd research questions. I also appreciate the excellent transcribing assistance of Olha Alekseeva, Maya Garbolinskaya, and Liz Moussinova.

I am indebted to William F. Kelleher Jr., for his engagement with this project, his many contributions to my intellectual growth, and the fine example he sets for an ethical anthropology committed to social change. I cannot begin to thank Catherine Wanner adequately for all the support she has offered me and my research in ways great and small. I thank all my colleagues in the Department of Anthropology at Indiana University for their ongoing support of my work, and especially Anya Royce for her unwavering friendship and stellar advice in matters ranging from research to teaching to gardening. I am also grateful to all the mentors, colleagues, and students who read various versions of the manuscript in its entirety and offered me invaluable feedback: Nancy Abelmann, Maryna Bazylevych, Heidi Bludau, Matti Bunzl, Wu Jung Cho, Joe Crescente, Clark Cunningham, Olga Filippova, Alma Gottlieb, William F. Kelleher Jr., Karen Kowal, Jacek Luminski, Anna Muller, Abby Pickens, Marian Rubchak, Brooke Swafford, Anna Urasova, and Catherine Wanner. Special thanks go to Marian Rubchak for her multiple readings of the manuscript. I also benefited from the insights of colleagues who read parts of the manuscript in various forms: Gina Bessa, Julie Fairbanks, Sandra Hamid, Pat Howard, Soo-Jung Lee, William Leggett, Amy Ninetto, Andrew Orta, David Ransel, Anya Royce, Jesook Song, Maria Tapias, and Elizabeth Vann. Special thanks are due to Rebecca Tolen, my editor at Indiana University Press, for her support of my work and her expert guidance, and to Rita Bernhard for her marvelous copy editing. Thank you also to Daphne Berdahl, Matti Bunzl, and Michael Herzfeld for their support of the book. I am also grateful to Bruno Rachkovski, Yury Sayenko, Paul Thacker, and the late Nikolai Zhdanov for allowing me to reproduce their beautiful photos, and to John Hollingsworth for his map of Ukraine.

My research in Ukraine was funded through a Fulbright-Hays Doctoral Dissertation Research Abroad (DDRA) grant from the U.S. Department of Education and an Individual Advanced Research Opportunities (IARO) grant from the International Research and Exchanges Board, with funds provided by the National Endowment for the Humanities, the U.S. Department of State, and the U.S. Information Agency. During various stages of writing I have received generous support through a Dissertation Grant in Women's Studies from the Woodrow Wilson National Fellowship Foundation and an American Fellowship from the American Association of University Women (AAUW), as well as a summer stipend from the Office of the Vice President for Research at Indiana University. None of these organizations is responsible for the views expressed, and all errors are my own.

Last but never least, my husband, Sasha Savytskyy, has contributed to my research and writing in many ways, and I am grateful for his patience, understanding, and steady support. Final thanks are due to our sons, Roman and Micah, who help us keep it all in perspective.

Portions of this book have appeared elsewhere in different forms:

Parts of chapters 1 and 2 appeared in "Civil Society and Healing: Theorizing Women's Social Activism in Post-Soviet Ukraine," *Ethnos* 70 (2005): 489–514.

Parts of chapter 2 also appeared in "Will the Market Set Them Free? Women, NGOs, and Social Enterprise in Ukraine," *Human Organization* 64 (2005): 251–264.

Parts of chapter 4 appeared in "Women and Development in Postsocialism: Theory and Power East and West," *Southern Anthropologist* 30 (2004): 19–37.

Note on Transliteration and Translation

Throughout this book I use the Library of Congress system of transliteration for Ukrainian and Russian. However, for purposes of simplification, I transcribe the Ukrainian letter "ï" as "yi" (an exception to this is the use of *Ukraina* in the text, not *Ukrayina*) and the Russian letter "ë" as "yo." When a Russian word or phrase is given, I indicate this by the abbreviation "Rus." If no indication is given, the transliterated word or phrase is Ukrainian. When both Ukrainian and Russian variants are given, they are distinguished by the abbreviations "Ukr." and "Rus."

Most words and names commonly used in English appear in their most familiar variants, usually transliterations from the Russian. I use Chernobyl, for example, rather than the Ukrainian *Chornobyl'*; glasnost rather than the Ukrainian *hlasnist'*; and perestroika rather than the Ukrainian *perebudova.* Other place names, however, are transliterated from the Ukrainian instead of the Russian: Kyiv (not Kiev); Kharkiv (not Kharkov); L'viv (not L'vov), and so on. Exceptions are made when presenting quotes and narratives from activists who referred to place names in Russian. In the text and bibliography I refer to published Ukrainian and Russian authors according to how they write their names in English.

I have assigned most key informants pseudonyms and spellings that correspond to their ethnic self-identification. For example, I use Svetlana for a woman who identifies as Russian, rather than the Ukrainian variant of this name, Svitlana. Alternatively, I use Vira for an informant who identifies as ethnically Ukrainian (but speaks Russian), instead of the Russian variant, Vera.

Direct quotes and words or phrases used by informants during interviews and casual speech are transliterated and translated according to the language used by the informant. All translations are my own, except where otherwise noted.

Note on the Purchasing Power of the Ukrainian Hryvnia (UAH)

In January 1999, when I began the research described in this book, one U.S. dollar was equivalent to 3.43 UAH. In July 1999 the official exchange rate was $1 = 3.95 UAH, and in August it was $1 = 4.27 UAH. By the end of my fieldwork in December 1999, one dollar bought 5.02 UAH. During 2005–2007 the exchange rate was also around $1 = 5 UAH. The official government minimum wage in 1999 was 73.70 UAH per month.

For a sense of how much buying power the UAH carried in Ukraine during my fieldwork, see Table 1, which contains a list of the approximate costs of some basic food and non-food items in Kyiv during 1999 and 2007. The prices of these items fluctuated according to their quality and place of purchase within Kyiv. These prices may differ from those of goods outside the capital city (some prices may be higher, some lower).

Table 1

ITEM	PRICE IN 1999	PRICE IN 2007
Kilogram of meat	7.06 UAH	32 UAH
Liter of milk	1.26 UAH	5 UAH
Bread (baton)	.70 UAH	1.50 UAH
Kilogram of potatoes	.40 UAH	2.75 UAH
One-way fare on city transport	.30 UAH	.50–2 UAH
Ukrainian-made automobile (Tavriya ZAZ 21028)	12,380 UAH	25,000 UAH

Women's Social Activism in the New Ukraine

Introduction: Women, NGOs, and the Politics of Differentiation

May 13, 1999. Today I am hoping to interview women directors of two different community organizations about their work, and it is fortunate that their offices are not too far from each other. My first meeting is with Ivana—she has agreed to take a lunch break from her supervisory job at the Kyiv city vocational education administration office.[1] I wait for Ivana outside the modest two-story, nineteenth-century building where she works, and watch the cars, trolleybuses, and minibus taxis creep by on the busy city street here in Kyiv's "Old Town," the modern city's oldest district. The old Soviet-made cars—Zhigulis, Moskviches, and gas-guzzling Volgas—present a sharp contrast to the new SUVs and Mercedes which cushion the city's business and government elites behind their darkly tinted windows.

Soon Ivana emerges from the building, rushes to greet me, and whisks me through the "control" desk at the building's entrance ("This girl is with me, she's from America"). She takes me on a quick tour of the offices, stops to talk briefly with several female office mates, and then we head outside for a chat. We sit in a quiet courtyard, in a gazebo (appropriately called a "little conversation house" [*besedka*] in Russian), sharing a chocolate bar as Ivana tells me about her life as a social activist. The lilacs are in bloom, and their delicious scent surrounds us. As we talk, I think about how much has changed for Ivana since we first met in February 1998 at a conference on women and children's health. She was then forty-seven years old and still teaching high school physics, but also running the nongovernmental organization (NGO) called Hope that she founded in 1996 to help disadvantaged teens, especially girls. Although the organization's original focus was humanitarian aid assistance (food, clothing, medicines) for impoverished teens, Ivana's increasing involvement in local NGO networks through seminars and workshops shifted her outreach activities toward what she called "enlightening" (Rus. *prosvetitel'skie*) or educational events. She concentrated particularly on providing teenage girls with sex education courses. This focus on education dovetailed well with Ivana's new job as an administrator in the city's vocational education division. She was very active in Kyiv's NGO community and had become a "trainer" (seminar instructor) for one of the international NGOs in Kyiv promoting NGO development among women. Although Ivana's work in the educational administration was very poorly paid (less than $30 a month), her position as a trainer provided the opportunity to earn additional income.

On that warm May afternoon, Ivana and I discussed many aspects of her so-

Figure 2. "Waiting." A woman in Kyiv, 1989. Photo montage by Nikolai Zhdanov.

cial activism, which she referred to repeatedly as her "calling." Our conversation meandered through both Russian and Ukrainian languages—Ivana, who considered herself ethnically Ukrainian, had grown up speaking Russian but was making a conscious transition to speaking Ukrainian at home with her family ("Ukrainians should speak Ukrainian"). She was required to speak Ukrainian at work, since she worked for the education administration.

We talked about the fact that the NGO sector in Ukraine seemed to be a "women's sphere," since the majority of NGO leaders we knew were women. Ivana said this was only natural; she believed that women were more suited for this "social work" because of their caring natures and their more sensitive and patient approaches to personal and social crises. On the other hand, she noted that women had fewer job opportunities after the socialist collapse in Ukraine, especially middle-aged women like herself, many of whom had been pushed out of their careers in education, science, and engineering when their jobs became superfluous during the transition to a market economy. The most poignant aspect of the interview, however, was Ivana's stories about how taking up an NGO leadership role had changed her own self-perspective. She told me that her organizational work had given her increased self-esteem and a greatly improved self-image. She was able to develop her own creative thinking and innovation skills, and learned to "see herself from the outside." Although it took her a while to join the inner circle of NGO experts in Ukraine, she gradually gained the trust of representatives of international foundations and donors. This support provided her with lucrative social networks and a language of transnational NGO phraseology; her speech was littered with references to "civil society," "grant making," and "fund-raising." Ivana underlined the important services she provided, both in her outreach activities through Hope and in her capacity as a trainer for those entering the NGO sphere. In this, she contrasted herself with "user" organizations whose leaders and members "just ask for handouts." Ivana clearly privileged a language of self-reliance and personal initiative.

Perhaps more than any other activist I knew, Ivana's story typified ways in which civic organizing simultaneously engendered changes in women activists' profession, expertise, and interests, and sparked personal transformations. Among my informants Ivana was unique in that her husband (a small business owner) and two grown children were also involved in her NGO, each contributing time and skills to the projects she developed. Still, she continually emphasized the "womanly" qualities that drove her social activism—her emotional nature, her commitment to motherhood, and her role as a nurturer.

I have detained Ivana too long and must rush to my next meeting. As I depart, she hands me a business card from her NGO, Hope, that features a sketch of a kneeling, naked woman holding the world in her hands. The symbol reminds me of the *Berehynia*, a pagan goddess and Earth Mother figure from ancient Slavic mythology whose image has been revived in Ukraine in recent years. For contemporary Ukrainians, the *Berehynia* represents women's traditional domesticity and role as keeper of the home hearth and protectress of the generational fire, but she is also seen as the guardian of the nation (Rubchak

1996:320).[2] Drawing as she does on her self-described "feminine" qualities of caring and protection to reach out to girls in crisis through education and assistance, I wondered: Does Ivana see herself as a *Berehynia*?

I wave down a minibus taxi, pay the driver 50 kopeks (about 15 cents), and within minutes reach the office of Our House, a mutual-aid association that supports large families in one of Kyiv's historical districts.[3] Having been here several times before, I easily find my way through the side door and the long corridor to the small room which Svetlana and Vira, the director and assistant director of the organization, rent from the state. A new commercial firm occupies most of the building, and Svetlana and Vira believe that the firm's owners want to purchase the entire premises, including the small ramshackle office of Our House. The young black-suited men who run the private company are members of Ukraine's new business elite, and they appear to do a brisk business. I say hello to Nadia, the firm's secretary. She is impeccably dressed as usual in a short, tailored suit and snappy shoes, and is freshly manicured with long polished nails, perfectly defined eyebrows, and shiny lipstick. I'm aware of my slapdash appearance as I pass by her desk in my long skirt and flats. The firm's recently remodeled modern, "Evro" (European) offices make the premises of Our House look all the more wretched—this small room has not seen a coat of paint in quite some time, and the weathered wooden window frames are disintegrating.

Seated in the small office I retrieve some cookies from my backpack, and Vira puts on water for tea. My conversation with Svetlana and Vira rings a very different note than that with Ivana. Whereas Ivana emphasized the energetic people she met and the skills she gained through her civic organizing, these two women relate how their efforts to draw attention to the needs of large families during this time of economic crisis are continuously rejected by state bureaucrats, potential "sponsors," and everyday people. They took up NGO leadership roles to serve the very category of persons to which they themselves belong— "mothers of many children" (three or more). Previously targets of special attention and assistance because they fall into a category of citizens designated as vulnerable, these women now feel acutely the state's economic retreat from their lives. State economic crisis, and concomitant reforms to introduce a free market economic system and dismantle the Soviet-era, cradle-to-grave social welfare system, have meant the overall reduction of benefits and subsidies for susceptible populations such as "mothers of many children." During our conversation that day, Svetlana and Vira spun out heartfelt stories about their lives and their organization, and offered personal vignettes of social suffering. (We spoke Russian, as Svetlana identified as an ethnic Russian and both Svetlana and Vira [who identified as ethnically Ukrainian] spoke Russian as their first language.)

The women became the directors of Our House during the mid-1990s, after losing their jobs and failing to secure other paid employment. Both were trying to support their three children; Vira was married, but Svetlana, twice-divorced, was currently single. For the "social work" they did, the women received no compensation save double rations of the humanitarian aid and subsidies they were able to procure for the organization's members. Both women were registered at the unemployment bureau in Kyiv, and they had taken courses to acquire skills so they could better compete in Ukraine's tight job market. Svetlana, who had a degree from a technical institute, took classes in management and had received a "manager certificate." Vira, who for many years had worked as a shop clerk, studied accounting. Despite these efforts, they were unable to find satisfactory work, largely, they believed, because, as women of "advanced" age (both were forty), each with three children, they were viewed as unreliable employees. In Svetlana's words: "I've got three kids, and I'm forty years old. I'm not going to squeeze myself into a miniskirt for a job interview now, am I?" Adding insult to injury, when the women registered at the unemployment bureau, they had been subjected to a demeaning IQ test. At the root of these testing procedures, they believed, was the stereotype of women with multiple children as "incapable" and "stupid."[4]

In contrast to Ivana, who recounted how NGO work had allowed her to "blossom," gain new skills, and pursue a range of avenues for career development, Svetlana and Vira described at length their harrowing run-ins with state representatives and businesspeople in their city district. Their stories emphasized the psychological trauma of being treated like "beggars" by potential sponsors. "Something inside you breaks," Svetlana told me. "That is the only way you can force yourself to ask for help. You have to become a broken person. At first, when they would turn us out and call us names, we would find a bench outside the office, sit down, and cry our eyes out." The women, however, had apparently learned to cope with such treatment. Svetlana continued, "Now it doesn't even faze us. Recently one businessman we approached for help called me a 'very insolent woman.' I thought about it for a while and then decided, I'll take that as a compliment!" But their newly toughened skin had not resulted in greater support for their charitable fund for large families. Unlike Ivana, the women were not plugged into the transnational NGO advocacy networks in Kyiv, and they did not have close working relations with other NGO leaders around the city. Moreover, they informed me, they owed the city more than $500 in rent arrears and were in danger of losing their office. Both were discouraged and uncertain that their NGO work was indeed worth it. They had hoped to help improve the lives of large, impoverished families in crisis (including their own), but no one seemed to value their work—neither the state nor international foundations nor local business sponsors. These entities dismissed their claims that large families, as a category of citizens hit especially hard by the market transition, were deserving of substantial entitlements from the state and support from local business structures.

By 2006, Svetlana, Vira, and Ivana were all living in quite different circumstances. Our House was unable to repay its outstanding rent; the meeting space was repossessed by the city administration in 2001 and subsequently bought up by their businessmen neighbors. Svetlana explained that the "scandal" over the premises actually began when she applied for a housing subsidy for her own family, which drew the attention of "the system" to her NGO work and the organization's bank account; eventually the office was wrested away by the city administration. Our House still exists, and Svetlana, now working from home, continues her NGO activities but in a limited way. For a time the women pondered strategies for revamping the organization's profile—perhaps changing it from a "fund" to a "center," which carries different tax implications, and refocusing the aim to serve needy families in general rather than large families only—but they have not carried out these plans. Svetlana now works as a counselor for a crisis hotline—for which she believes her NGO work with disadvantaged populations prepared her well—but Vira remains unemployed. Svetlana's counseling job, which involves twenty-four-hour shifts, is physically challenging for Svetlana, who is overweight and has poor arterial circulation. In fact, she suffers from serious health problems requiring surgery but can afford neither the surgery nor time off from work for recovery. Svetlana's monthly salary is $100, well below the average nationwide salary of $220 per month.[5] Because her bleak employment history means that she has contributed very little to the state pension fund, she expects to receive only a small pension upon her retirement. Her three children still live at home, and she recently became a grandmother. Looking back over her NGO career, Svetlana says, "I now realize that you should become well-provided for yourself before trying to help others." But, she admits, "I failed to take my own advice." Unlike Ivana, who saw NGO work as her calling, to Svetlana it is her cross.

Yet Ivana's life took quite another turn. In late 1999 she went to work for a local institute as a lecturer, until tragedy struck her family. She herself fell ill with cancer in 2002, the same year that her grown daughter was killed in an automobile accident. The shock of her own illness and subsequent surgery, and especially her beloved daughter's death, immobilized Ivana, and for almost two years she was unable to work. Afraid to be alone, she required constant companionship. By 2003, however, Ivana had managed to recover, and she became a marketing representative for a major publishing house. By 2006, she had become the director of one of the publisher's Kyiv divisions. Ivana continues to work with her NGO Hope, and she also established a new NGO that combines her interests in education and publishing. Ivana acknowledges that her NGO work helped her develop the social networks and organizational and interpersonal skills necessary to make it in the business world. She has been able to effectively wield this social and cultural capital to become a successful manager and businesswoman, while continuing to pursue her "calling" of social activism, even in the wake of successive personal tragedies.

Ivana, Svetlana, and Vira are just three of the thousands of women who have taken up leadership roles in various types of civic organizations in Ukraine since Gorbachev, in the mid- and late 1980s, loosened the reigns on the right of Soviet citizens to associate freely. Their contrasting experiences raise important questions about the nature of Ukraine's postsocialist "third sector" (as the NGO sphere is called in transnational "development-speak") and about the impacts on women of the collapse of the socialist system and the introduction of a market economy. Why have women flocked to the nonprofit sector, and what accounts for the starkly different life and career outcomes of women such as Ivana and Svetlana? Why was Ivana able to rise through the ranks of the state educational system and international development foundations finally to launch a career in business, while Svetlana remained marginalized and impoverished? Why was social activism a "calling" for one woman, and a "cross" for another? Why did the women speak in such contrasting terms about their social justice struggles, and why were their efforts evaluated so differently by state and business elites?

Postsocialist Politics of *Dyferentsiatsiia*

Just like millions of other people in post-Soviet Ukraine, Svetlana and Ivana found themselves in the crosshairs of processes of *differentiation,* as criteria for productive citizenship are reworked, and the rights and needs of various categories of citizens redefined. These women's social justice struggles and their uneven success highlight some of the social costs of economic reforms centered on marketization, privatization, and welfare reduction, policies that entail a reevaluation of citizens' productivity and deservedness, and a dramatic rearrangement of the state's acknowledged responsibilities toward different groups of citizens. The claims of people like Svetlana, who called upon the Ukrainian state to provide the same level of social protection she had enjoyed as a "mother of many children" in the Soviet Union, have become increasingly devalued as the state is pulled back and social problems become privatized. By contrast, Ivana's language of "self-reliance" and initiative resonates well with the new neoliberal reforms to scale back the social safety net and promote entrepreneurship and active citizenship.

Although "differentiation" is a scientific term in sociology, it was never widely used in the Soviet Union—and was, in fact, forbidden—given the official ideology of a classless society and social equality. Today, in Ukraine, the term is used primarily in scientific circles (as in references to "the differentiation of society"), and in official government documents and speeches on social welfare reforms. I first heard the word "differentiation" (Ukr. *dyferentsiatsiia*) in 2005 when I was in Kyiv talking to a friend who receives a disability pension after suffering a spinal cord injury. As a lawyer, he is very well informed about social politics, and during our conversation he began to reflect on how social welfare reforms proposed by the new administration of President Viktor Yushchenko would affect him personally. He mentioned recently adopted legislation that would lead to a reassessment of the status of all citizens who receive disability pensions; the reevaluation would focus especially on citizens' capacity to work. Unlike current regulations, the new rules would prohibit some categories of disabled persons from working and simultaneously receiving a disability pension. A concomitant "differentiation" of pensions was also planned for the disabled and for war veterans, based on individuals' work histories and salaries at the onset of disability.[6] My friend summed up the situation thus: "It looks like they're telling us, 'We just realized that you want too much.'" As I read more about social welfare reform I found that the concept of "differentiation"—separating groups and individuals according to new criteria, standards, and calculations of need and entitlement—now litters official documents and proclamations issued by President Yushchenko and the Ministry of Labor and Social Policy. Other notions that pepper these documents include "personification," "personalization," "individualization," and "reclassification." These may be indigenous concepts in the sense that they are used in the Ukrainian lexicon (in officialese, at least), but they also reflect the influence of processes of globalization on Ukrainian social reforms, especially the language and mechanisms of the global market economy.

Although the language of differentiation had not yet gelled in the late 1990s when I conducted the bulk of my fieldwork for this project, it became clear, as I thought more and more about this concept, that processes of differentiation were certainly already under way during those years. In fact, many of the NGO activists I knew were waging social justice struggles precisely to stave off and protest differentiation, which they found antithetical to ideas of social equality that they and many people in postsocialist countries hold dear. As I reread interview transcripts, perused the literature published by international NGO development organizations active in Ukraine (handbooks, newsletters, project reports), investigated emerging social welfare and pension reforms, and conducted follow-up interviews with key informants, I began to ponder the various types of differentiation to which the social activists I knew had been subjected. I identified three major vectors of differentiating processes that affected their lives and their advocacy efforts:

1. differentiation driven by social welfare reform and the reevaluation and recategorization of citizens in official state discourse and policy
2. differentiation driven by international and local NGO development initiatives in which certain types of claims and organizational forms were privileged over others
3. differentiation as an interpersonal phenomenon driven by activists' changing perceptions of their own personal and social worth and that of others.

The politics of differentiation are brought into especially strong relief when we train our lens on civic organizations, whose leaders and members launch social justice struggles that both stave off and perpetuate all these differentiating procedures. As much as NGOs are providing a much needed safety net for vulnerable populations in Ukraine, they are also agents of differentiation, especially those NGOs based on Western models.

This book concerns women's social activism in the new Ukraine and the processes of differentiation that have both motivated and resulted from women's NGO activities. It explores not only the very different life circumstances that have compelled women in post-Soviet Ukraine to engage in NGO activism but also how and why some women have emerged from NGO work as successful entrepreneurs and bureaucratic cadres whereas others remain marginalized from power. The life stories and personal narratives of women activists are windows onto the changing and competing ideas about entitlement, social justice, and social worth that inform local understandings about post-Soviet persons and collectives during the "democratization" of Ukrainian society. As such, activists' contrasting experiences show how the privatization of social problems, and the increasing emphasis on self-reliance and the entrepreneurial spirit, result in the privileging of certain citizens' claims over those of others. This differentiation occurs at the nexus of Ukrainian policies for economic and institutional reform, transnational NGO advocacy networks with their civil society building programs, and the little histories of local NGOs and their leaders, whose personal lives are inextricably tied up in their advocacy work.

Processes of differentiation have had an especially marked impact on women, which is reflected not only in macroeconomic indicators and unemployment statistics (which generally show women to be the losers of "transition") but also in the large numbers of women who have sought refuge in NGOs as a forum to advocate for marginalized populations and eke out a meager living.[7] In the context of economic reform and the shrinking social safety net, it is mostly women who have been left to pick up the pieces of the disheveled social welfare system; women have been compelled to engage in the care and defense of marginalized groups whose concerns and demands are increasingly delegitimized in the neoliberal moment. Barbara Einhorn describes this situation as a "civil society trap," since so many women have been ushered into the low-prestige, low (or no)-paying ghetto of NGO grunt work (2000:110).[8] Across the former Soviet Union, women generally appear to dominate the NGO sphere.[9] Despite popular assumptions that this is also the case in Ukraine, a recent survey of 610 civil society organizations in Ukraine showed no significant gender differences in NGO leadership (51 percent were directed by women, and 49 percent by men) (Palyvoda, Kikot, and Vlasova 2006:92). There were some regional variations, with greater percentages of NGOs being led by women in Western and Eastern Ukraine, and men dominating in Central Ukraine. However, the types of NGOs commonly associated with women differ significantly from those associated with men. In Ukraine, women tend to head social organizations that serve the interests of women, children, and families, and those that focus on "solving social issues"; women are believed to possess "natural" roles as mothers, caregivers, and guardians of the home and nation.[10] Many women-led organizations are "mutual-aid" associations (*hrupy vzaiemodopomohy*) that are simultaneously a support group and a humanitarian (charity) organization. Like Svetlana and Vira, scores of NGO directors are themselves members of a marginalized category (large families, the elderly, the disabled) and may engage in NGO work as a form of precarious employment as they wage social justice struggles to help themselves and others. Men, on the other hand, are more likely to direct NGOs associated with human rights, civic education, politics, the state, and the economy, which represent much more prestigious and lucrative spheres than children's issues and "solving social problems" (Palyvoda, Kikot, and Vlasova 2006:92).

By now it is no secret that market reforms in postsocialist states have left women economically and socially vulnerable; so much has been written on this subject that women's tough luck after socialism has become an expected and seemingly natural outcome of "transition."[11] Thinking about differentiation may help jar us out of the assumption that extreme social disruption (for women, especially) is an inevitable, natural, yet temporary by-product of market reform. In this, perhaps an analysis of differentiation processes constitutes an antidote to the ideology of "transition," which has proven dangerous for how women are positioned by governments, the international community, and scholars. As Tatiana Zhurzhenko (1998:110) pointed out:

> The concept of the transition economy justifies the disintegration of society and the social costs accompanying market reforms, including the worsening of the situation of women and other vulnerable social groups. The transition period is usually regarded as a natural and inevitable stage when the market mechanisms, which supposedly will guarantee the social equity and welfare of all members of society, have not yet formed. In this way the ideology of transition is itself a part of the mechanism generating the social and economical marginalisation of women in contemporary Ukraine.

Honing in on differentiating processes reveals that this marginalization and disintegration is anything but natural and inevitable. On the other hand, differentiation produces both winners and losers, and some of the former are certainly women as well. Tracking differentiation thus also sheds light on processes of social mobility by documenting the stories of women who have succeeded in the realms of civil society, business, and government (Ghodsee 2005; Johnson and Robinson 2007).

More broadly, then, exploring different trajectories of women's social activism also reveals some of the contradictory effects the postsocialist transition has had for women's lives. Although some women seem to have sought refuge in NGOs from processes of marketization, others have undertaken NGO leadership work as a stopping-off point or a trampoline to careers in business. And although many women seem to have found a niche in Ukraine's NGO sector, prompting some to describe Ukrainian civil society as having a "woman's face," women's representation in the official political sphere has plummeted since Ukrainian independence in 1991. At the same time, some women have managed to springboard themselves from NGO leadership to positions in the government administration.

The ethnographic approach is well suited for exploring the factors that have compelled women to engage in civic organizing in the wake of postsocialist collapse, and for understanding what accounts for women's very different experiences of such activism. The stories of women like Svetlana and Ivana help us track some of the strategies that women have used to cope with their own social dislocation, and to understand and evaluate their differential success. Along the way, the stories these activists tell about their lives reveal the complex negotiations women have made to re-imagine and reconstitute themselves as women, mothers, workers, and citizens in a postsocialist, postcolonial state. To begin to understand the postsocialist politics of differentiation that are telescoped in the experiences of the NGO activists profiled here, it is necessary to outline the emerging politics of social welfare reform and claims-making in post-Soviet Ukraine.

Cradle-to-Grave Has One Foot in the Grave?

The Soviet welfare system provided universal benefits including old-age pensions, disability pensions, health care, child care, family benefits, education, housing, and others. This is the system Ukraine inherited upon national independence in 1991. Within existing welfare programs there are twenty-three separate benefits, eleven of them relating to child care or maternity. Examples include unemployment benefits, subsidies for housing and fuel, benefits for large families, Chernobyl compensation, a child leave benefit, and temporary disability. The social welfare system is widely utilized; in the late 1990s, 73.7 percent of households received at least one benefit (Whitefield 2003:407–408). In fact, in Ukraine in 2005 more money was paid out in social assistance than in wages.[12] Social welfare has been recognized by some political actors (and the international development community) as a drain on state coffers and in critical need of reform; others (such as former prime minister Yuliia Tymoshenko) have sought to increase social support to the needy in what are perceived by many observers as populist efforts to attract votes and support. Indeed, a strong element of populism characterizes social welfare reform; competing political factions make promises and adopt legislation to appeal to constituents and attract popular support. This phenomenon was evident during the early parliamentary elections in September 2007. All the major parties promised significant increases in pensions, salaries, and social payments, but mechanisms for funding these increases were not fully explicated.

Welfare reform is one of the most contentious political issues in the new Ukraine (as anywhere), since such reforms involve a dramatic rearrangement of the relationships between state institutions and different categories of citizens. Via the cradle-to-grave system of social welfare, the Soviet state supplied citizens with the necessities in return for furnishing low wages and acquiescence. This system inculcated an ethos of entitlement among citizens, who looked to the state as a provider of security, services, and benefits (Lipsmeyer 2003). Today, these perceptions are running up against a new model of entitlement and "needs," which are being defined not through a lens of state socialism but rather through neoliberal economic theory promoting privatization, liberalization, and deregulation. The marketization of the Ukrainian economy appears to be leading—in a meandering and contradictory fashion—to the trimming back of social welfare systems and an ongoing politics of differentiation.

Examining emerging social programs and welfare reforms is like tracking a moving target, since reforms are a work in progress and policies keep shifting with the changing political landscape. Although the general system is in place and legislative changes have been adopted, budget deficits have stalled the reform process and reforms are being implemented slowly if at all. President Yushchenko's dissolution of Parliament in April 2007 further stymied the reform process.

Much pension reform exists on paper, but the government cannot afford to keep its promises. In 2005, for example, the Pension Fund of Ukraine was running a deficit of 14.7 billion UAH (the hryvnia, the Ukrainian currency; almost $3 billion) for pension payments to be paid out by the state; by March 2006 the deficit was 16 billion UAH ($3.2 billion) (Cabinet of Ministers of Ukraine 2005).[13] All too frequently reforms exist in declaration only, never to be followed through. Just one example is the IPRI plan, or the "Provision on the individual program of rehabilitation and adaptation of the invalid."[14] The Ministry of Health approved the IPRI in 1992, a plan designed to integrate economic and social concerns into a rehabilitation process that has heretofore focused primarily on the medical and technical problems of the disabled. However, a mechanism for funding the IPRI process was not approved until 2003, and the program has still not been implemented (Marunych et al. 2004; Poloziuk 2005). Therefore, a full fourteen years after the adoption of this legislation, many people with disabilities are still waiting for their IPRIs.

Although it is widely recognized that Ukraine's social welfare system needs a dramatic overhaul to remain viable, no politician, of course, wants to be the grinch who pulled the plug on welfare. So reforms are couched in positive terms about alleviating poverty and increasing support to the needy, though the actual outcomes of newly emerging policies are still quite ambiguous. On the surface, there has been an apparent increase in social spending in recent years. During 2005, public wages were increased by the Yushchenko administration (especially those of state employees, which increased 57 percent), and social welfare spending was ratcheted up by as much as 73 percent (Kuzio 2005). In February 2006, President Yushchenko boasted that during his tenure real income had increased by 20 percent, wages had gone up by 34 percent, and pensions and the minimum wage increased. Large families received a three- to twelvefold increase in benefits, and a childbirth incentive was introduced offering families up to 8,500 UAH (roughly $1,700 in 2006) upon the birth of a child (National Information Service Strana.Ru 2006).[15] In 2005, retirement pensions were increased and indexed to the minimum monthly wage (332 UAH, or $66), and the average retirement pension reached 383 UAH ($77). Not mentioned in these proclamations, however, are the budget deficits that make it difficult, or even impossible, to fulfill these promises. For example, it has been suggested that, in order for the government to make good on its promise to pay out increased retirement pensions, it still has to come up with 64–65 billion UAH ($12.8 billion).[16] Overall, in official pronouncements and the speeches of state officials, discussions of social politics are detached from the broader political economy. Ongoing inflation and higher costs of utilities, transportation, communication, and other services eat up any increases in wages and pensions, making references to "increased social support" of citizens circumspect at best.[17] Recent measures have been taken to index social allowances and pensions to the minimum monthly wage to prevent the effects of inflation, but it is unclear whether these will be feasible, at least in the short term.

When it comes to social spending, key political actors sometimes give with one hand while taking with the other. Although in 2007 President Yushchenko vowed to increase wages, pensions, and social payments in 2008, his secretariat simultaneously developed an initiative to decrease total contributions to social funds (N. Iatsenko 2007). Similarly, during his 2006–2007 term as prime minister, Viktor Yanukovych oversaw the withdrawal of more than sixty social assistance programs. Nevertheless, during the parliamentary election campaign of 2007, his Party of Regions promised significant increases in social spending. Alongside pronouncements of increased social spending and support for the poor runs a neoliberal language of reform that focuses on streamlining social institutions, making social service provision more "humane," and bringing social insurance in line with European standards. In November 2005, an agreement was signed with the World Bank providing almost $100 million for the Project on Improvement of the System of Social Assistance to overhaul the system of social welfare; the agreement was ratified by the Verkhovna Rada (the Ukrainian Parliament) in February 2006. The influence of "structural adjustment" strategies, which since the Reagan-Thatcher era have been tied to worldwide development aid, is clear in this document and others. In official documents and reports, Ukrainian social welfare reforms are presented in the language of "differentiation," "personification," "activation," and "individualization." The system of universal benefits is called a "passive" system, whereas reforms (such as targeted assistance) are said to create an "active" system of social welfare. Motivating citizens to become self-sufficient is a key component of reforms. For example, the Ministry of Labor and Social Policy reports that disability policy has changed from one of "social welfare" (*zabezpechennia*) to one of "social insurance" (*zakhyst*). The former is associated with a "passive" function, whereas the latter is said to "insure [the disabled] equal opportunity to realize their life needs and potential." In contrast to universal benefits offered in the Soviet welfare system, today social assistance is differentiated according to length of work service, salary at time of retirement or onset of disability, one's former profession, and so on. For instance, although pensions for all retirees rose in 2005, pensions were differentiated according to the years one had previously worked and the salary one received. If before pension reforms 83 percent of retirees in Ukraine received identical pensions, after the implementation of differentiation policies just 44 percent were slated to receive identical pensions (Myronivs'kyi 2005). Although the major parties in the September 2007 parliamentary elections promised increases in pensions, their platforms also emphasized differentiation, privatization, and personalization through the eradication of "pension egalitarianism" and the development of private pension insurance and personal accumulative retirement accounts. All this is indicative of new procedures to reevaluate citizens and their claims to state assistance, a process fraught with difficulties such as lack of institutional space and qualified inspectors, and inadequate means to verify documents and salaries.[18]

Along with differentiation, "targeted assistance" (*adresna dopomoha*) is an emerging mantra of the Ministry of Labor and Social Policy. Targeted assistance was first introduced by former president Kuchma in his plans for reforming the social insurance system, which he called a "Soviet relic," and he used the term *adresna dopomoha* in his Fighting Poverty initiative. Today, targeted assistance programs, which use new criteria for determining the scope of social assistance, are replacing the Soviet-era universal system of privileges to certain population categories. Primary among these criteria is needs testing. One pertinent example of the evolving politics of targeted assistance and differentiation is the ongoing shifts in state policy toward large families.

In the Soviet Union, large families—those with five or more children, and later those with three or more children—were eligible for a range of social allowances, including a large family benefit for each child and subsidies for housing and fuel. In the late 1990s, children in a qualifying family each received an allowance of 70 UAH ($20) per month. In 1999, President Kuchma adopted, by decree, the document Measures on the Improvement of the Situation of Families with Many Children, legislation that represented a retrenchment of state support for large families. The decree stated that in conditions of the market transition in Ukraine "the support and care of children depends significantly more on parents than on the state. The role of the family in life-preparation and rearing of children is increasing. This reorientation changes the function of the family and affects the demographic situation in the country" (Koval's'kyi 2002:178).[19] State benefits were all but withdrawn, and emphasis was placed on surveillance and "educational work" among families with many children. As Tatiana Zhurzhenko notes:

> This document does not provide for the rise of family allowances, as one should suppose, but only for "timely payments and the liquidation of debts." It mainly deals with the collection of information on these families and educational work among them. In fact, this is an attempt to mobilize the relics of the system of nonmonetary privileges and state services for the children from these families (e.g., free school uniforms and breakfasts). In comparison with Soviet times, the motive for special attention to families with many children is not the encouragement of birthrates but the recognition of the fact that the number of children is the main factor in family impoverishment, and that this category of families is the most vulnerable. (Zhurzhenko 2004:40–41)

The decree redefined the "needs" of large families. No longer were these families "deserving" of state assistance as a reward for their increased fertility. Rather, they were in need of educational work to ward off poverty (a condition they evidently brought upon themselves). Herein lay the seeds of the accusation that Svetlana and Vira once told me others were hurling at them: "They are giving birth to the poor." In 2005 and 2006, however, social politics toward large families shifted somewhat as plans for "targeted assistance" were refined under President Yushchenko's administration.

The World Bank–supported Project on Improvement of the System of Social Assistance is designed to streamline the social insurance system and "establish in Ukraine an effective, new organization of targeted assistance for the poorest groups of the population," including families with three or more children.[20] This agreement was followed in March 2006 by a change to the Law on State Social Assistance to Poor Families offering each child in families with three or more children under the age of sixteen (under eighteen if in school or attending a university) a 20 percent increase in monthly pension benefits.[21] (If a child ages out of the system, leaving only two children under age sixteen [eighteen], the family no longer qualifies as a "large" family.) Legislation, still in the pipeline (proposed changes to the Law on Defense of Childhood), proposes to offer large families special access to housing loans to improve their living situation.[22] Earlier, in March 2005, legislative changes were adopted that grant women who have borne five or more children, and have reared each of them to at least age eight, the opportunity for early retirement at age fifty instead of fifty-five.[23]

These reforms seem to offer increased support and state assistance to large families, who are acknowledged as an especially vulnerable segment of the population. It is important to note, however, that recent changes involve a process of differentiation and a specific language of productivity in line with neoliberal market reforms. Unlike Soviet-era programs, these benefits are couched not in a language of "entitlements" (*pil'hy*), but in a language of "assistance" and "poverty alleviation." There are incentives for children in large families to study longer (they may receive benefits until they are eighteen if they do so), and large families are offered access to housing loans rather than increased housing subsidies. The provisions entailed in legislation offering mothers of five or more children early retirement (they must have these children in the household until they are eight years old) ensure that children are raised by families at least until school age and that families do not simply produce children and abandon them to receive state benefits. Crucially, the Ministry of Labor and Social Policy makes it clear that targeted assistance will be extended to families who are poor "not by their own fault."[24] Overall these reforms tend to follow Kuchma's line of "educational work," with emphasis placed on surveillance and stimulating the poor and vulnerable to active citizenship. Furthermore, the language used in official documents on social insurance reform sometimes casts large families in a negative light; for example, large families are lumped with "problematic" (*neblahopoluchni*) families, and "impoverished" (*malozabezpecheni*) families, implying that large families are also likely to be problematic, impoverished, or both.

One of the most striking new social assistance programs implemented by the Yushchenko administration has been the payment of up to 8,500 UAH ($1,700) upon the birth of a child.[25] This represents a twelvefold increase in assistance to families with newborns. The program, introduced in 2005, was presented by the then prime minister Tymoshenko as a response to the ongoing demographic crisis in Ukraine, and as a birth incentive for those who feel too financially insecure to have children. In a context of ongoing economic hardship, "children have become a luxury" (Wanner and Dudwick 2003), resulting in a low total fertility rate (births per woman) of 1.1 from 2000 to 2005, and a negative annual population growth rate (−0.1 during 1975–2003, and a projected −1.1 during 2003–2015) (United Nations Development Programme 2005:232). The childbirth allowance was designed to provide a minimal standard of living (*prozhitkovyi minimum*) for the child during his or her first six years of life. The childbirth incentive is one of the few new social programs that has actually been financed and implemented, albeit with delays in payouts. The childbirth allowance unfolds in stages: 3,384 UAH ($677) is paid out immediately after the birth, with the remainder offered in installments over the course of twelve months. Amid skepticism that the childbirth allowance could easily be abused, since individuals might have children merely to receive this considerable sum and quickly abandon their offspring, Tymoshenko was quick to assure the public that "problematic" (*neblahopoluchni*) families would receive the payouts under the supervision (*pid nahliadom*) of city administrators, thus insuring that the money be used for the child's needs.[26] This "supervision," which apparently would be unevenly applied to only families deemed "problematic," is representative of the discourse of differentiation that drives strategies for reforming the social welfare system.

My acquaintances who have received the childbirth incentive are grateful for this financial assistance, but they acknowledge that it "will only go so far, and then we're on our own." In many ways, the program reflects the overall trend of the personalization of social problems such as the demographic crisis: as Alexandra Hrycak points out, the Ukrainian state has failed to invest in basic infrastructural improvements to make it possible for more citizens to start families (and improve women's health) (2001:147). Instead, thus far solutions include temporary measures such as the childbirth incentive payouts. This program is an example of the rise of what Tatiana Zhurzhenko calls "neofamilism" in post-Soviet Ukraine, a critique of the totalitarian communist past that political actors use to hone in on the reproductive function of the "traditional family" and agitate for the reestablishment of proper gender roles in the family (2004). Of course, it is curious that these efforts to rectify Ukraine's demographic crisis and support families become more ambiguous in the case of large families, who are not offered the real increases in assistance one might expect, given these families' contributions to demographic growth. Large families generally are treated more as a population at risk for poverty than as contributors to the "genetic pull" or "gene pool" (*genofond*) of the nation, a common expression in popular and scholarly discourse. Indeed, a perusal of the demographic literature in Ukraine (which includes copious discussions about the "ethnodemographic" situation) reveals more than a hint of a pseudo-academic eugenicist narrative.

Thus, alongside increased monetary support for the retired, the disabled, impoverished families, families with newborns, and others flow new procedures for reevaluating the criteria citizens must meet to be eligible for social assistance, and for differentiating claims based on these criteria. Therefore, although the Yushchenko administration ushered in significant increases in social spending, it is unclear how long such generous social welfare policy will be sustained, and whether promises of increased spending will ever be carried through, given the populist nature of these proclamations, budget deficits, and the changing winds of Ukrainian politics. Tymoshenko was ousted from the position of prime minister in 2005 presumably owing in part to dissatisfaction with these very increases in social spending, and the sharp decline in GDP growth during 2005 (from 12 to 3 percent) has caused many to reevaluate these reforms. The strategy of differentiation that has been put in place may have the eventual effect of shrinking social spending overall while increasing some areas of spending through targeted assistance programs. Or, to the contrary, welfare expenditures may continue to increase, and welfare rolls may rise as well, even as the Ukrainian state works with ever narrower definitions of need—a situation Lynne Haney (2002) has documented for Hungary during the 1990s. In any case, excavating changes in social policy provides a view onto changing citizenship models and processes of differentiation in postsocialist states such as Ukraine, and sheds light on how various categories of citizens are weathering these changes.

Civil Society for Whom?

The processes of differentiation outlined here had real effects on the lives and organizing strategies of many of the social activists I knew in Kyiv. Several of the groups in my study were convened for the express purpose of stemming the tide of social welfare reform by lobbying for the interests of certain vulnerable groups, and lending aid to those who were falling through the holes in the disintegrating social safety net. Romashka was an organization that served fifty children with cancer and their families by providing social support from families going through similar trials; aid in the form of medicines, food, and vitamins; and assistance with medical bills. Svitanok was an umbrella organization for sixteen NGOs for women with disabilities throughout Ukraine; the organization coordinated a range of activities including seminars, a journal, and fund-raising for women's groups. Two NGOs—Lily of the Valley and Chernobyl Children Rescue—provided humanitarian aid, health care assistance, and health trips to Chernobyl children. The NGO For Life served Kyiv's population of elderly retired women, and an NGO called Equus focused on the rehabilitation of children with cerebral palsy utilizing equine-assisted therapy. Lotus served two hundred persons with spinal cord injuries in Kyiv by providing social and psychological rehabilitation services; humanitarian aid in the form of wheelchairs, medicines, and supplies; and self-care resources. (My study also included one nonprofit cultural organization whose members strove to instill a sense of patriotic pride in Ukrainian youth through dramatic performances.) Many of these groups were involved in lobbying efforts to recapture entitlements that certain categories of citizens had enjoyed prior to the Soviet collapse, or to secure new ones. Those government officials and other social actors (including some NGO leaders) who had taken up the neoliberal banner of progress, modernization, and a scaled back social safety net shunned those who clung to what were perceived as Soviet-era ideas of needs and entitlement. Additionally, "entitlement organizations" such as Our House that were outside the loop of international NGO development projects (which also promote ideas of self-sufficiency, sustainability, and individual initiative) were devalued by some local activists and NGO experts as "Soviet," "lazy," "freeloaders," and so on. Critiques of entitlement organizations were extended to their leaders and constituents, who were seen as asking for handouts instead of working. Entitlement groups were assessed negatively not primarily because members tended to be poor but because they articulated their needs in a fashion perceived as outdated (read: Soviet).

For several reasons, NGOs are especially good sites to track postsocialist processes of differentiation. First, many NGOs in Ukraine have been formed precisely as a refuge and resource for dispossessed groups of citizens who are struggling to regroup and recoup in the wake of the reordering of state priorities and the withdrawal of social welfare benefits. The drama of differentiation that is occurring at all levels of post-Soviet Ukrainian society plays out in particularly poignant ways in NGOs, where individuals and groups of citizens are struggling to have their voices heard, their claims recognized, and their social worth reaffirmed. The shifting postsocialist politics of recognition and redistribution (Fraser 1997) thus resonates through the everyday efforts of NGO activists to carve out a space for themselves and the groups they represent in the changeable social landscape. By paying attention to the claims launched by particular groups of citizens, and assessing the factors that make claims successful or not, we can track processes of differentiation as certain claims are valued over others and as activists seek new ways to articulate their rights and needs. This investigation also interrogates the class politics of civil society in postsocialist states, an aspect of "democratization" that has been overlooked by anthropologists and others studying the region. This lack has been noted by Martha Lampland, who writes:

> With all the talk about the rejuvenation of civil society, it is curious that the class politics of civil society are rarely broached. The rhetoric of socialist empowerment of the working class clearly has contributed substantially to the dismissal of class analysis among former socialist citizens. But this fact does not excuse Western analysts—particularly those so keen on the rebuilding of civil society—for their consistent failure to analyze the differential participation of various social groups in the new world of politics and community. Questions need to be asked: Civil society for whom? Who shall be heard in the new community of citizens, and why? (Lampland 2000:213)

I see this book as an answer to Lampland's challenge. My focus on differentiation—illustrated here ethnographically via the contrasting histories of NGO leaders like Svetlana, Ivana, and others, and by examining shifting state welfare policies and the politics of international NGO development—speaks directly to the changing politics of class in postsocialist countries.

Second, NGOs provide a window onto the changes taking place at the state and market levels that drive postsocialist processes of differentiation. Although it is often assumed that NGOs comprise a sphere ("civil society") that is detached from the state and the market, in fact NGOs in Ukraine and elsewhere frequently intersect with state and market forces. NGO activists often make claims on the state, seek out business ties for funding, and may be involved in market activities themselves. These interactions inevitably entail negotiations over the rights and needs of citizens, and thus provide further clues to the differentiating processes that shape contemporary Ukrainian society.

Third, NGOs are an important site of globalization where international development strategies intersect with local understandings of citizenship, social welfare, and the state. Market reforms are driven by neoliberal visions of the free market with minimal state interference, and by discourses of entrepreneurship, initiative, and self-reliance—a vocabulary that has also steered many recent international NGO development initiatives. This way of ordering the world contrasts sharply with the ethos of entitlement and desire for a strong state found among many Ukrainian citizens, and especially among many NGO activists who represent marginalized groups. The ability or inability to tap into this can-do rhetoric serves as a major differentiating factor between Ukrainian NGOs seeking recognition from international donors. Further, the transnational NGO industry has been a source of support and employment for a significant number of Ukrainian activists. The economic, cultural, and social capital provided by such connections play a big part in the success of some NGO professionals (e.g., Ivana), whose stories are very different from those with little or no access to international "transition aid."

Finally, the little histories of NGO activists, who carry out their advocacy work at the intersection of numerous, often competing influences (personal circumstances, local conditions, national/state projects, international interventions), are especially fertile ground for understanding postsocialist change, and processes of differentiation in particular. By comparing the life stories and organizational histories of women such as Ivana, Svetlana, and Vira, and by tracking their interactions with state officials and institutions, international foundations and development workers, and other local NGO activists, we can better understand not only why the voices of some NGO activists are privileged above others but also how ideas about citizenship, deservedness, and social worth have shifted in the postsocialist milieu.

Activists' life stories also reflect differentiating processes. Focusing on processes of differentiation thus allows me to bring up another important aspect of social activism that has been underexplored in existing studies of postsocialist civil societies: the personal transformations that social activism engenders. As they carry out social justice struggles, activists are compelled to navigate and enact new citizenship models and locate themselves in a rapidly changing society, all of which entails a reevaluation of one's self in relation to others. As these women endeavored to remake the worlds around them, they took up various narratives that allowed them to account for their actions and reconstitute themselves as persons. The reassessment of self-worth and personal purpose experienced by social activists is one of the less recognized aspects of NGO work (Edwards and Sen 2003), but it is arguably just as crucial for engendering social change and remaking postsocialist citizens as the institutional changes tracked by conventional studies of civil society.

These processes are not easily captured by standard approaches to understanding civil society, which fail to explain the interconnections between political, social, and personal change revealed in these activists' life narratives.[27] Although conventional notions of civil society—as a "democratizing" space where citizens can convene outside the watchful eye of the state, as a mediating force between the individual and the state, or even as an alternative economy— may describe aspects of these activists' experiences and motivations, such formulations cannot encompass the complex intersections of agency, power, and personhood that their stories entail. Analyzing institutional culture, collective action frames, transnational advocacy networks and so on are important for understanding postsocialist civil societies, but we should not lose sight of the human face of the NGO sphere, the individuals who populate it, or their stories. The problem with existing models of civil society, and with many critiques of these models, is that they flatten out the experiences of the people who inhabit this sphere. NGO activists are often reduced to either modern-day Robin Hoods sacrificing themselves for the greater good, or savvy and cynical opportunists playing the civil society game as a stepping stone to bigger and better things. The power of the ethnographic approach is to breathe life into "models" and "sectors" by exploring the lived experiences and life stories of flesh-and-blood actors who engage in NGO work.[28] This provides us with a more nuanced picture of social justice struggles, institutional change, and the effects they have on individual lives.

Studying Over

> When you asked me all those questions, I had to get inside myself, and dig down to things that are sometimes painful to touch. Why? A person tries to avoid all the sharp corners, out of instinct. The need for self-preservation makes him avoid them. And here I had to dig down deep inside. It helped me a lot. It helped me later on, and it helped improve my sense of self [Rus. *samooshchushchenie*], I guess. I confirmed some things for myself, calmed myself about others, and reconciled myself to other things.
>
> —Zoia, summer 2002

Zoia was the director of Lotus, an NGO organized to support persons with spinal cord injuries in the city of Kyiv. As the single mother of a son, Sasha, who injured his spine in an accident as a young teen in the early 1990s, Zoia initially formed the organization as a survival strategy for her own family. During that time, the pension Sasha received as a disabled individual, and the pension Zoia was offered as his caregiver—she left her engineering job to take care of him—was so small that it was not even worth Zoia's time to take a bus across town to collect the money. In conditions of health care collapse, Zoia struggled to organize adequate medical services and secure material assistance for her son and other people with disabilities. She regularly saved lives by intervening in the care given to persons with spinal injuries, especially young people from disadvantaged and troubled backgrounds. These rehabilitation efforts were often enacted as critiques of the state for its disinterest in providing adequate care and support for the disadvantaged. Zoia frequently repeated, "We are carrying out the work of the state. These efforts should be the state's responsibility." Zoia's social activism had spread well beyond Kyiv, and Lotus, in her words, "warmed up" (Rus. *obogrel*) practically all of Ukraine. Zoia happened to live a short walk from the apartment I rented in Kyiv during 1999, and we spent considerable time together. We talked a lot about her NGO work, but we also got together to relax, have fun, and share stories. Some of my fondest memories of fieldwork are our trips to Kyiv's "Bird Market," where Zoia gave away the yawning black kittens her favorite housecat regularly produced. I also cherished eating watermelon on her balcony, and watching a solar eclipse through a special telescope Sasha rigged up.

During the summer of 2002, Zoia reflected upon the life history interviews I had conducted with her during 1998 and 1999. My questions about her life had caused her pain at times—she had been forced to revisit her spoiled marriage, and the tragic accident that nearly killed Sasha and left him in a wheelchair. But she relived happy times as well—her childhood in a Siberian town, her son's precocious boyhood antics, her years as a student and a young bride, and some glorious love affairs. She became interested in her family history (about which she knew very little, since she was from an exile family), and contacted some distant relatives to learn more about her genealogy. My questions about her past led Zoia to pull out all her old black-and-white photographs, which she subsequently scanned so they could be properly preserved. She sent me home with hundreds of digital photos, treasures that adorn the walls of my home. She revisited the poetry she had written during the 1980s and 1990s, and gave me her poems as a "window into her soul." Gifting me her life history had been painful and rewarding for Zoia, and the exercise reverberated for both of us long after our work together was "finished."

Zoia was one of eleven NGO activists with whom I worked closely to gather ethnographic data for this study for one year in 1999 and during follow-up research in 2002, 2003, 2005, and 2006. My attention was drawn to the work of mutual-aid associations and other NGOs during my research on the effects of the 1986 Chernobyl nuclear disaster (Phillips 2002, 2004), and I began to pay more attention to how civic groups and their leaders were stopping up the cracks in the disintegrating social welfare system. After establishing contact with a few NGO directors, I asked informants such as Svetlana and Vira, with whom I had established good relations, to introduce me to other women social activists they knew. I tried to include a broad range of organizations in my study while keeping the number of organizations and key informants manageable. Eventually I settled on ten organizations and eleven activists (the directors and assistant directors of those organizations) as the major sources of information for my project. I chose mainly civic organizations structured as mutual-aid associations; most of the groups had a fixed membership made up of persons and families with common concerns, and they were founded on the city level. This distinguished them from larger regional or all-Ukrainian organizations with no fixed membership, and I hoped that focusing on small city-based organizations would allow me to conduct participant observation more readily. Only two of the ten organizations were founded on a specifically women's platform: Svitanok, which served disabled women, and For Life, made up of women retirees. No high-profile "political wives" (wives of prominent politicians, who head some of the most powerful women's groups in Ukraine) were directly consulted for this book, and the very broad spectrum of civic groups making up Ukraine's "third sector" is not surveyed. In a situation where civic groups might include ecological organizations, sports clubs, associations of dog lovers, anti-abortion activists, veterans of World War II, and neo-Nazi groups, the concentration on "mutual-aid associations" here makes for a relatively narrow focus.

During fieldwork in 1998 and 1999 I visited the offices of various organizations and frequently took part in the groups' activities in order to carry out participant observation with organizations and their memberships as a whole. I also audio-recorded unstructured and semi-structured interviews with the directors and assistant directors of the organizations. Interviews and conversations were conducted in Russian or Ukrainian (and often a combination), depending on informants' language preferences. I translated many of the recorded interviews into English; others were transcribed from the Russian and Ukrainian by assistants. Semi-structured interviews were conducted based on an interview guide or a list of questions and topics that I wanted to cover during the conversation. These interviews were designed to elicit narratives from key informants concerning the history of the organization; the organization's leadership structure, main activities, goals, and plans for the future; the group's networking strategies and relationships with the Ukrainian state, international foundations, and other civic organizations; past and current sources of funding; and the organizers' personal histories of participation in social activism. Another important aspect of my research was the collection of life histories from key informants. These life history interviews were designed to go beyond the period of the women's activism to determine how activism fit into their lives as a whole. Several interviews with American and Ukrainian representatives of international development organizations in Kyiv were conducted (in

English) during the summers of 2002 and 2003. I also gathered information on relevant topics from sources of mass media such as television, newspapers, journals, and the internet, and I also consulted a range of Ukrainian scholarly publications.

The study was complicated by my choice to conduct research in an urban setting among people who, by definition (social activists), were extremely busy. Although I was not studying up in the traditional sense (Nader 1969), I was studying over, to borrow a term introduced by Lisa Markowitz to describe research on the "NGO world" at home and abroad (2001:42). My key informants, all leaders and public figures in some sense, had many demands on their time. Talking to me was often not a top priority for them, so I had to get used to interviews being canceled, put off for weeks at a time, or cut short. One activist, Mariia, was an expert at briskly ending my phone calls before I could arrange a meeting. Once, after we had exchanged our greetings and a few pleasantries, she quickly said, "Okay, then, all the best," and hung up the receiver.

Many days were spent waiting by the phone, answering calls from an activist every few hours who would repeatedly delay our interview because more pressing obligations had come up. Ironically, however, when at times I gave up and neglected to call for a few days or weeks, some informants felt neglected. Because of the constraints on their time, some women were rarely able to engage in the informal get-to-know-you chitchat that has become part and parcel of what I think of as participant observation, especially in Eastern European societies where socializing in the home (often around a table) is often so important to sociality. As I wrote in my field notes, "These are not the tea-drinking type of informants." This meant that I failed to get to know some activists as well as I would have liked, even though I became very close friends with others. I conducted follow-up interviews with several activists during the summers of 2002, 2003, and 2005, and in early 2006 I carried out further interviews with four key informants via telephone and electronic mail.

Although extensive interviews for this study were conducted with eleven NGO activists, in the discussions that follow I focus primarily on the stories of four activists—Svetlana, Ivana, Sofiia, and Maryna—whom I came to know especially well, and whose lives best reflect differentiating processes after socialism as refracted through the NGO sphere and individual women's lives. Although I cannot claim that their lives are representative of the experiences of Soviet women, post-Soviet Ukrainian women, NGO activists, or any other group for that matter, I do believe that these women's stories serve as useful prototypes for the different possible life trajectories of post-Soviet women in general, and social activists in particular. I have thus chosen to unfold my arguments through the little histories of these women, who are such capable guides to the world of NGO organizing and the politics of differentiation. Admittedly, their contrasting stories and differential success in making claims and forging successful career paths bring the politics of differentiation into especially vivid relief, at the risk of masking the middle ground and downplaying the many ambiguities and contradictions of the "transition." This is a risk I am willing to take in order to present these women's stories, which are an important chapter in the saga of "democratization" in postsocialist Ukraine.

In chapter 1, I invite readers on a walking tour of Kyiv, and I outline Ukraine's history and contemporary political economy to situate the lives of the NGO activists whom we shall get to know. Their experiences are further contextualized in discussions of women in Ukraine during and after socialism, especially in terms of work, social welfare, and politics.

In chapter 2, Maryna ushers us into the world of NGO organizing and helps us explore the post-Soviet "NGO boom," or the rapid expansion of civic organizing in Ukraine. We examine the history of women's organizing in Soviet and post-Soviet Ukraine, and I invite readers along to a "training" seminar on women and leadership as an example of international NGO development interventions to promote women's civic organizing. Ivana also guides us through these interventions as we examine the ideologies on gender, leadership, and individualization that mark and mobilize differentiating processes in the transnational NGO advocacy sector.

Maryna, Vira, and Sofiia are profiled in chapter 3 on claims and class. Their stories are indicative of new forms of class differentiation in Ukraine, and they shed light on the shifting definitions of "needs" and entitlement in postsocialism.

In chapter 4, we follow Ivana through the twists and turns of her career, in an exploration of the upward mobility that NGO leadership offers some women. Ivana's life history reveals the various factors that have shaped her worldview and life strategies, not least among them ideologies of women's empowerment, self-reliance, and positive thinking. The stories of all these women are revisited in the final chapter, the conclusion.

"If we don't do it for ourselves, who will?"

September 24, 1999

"There's a saying: 'I started making soup but I ended up with something else,'" laughs Sofiia, as she looks across the table at me with her piercing blue eyes. I'm relieved that Sofiia turned out to be so warm and approachable; during our initial conversation over the phone she came across as a real tough cookie. As I sat cross-legged on the brownish-orange carpet in the apartment I'd rented in Kyiv, holding the receiver to my ear with my shoulder and furiously scribbling down notes, Sofiia grilled me for half an hour about my research plans. She made it clear that if she were to participate in my research that she would expect something from me in return. I was reminded of Basha from *Number Our Days* who asked Barbara Myerhoff (1978), upon meeting her at the Jewish Community Center, "So what do you want with us here?" Basha quickly followed this with another question: "And what will you do for us?" Myerhoff offered to teach a class; I offered to translate documents and letters into English, to videotape the organization's events for their archives, and to try to make myself generally useful.

Sofiia was born in 1937 in a small village in Central Ukraine, in the Pale of Settlement, making her sixty-three years old when I first met her in 1999.[29] She never knew her father, who disappeared during Stalin's terror when Sofiia was an infant.[30] Before World War II, 82 percent of the village's population was Jews; by war's end the number of Jews was estimated at less than 1 percent. One of Sofiia's most vivid memories is fleeing with her mother during the war—mostly on foot—to reach a safe haven with relatives in Siberia. Her grandparents stayed in the village; they said they were "in good relations with everyone" and did not fear for their lives. They were shot with eight hundred other Jews in a forest near the village and buried in a pit they had been forced to dig themselves. After the war Sofiia and her mother returned to live in the village, and Sofiia remembers walking around the forest and stumbling upon bones, traces of her fellow villagers. Foxes had dug up and eaten the remains, leaving bones strewn throughout the woods. "We walked through the forest and my mother would point them out: There's a leg, there's a finger." Were the scattered bones of her grandparents right under their feet? Sofiia wondered.

When Sofiia was in fourth grade she and her mother moved to Kyiv. As a Jew, Sofiia's mother was denied employment in the city proper, so she traveled to a town outside the city every day where she worked as a janitress. Sofiia moved back to Kyiv as an adult, after studying at a technical institute in Siberia, and has lived there ever since. She never married and has no children; Sofiia describes herself as *odinokaia*, a Russian word that can be translated either as "single" or "lonely." Sofiia had been active in the Communist Party, and she served as Trade Union representative at her place of work, but she never rose very high in the Party ranks. She attributes this to two factors: her unwillingness to "act as a doormat" for other people; and her "data," meaning that her "nationality" was considered to be Jewish.[31] She frequently describes ways in which she has been discriminated against because of her "data," especially in terms of education and employment.

After reading in a Kyiv newspaper about the NGO Sofiia founded to protect the interests of elderly women, I expected her to be "grandmotherly." Though neither a grandmother nor a mother, for that matter, she is a born organizer who knows what she wants. The "soup" she referred to is her NGO, For Life, which began in 1988 (when she was fifty-one years old and still working as an accountant), with Sofiia doing a few good deeds for individual lonely retirees. I ask her to recall that time and think about her reasons for becoming involved in pensioners' affairs. She answers quickly: "I didn't like the way the elderly were being treated, by both the government and the population at large. And I told myself, 'You are going to be old one day, too. So if you don't like how the elderly are treated now, change it!'" She believed that a formal organization was needed to address the increasing marginalization of the elderly, who were becoming impoverished and ill as a result of government reform and the economic crises sparked by perestroika (Gorbachev's plan for "restructuring"). And she added:

> Conditions for pensioners have steadily worsened since perestroika and independence. The monthly pension I've received since I retired in 1995 has gotten smaller and smaller. In 1995, $1 was worth 65 kopecks. I had a pension of 120 [rubles], which was $200. Today the exchange rate is $1 to 5.18 hryvnias.[32] So if my pension is 106 [hryvnias], that means I get $25. Do you see the difference? The goal of our fund is to teach these women to hold their heads up, to refuse to be brought to their knees. To be able to say: "I deserve better."

Sofiia began attracting her friends to the cause, and she also became involved in a Jewish organization in the capital city. When she left that group over conflicts with the leadership about keeping kosher and observing ritual practice (Sofiia did not), and the way women in the organization were treated, several of her female friends left with her. Sofiia, along with her friends, registered For Life, a charitable organization whose membership in 1999 hovered around 150. All the members were at least fifty-five years old (the retirement age for women in Ukraine), and 90 percent were women.[33] "We have a core collective of twenty-five or thirty women," Sofiia explains. "Most of them have been through training courses and are certified volunteers. These are the women who attend weekly meetings and help me with the real work of the organization."

I glance around the office, a small room crammed with several tables, an assortment of mismatched chairs, and a makeshift bookshelf that groans under the weight of myriad vases, books, knickknacks, and a samovar. For Life clearly needs more space—how could twenty-five women possibly fit comfortably in this small room? As if reading my mind, Sofiia continues: "I stood in line at the Kyiv City State Administration (*DerzhAdmin*) every day for seven months until they bequeathed us this office." Now she has assumed a new task—to persuade the city government to grant the organization larger premises. To this end, Sofiia has addressed Mayor Omelchenko and President Kuchma by letter. So far, no response.

Some of the NGO's activities center on procuring humanitarian aid for members in the form of food, clothing, and medicines, but Sofiia clearly prefers to emphasize the group's mission to stimulate pensioners to remain independent and pursue an "active" lifestyle. I take note of a hand-painted banner that stretches across one wall of the office. Emblazoned across it in Ukrainian in bright blue, capital letters is the slogan, "If we don't do it for ourselves, who will?"[34] In addition to weekly business meetings, Sofiia organizes lecture series, art classes, and excursions for members, as well as musical events and monthly birthday celebrations. Sofiia also stresses the importance of providing "social defense" for the group's members, defense she characterizes as material, psychological, physical, and legal in nature. Members tirelessly engage in letter-writing campaigns and other lobbying efforts, and they brief one another on legislation in the pipeline that will affect the lives of retirees.

I notice a poster commemorating 1999 as the United Nations "Year of the

Figure 3. "Kindred souls." An elderly woman asks for alms in Kyiv's Podil district, 1990. Photo by Bruno Rachkovski.

Elderly" hanging on the back of the door, which Sofiia has pulled shut to insulate us from the noise of people talking loudly in the hallway. Sofiia quips: "To designate just one year to honor the elderly, well, it seems pretty pitiful to me." She informs me that For Life was recently approved for a $20,000 grant from the UN, which will allow the group to take care of members' personal needs (eyeglasses, prescriptions, food), update office technology (install a telephone, fax, television and VCR, scanner, photocopier, and new office furniture), and, most important, establish a volunteer center to train volunteers to provide services to Kyiv's elderly population. I ask Sofiia whether she feels that elderly persons are discriminated against by the Ukrainian state. "What kind of question is that? That is why I am constantly in bad relations with them." "With whom?" I ask. "With the men in power. The government calls us *nakhlebniki* [Rus., beggars, literally "people who beg for bread money"]. Bureaucrats are notorious for their abuse of the elderly." Her characterization indicates that the elderly are abused because they draw on an ideology of entitlement, one that is construed as outdated and Soviet. I recall a conversation I had with a Ukrainian colleague a few days ago. This man (no youngster himself) commented that the population of Kyiv is dominated by elderly pensioners (many of them military veterans) who tend to be "conservative," and who vote for the Communist Party in elections. He said, "This is what is keeping us out of Europe; this is what is holding up our progress toward becoming a democratic society." Elderly people, it seemed, were seen by many as synonymous with an outdated socialist ideology and way of life. Sofiia would have none of this. As I turned to leave, she handed me a printed invitation: "You come to the special event we are holding in two weeks' time. It is called 'My Years, My Wealth,' and it's an opportunity for our girls [her fellow retirees] to reflect on their life's accomplishments. We are inviting government officials, and we will prove to them that the elderly do not eat bread in vain. We are going to teach them that they must bow to each elderly person who walks by." I promise to be there, video camera in hand.

January 15, 2000
Dear Sarochka,
   Happy New Year! Has anyone written you yet during this millennium? Wishing you all the best days and years of your life . . . I'm finishing up my treatments at a sanatorium, near Uzhhorod. There's excellent mineral water here but I'm only taking a few treatments on the orders of my cardiologist in Kyiv . . . What else is new? We are fighting to keep our office. If only one project would go through, I'd be happy. Maybe we don't know the people on the grant committees well enough? Where we do have contacts, no one is interested in the theme of old age, and we didn't even get an answer from the agencies where we did send applications. So far we haven't been able to find a long term and reliable sponsor. . . .
   We are dealing with the most sensitive issue, and the less prestigious. No one wants to be old (when people look at us they see themselves in

the not-too-distant future) or to defend the elderly. I refuse to give up. If I am able to implement just one positive change in the state's treatment of the elderly, I will feel that I have done my part. . . .

Best wishes for the holidays from all the women at For Life.

Sofiia

April 27, 2002
Dear Sarochka!

All best wishes to you and your family. I received your letter when I got out of the hospital. I read it aloud at our last meeting. There was so much to do, and we were trying to do it all before the elections, so I didn't have time to get my thoughts together and answer you right away. Now about us, your favorite ones [Rus. *Teper' o nas liubimykh*]. . . . Our new office is in the center of Kyiv, and it's twice as big as the old one. It has a good aura. You'll see it when you visit this summer. . . .

We didn't create the volunteer center. There's a big, nonsensical battle going on. Two organizations that don't even have their own volunteers, and have never worked with volunteers, but who do have powerful connections and financial resources, announced to Ukraine and the world that they are founding a center for volunteers. . . . Meanwhile we continue to work from our own experience and, unfortunately, without money. . . .

Elderly people can only be active, and tackle their personal problems and the problems of old age in general, in their own united collective. That's the only place they can feel like they still have strength. The work we do gives people their health back, and renews their energy. It's hard to get people going when they've been stripped of their will, and taught to sit and wait while others make decisions for them and give them what they need. But there are those energetic individuals—natural born leaders—who get inspired and really take to it. But the state still doesn't recognize our work, and looks down on us. Even so, it is so rewarding to see people's eyes starting to wake up, starting to shine. . . .

Hello from the girl-activists [Rus. *Privet ot devochek-fondovtsev*].

Sofiia

1 All Aboard the "Titanic Ukraina"

Kyiv, the Heart of Ukraine

To understand the lives of women like Ivana, Svetlana, Vira, and Sofiia, we first need to become familiar with the settings in which they lived and worked. Kyiv is Ukraine's capital city of around 2.6 million situated on both banks of the Dnipro River, Ukraine's largest waterway. Kyiv is the political and commercial heart of Ukraine and by far the largest city. Much of the world came to know Kyiv through compelling images of the Maidan Nezalezhnosti, or Independence Square, where up to a million protestors weathered the winter cold for seventeen days to challenge election fraud during the 2004 presidential elections. Media coverage of the Orange Revolution captured the sea of orange-clad and beribboned protestors, and the "tent city" where some protestors camped out, as well as the strange amalgam of built structures that make Kyiv a city of contrasts: ancient monasteries and churches, low-slung pre-Soviet buildings (former private homes of merchants and other local elites), imposing Stalinist structures, towering high-rise cookie-cutter apartment buildings, and the maze of statues, monuments, fountains, and other structures that now litter Independence Square.

Revolution or not, Independence Square (formerly Lenin Square) is always bustling with people. Located in the heart of the city center, the square is a hub for shopping, access to services such as Kyiv's main post office, and tourism. The square is bisected by Khreshchatyk, the wide street that has been Kyiv's main downtown thoroughfare for the last hundred years. Most of the street was destroyed during the Nazi occupation of Kyiv in World War II—only one block survived—but it was rebuilt by the city's residents. One side of the square is flanked by five tall Stalinist buildings, former apartment buildings and sites of government that now also sport stores, restaurants, and hotels, and are bedecked with neon advertisements for beer, banks, and construction companies. Narrow streets snake past each of these buildings, ascending up a steep hill to connect the Maidan with an equally grand venue—Sofiia Square, which boasts the ancient St. Sofiia's Cathedral at one end and the newly reconstructed St. Michael's monastery at the other. A beautiful yellow two-story prerevolutionary building stretches along the square. One of my friends lived in a communal apartment here in 1995 when I first visited Kyiv, but a few years later all the residents had been "bought out." Developers offered families private apartments (and more square meters) in other parts of the city, and the communal apartments were turned into offices and stores. In the middle of Sofiia Square stands a bronze monument (completed in 1888 by Mikhail

Mikeshin) to Bohdan Khmel'nyts'kyi, who led the Zaporozhian Sich (Cossacks) in the 1648 Ukrainian uprising against the Poles, and through the 1654 Pereiaslav Agreement, accepted the Muscovite tsar's overlordship of Ukraine. The Hetman's mace in his hand still points toward Moscow. (Khmel'nyts'kyi's legacy is debated by Ukrainians; some see him as a great liberator who roused Ukrainians to national statehood, whereas others mourn Muscovy's subsequent domination of Ukrainian lands.) Nearby is a monument to the saints of ancient Rus'—Saints Cyril and Methodius (inventors of the Cyrillic alphabet) and Andrew the Apostle flank Olha, the first Christian ruler of Rus'. Turning left from the square onto a small side street, one passes several foreign embassies behind dark-paned security booths, as well as a state-run newspaper stand. After navigating a busy crosswalk, the street widens slightly and accommodates outdoor cafes with small umbrella-covered tables, where city dwellers and visitors to the city drink beer, soda, and vodka with snacks such as nuts, chips, and open-faced sandwiches. Further along the cobblestone street, which winds and descends down a steep hill, are street vendors selling original artwork, jewelry, handmade souvenirs (wooden spoons, embroidered Ukrainian blouses and towels, painted nesting dolls), Soviet watches and coins, propaganda posters, Che Guevara T-shirts, and many other treasures. This is Andriyivskyi uzviz (Andrew's descent), familiar to tourists as the quaint "historical street" leading down to Kyiv's Podil district, one of Kyiv's oldest neighborhoods. Located on the banks of the Dnipro river, the Podil was the birthplace of industry and trade in the city. In times past, Andriyivskyi uzviz was a creative center of Kyiv, and many famous writers and other cultural figures lived here, including the writer Mikhail Bulgakov, the cinema director Ivan Kavaleridze, and the medical professor Theofil Yanovsky.

Back on the Maidan, one can cross Khreshchatyk Street to access the other half of the square. This was once the site of a gigantic statue of Lenin, situated in the foreground of the towering Ukraina hotel. The statue, which was built directly into the largest and busiest subway station in Kyiv in 1946, was defaced during the failed putsch of August 1991 and was subsequently removed. This part of the square still sports a cascading fountain where, in the summertime, hot and tired walkers might dip their feet, as well as several newly erected statues depicting images from Ukrainian folklore. At the far end is an elaborate mirrored entrance to a new shopping mall. Most of the two-story shopping center is located underground, accessible via several entrances from the Maidan itself and from the smoky and close passages that connect the square to the Maidan Nezalezhnosti subway station. Such underground shopping venues now proliferate in the city, where practically every subterranean street crossing is jam-packed with kiosks, street vendors, and high-end shops. The underground passages around the Maidan are particularly busy with street musicians, panhandlers, and other entrepreneurs targeting Ukrainian and foreign tourists. Young Roma women hold babies and ask for money; elderly men and women collect coins in worn-out caps and sell small bouquets of homegrown and wild flowers secured with lengths of thread. Nuns singing hymns hold out collection boxes adorned with icons and Orthodox crosses; students from the nearby Kyiv Conservatory entertain passers-by with a lively jazz tune. Street-corner capitalists offer everything from furniture suites to shower caps, and the homeless and destitute reveal horrible sores and bloody cracked feet as they ask for alms. One elderly woman dressed all in black with huge plastic eyeglasses holds a sign reading, "Donate money for my coffin." Another woman's sign says, "My son is in prison. He is dying of tuberculosis. Please help save his life!"

Back outside, the wide Khreshchatyk Street, lined with chestnut trees and imposing Stalinist buildings—home to state institutions (such as the Kyiv City Administration building), stores (the huge Soviet-era mall called the TsUM, or Central Universal Store), and the residences of former and current government and cultural elites—leads to the famous and colorful indoor Besarabs'kyi market (commonly called the Besarabka). Here the prosperous shopper can buy pomegranates from the southern Caucasus, sturgeon from northern Russia, and everything else in between. Opposite the Besarabka stands the only remaining statue of Lenin in Kyiv (and one of the few left standing in Ukraine), whose pedestal is often adorned with bouquets of red and white flowers, offerings from those who mourn the downfall of communism.

On weekends and holidays, Khreshchatyk is closed to traffic and is transformed into a wide pedestrian street filled with vendors, street performers, and people on a stroll. Walking to the other end of the street brings one to a viewing area overlooking the Dnipro River, presided over by a huge monument to "People's Friendship." It is a huge silver-hued arc reminiscent of a steel rainbow that stretches over the plaza, under which stand two muscular men holding a banner decorated with the Soviet star, crest, and hammer and sickle. In both Russian and Ukrainian the pedestal used to read, "In celebration of the unification of Ukraine with Russia." "With Russia" has been scratched out.[1] From here one can look across the Dnipro to the Left Bank, a newer district of the city where uniform concrete apartment buildings stretch on and on out of sight. The plaza also offers access, through a series of stone stairways, to one of the city's many parks and outdoor concert venues. Indeed, Kyiv boasts forty-one natural and artificial forest-parks and parks, and Kyivans claim that their city is one of the five "greenest" in Europe. Meandering through the series of parks brings us to the building of the Ukrainian Parliament and the sky-blue, baroque-style Mariyins'kyi Palace, designed by Bartolomeo Rastrelli and constructed in 1750–55.

Although the social activists I knew in Kyiv enjoyed strolling around the city center when they had a snatch of free time, most did not live in the fashionable central and historical districts. They were more likely to live in newer (but less well kept), more affordable areas far from the city center, such as Sviatoshyn, at the extreme west end of one of the city's three subway lines, or in the Left Bank neighborhoods of Darnytsia, or the rather desolate Kharkivs'kyi masyv ("housing unit"). Some lived in *khrushchovky*—five-story buildings that were mass-produced, and hastily and poorly constructed, as "temporary" housing during Krushchev's housing reforms of the 1960s and never vacated; others

Figure 4. Entrance to Teatral'na subway station in Kyiv, with a view down to Khreshchatyk, 2005. Photo by Paul Thacker.

lived in the high-rise, nondescript and indistinguishable concrete apartment buildings ubiquitous in the former Soviet Union. Their living conditions varied, but many of my acquaintances' apartments were in a constant state of *remont* (repair)—some were involved in necessary maintenance such as replacing outdated and faulty plumbing, patching old wood floors, and making cosmetic renovations such as painting and hanging new wallpaper. Others with more means tore down walls, installed new appliances, and remodeled bathrooms. All my informants owned their apartments—they had received them from the state during the Soviet period and had "privatized" them after Ukrainian independence in 1991—but it was also common for people to rent apartments, especially newcomers to the city. The high and ever-rising cost of apartments in Kyiv meant that grown children often lived at home and started their own families there, which made for some very crowded living spaces.[2]

My friend Lidiia's experience was quite typical: Lidiia and her husband had been separated for some years, and in the late 1990s she lived with her teenage son, Myron, in a cramped one-room apartment (consisting of a living room, a tiny kitchen, and a toilet). There was hardly room to turn around, as the apart-

Figure 5. Kyiv, city of contrasts. Photo by author.

ment measured a mere 26 square meters. In the living room Lidiia and Myron had managed to cram two pull-out couches, a wardrobe, a table, a computer and chair, and two large bookshelves. The only space left for Myron's collapsible bicycle was a corner of the small toilet—it hung from the ceiling over the commode. Lidiia spent three hours a day in public transport making her way to and from work at a research institute. She had to use three kinds of transport—the tram, the subway, and finally a bus. "I devote that time to the transport God," she laughed. In 1998, Lidiia's meager salary was $45 a month, but she only received about $15 a month because of the funding crisis in Ukraine's research and development sector. A full half of this amount went to pay for public transport to and from work. So Lidiia took on odd jobs tutoring and teaching piano lessons to support herself and her son.

Lidiia's experience of sudden poverty was common for many in Ukraine during the 1990s, when economic crisis gripped the newly independent country. In 1990 and 1991, runaway inflation caused many in Ukraine (including Lidiia) to lose their entire life savings in only a few short weeks. From the early 1990s until 2000 the Ukrainian economy was in shambles, with persistent declines in real

GDP and surging inflation of at least 10 percent per year (including an unfathomable inflation rate of about 10,250 percent in 1993) (Kravchuk 2002:3). Poverty in Ukraine increased from 2 percent in 1987–88 to 63 percent in 1993–95 (Milanovic 1998). The country's economy worsened steadily during the 1990s, and Ukrainians were dealt a second blow in the fall of 1998 by a worldwide economic dip that resulted in a devaluation of the Ukrainian currency of nearly 60 percent (D'Anieri, Kravchuk, and Kuzio 1999:202). The crumbling of state socialism spurred the disintegration of the Soviet-era pillars of social support for citizens, such as guaranteed employment and social inclusion, subsidized prices, free high-quality medical care, and enterprise-based social welfare benefits (Iatridis 2000:4). In 1991, there were only sixty-eight hundred registered unemployed in Ukraine, but the number of official unemployed had risen to more than a million by the end of 1998 (Kravchuk 2002:26). Three-quarters of the unemployed are women, and Svetlana's experience of the economic crisis and sudden unemployment was typical for many women in Ukraine after the fall of socialism.

Before perestroika and Ukrainian independence, Svetlana worked at a factory and supported herself and her three children single-handedly. In the economic crash of the early 1990s, however, she lost her entire life savings of 3,000 rubles, money she had saved to secure the future of her three children, whose fathers had abandoned them.[3] At that time she was on maternity leave with her youngest daughter and subsequently was made redundant at the factory. Without a job or her savings, her situation deteriorated quickly. Svetlana often recounted the difficulties of living with her three children in a one-room apartment; they all slept together on a pull-out couch. On several occasions Svetlana described her living conditions to me, but she did not invite me to visit her apartment. I understood that she was embarrassed, fearing judgment from a relatively well-off foreigner. By 1999 she had sold most of her furniture, leaving only a bureau she had found at a secondhand store, a worn divan, a refrigerator, and an old television on the floor. Svetlana blamed the postsocialist transition not only for turning all the money she had saved into "soap bubbles" but also for wounding her sense of social worth as a mother and a worker, transforming her almost overnight into a marginalized person. Recalling the tumultuous economic crisis of the early 1990s, Svetlana once said:

> My money turned into trash, and I became destitute . . . I was hysterical. I lost consciousness. My heart began to hurt, and I lost the feeling in my arm, from terror. And then I told myself . . . I always get scared, but I survive somehow. I'm not going to get scared anymore. I will just live. And when we had the opportunity, we [families with many children] united together, because we were all in an identical situation: we became destitute all at once. It was a widespread hysteria. Not only large families, but everyone in the country—we were all in hysterics.

Svetlana thus criticized the government's failure to take responsibility for its citizens, argued for the importance of strategies of collective action, and described her own somatization of social crisis (heart pains, a numb arm). She repeated the self-descriptor "destitute" several times, indicating what a blow sudden impoverishment was to her sense of self-worth. Although one goal of Svetlana's civic organizing was to ensure the survival of impoverished families like her own by procuring humanitarian aid, she also strove to reeducate Ukrainian bureaucrats and the public about the social worth of large families. Socialist collapse in Ukraine produced economic crises and social suffering that made the work of mutual-aid associations and other charitable groups especially necessary, and it was in response to these economic and social crises that the women activists I knew had joined and organized NGOs to support vulnerable groups that were most affected—large families, single mothers, retirees, and the disabled and chronically ill. These efforts are taking place in a country with a long history of social turmoil and political instability, a context that must be understood before post-Soviet women's social activism can be put in proper perspective.

Shifting Terrain: From Ukrainian Independence to the Orange Revolution and Beyond

In some interpretations, the literal meaning of *Ukraina* is "borderland," a notion that describes well the nature of the historic geographical and geopolitical positioning of Ukrainian lands. Serving as a frontier between east and west and north and south, Ukraine has historically been an important center of trade. During the height of Kyivan Rus' (980–1132), Ukrainian lands lay along strategic trade routes between centers such as Constantinople and the cities of Rus' to the north. During the twelfth and thirteenth centuries the city of Kyiv was part of the Krakow-Prague-Regensburg trade route (Subtelny 1994:47).[4] The area's strategic position made its peoples susceptible to conquest by competing groups. The frequency with which Ukrainian lands have been occupied by non-native peoples has prompted the historian Orest Subtelny to refer to Ukrainians as a "historically stateless people who have been locked in quasi-colonial relations with outside ruling powers throughout history" (1994:xiii). Areas of contemporary Ukraine have been claimed variously by Greeks, Ottomans, Tatars, Poles, Lithuanians, and Russians.

Until the fall of the Soviet Union in the early 1990s, Ukraine was one of the fifteen republics that comprised the Soviet Empire (1921–91 for central and eastern Ukraine; 1939–91 for the western Ukrainian territory of Galicia). Like people in all the Soviet republics, inhabitants of Ukraine were subjected to a program of "Russification." This included an educational system designed to inculcate a Soviet consciousness in all citizens of the Soviet Union through a Russian-oriented curriculum that was standardized and highly politicized. The Ukrainian Soviet Socialist Republic was given certain privileges by its Russian "big brother" (Ukrainians have been referred to widely as "Little Russians") but remained "second among equals" (Lewytzkyj 1984:5). As Catherine Wanner notes when describing the Soviet educational system, "The second-class treatment that national and local cultures often received in Soviet curricula triggered

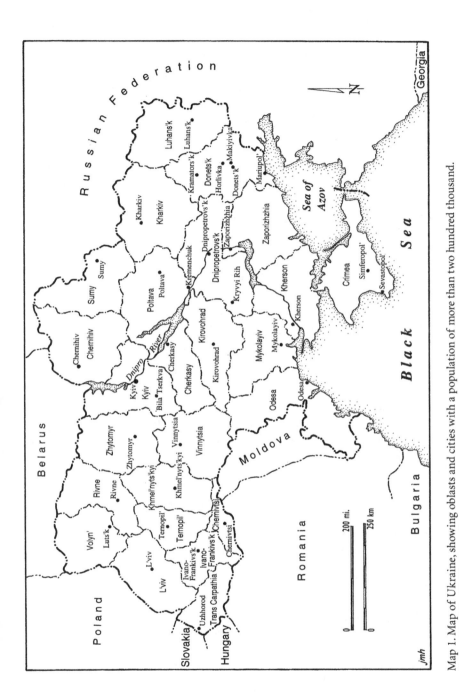

Map 1. Map of Ukraine, showing oblasts and cities with a population of more than two hundred thousand. Created by John Hollingsworth.

alienation, a poignant awareness of otherness, and often a sharp politicization of ethnicity" (1998:81). When Gorbachev's policy of glasnost, or "openness," made criticism of the Soviet system possible in the late 1980s, "this reservoir of ethnic resentment, long percolating among certain groups or among certain sectors, such as the intelligentsia, flooded the political scene in the late 1980s once weaknesses in Soviet power were detected" (Wanner 1998:81).

In this atmosphere of discontent (and also in response to the 1986 Chernobyl disaster) the Popular Movement for Restructuring in Ukraine (Rukh) was organized in 1989. Rukh's program centered on upholding the sovereignty of the Ukrainian republic; promoting the Ukrainian language and culture; focusing on ecological issues; and democratizing the social, political, and economic systems. Opposition parties also began to form in the late 1980s, namely, the Ukrainian Democratic Union (which later became the Ukrainian People's Democratic League), and the Ukrainian Christian Democratic Front. The Ukrainian Language Society and the Writers Union of Ukraine were also dedicated to raising Ukrainian national consciousness during this period. After the 1991 Moscow Coup, Ukrainian independence was declared on August 24, 1991, an act that was sealed by a national plebiscite on December 1 of the same year in which 90 percent voted in favor. At the same time, Leonid Kravchuk was elected as independent Ukraine's first president. Kravchuk adopted many of Rukh's programs of Ukrainianization in culture and education but failed to initiate far-reaching political or economic reforms. He did not dissolve the existing (Soviet) Parliament, did not ban the Communist Party, and operated through elite bargaining and divide and conquer in a neo-Soviet style of politics (Wilson 2005b:36). In early elections in 1994, Kravchuk was defeated by the former prime minister Leonid Kuchma, who finally launched Ukraine's first program of economic reform. However, large-scale privatization of national assets in Ukraine, which only got under way in the late 1990s, was a corrupt affair and resulted in the emergence of regional clans of oligarchs who continue to control Ukraine's major industries and media outlets. Kuchma was elected for a second term in 1999, even though during his presidency the country's economy worsened considerably, corruption at all levels was rampant, and the industrial sector stagnated. In 2001, his administration was further marred by a scandal involving the murder of journalist Hryhorii Gongadze, the editor of an internet newspaper (www.pravda.com.ua) who filed an exposé about one of Kuchma's close allies, Oleksandr Volkov. Gongadze's decapitated body was found and identified in early 2001, and Major Mykola Melnychenko, an officer in Kuchma's Security Service, reported that he had secretly taped conversations taking place in Kuchma's office implicating him in Gongadze's murder. At the time of writing, "Kuchmagate" has still not been resolved.

Meanwhile, in 2000, Viktor Yushchenko, the former head of the Ukrainian National Bank, was appointed prime minister and presided over the first successful economic reforms in independent Ukraine. In December 2004, in a dramatic election that went three rounds and was sustained by seventeen days of protest that have come to be known as the Orange Revolution, Yushchenko defeated Kuchma's (and Russian President Vladimir Putin's) hand-picked successor, Viktor Yanukovych, to become Ukraine's third president. For a time, the events of the 2004 Orange Revolution fueled scholarly discussions about the relative strength of Ukraine's civil society and the triumph of democracy in the beleaguered country, but the unraveling of the Orange coalition, ongoing political turmoil, and widespread dissatisfaction with Yushchenko's performance dampened this optimism. The Orange Revolution does appear, however, to have had a galvanizing effect for many in Ukraine, who now see themselves as capable of organizing for political change and ousting corrupt regimes. It signaled real hope for some that they might finally disembark from the "Titanic Ukraina," the tongue-in-cheek axiom of popular comedian Andrii Danylko (as his popular character, the brusque yet loveable train car attendant Verka Serduchka) that seems all too apt in light of the multiple crises that have plagued the country since independence in 1991.

The post–Orange Revolution period has been one of continued political turmoil. Yushchenko's popular co-revolutionary, Yuliia Tymoshenko, became prime minister in early 2005, but her government was dismissed in September 2005. In preparation for the 2006 parliamentary elections, Tymoshenko organized the Bloc of Yuliia Tymoshenko (BYuT). Even though her party received 22 percent of the vote, her aspirations to regain the position of prime minister were foiled when the Orange coalition fell apart, a majority coalition (Coalition of National Unity) was formed by the Party of Regions and other parties, and Viktor Yanukovych was sworn in as prime minister. Eight months of power struggles between President Yushchenko and Parliament ensued. The political crisis peaked when Yushchenko dissolved Parliament in April 2007 and called for early elections, which took place in September 2007. As the only major opposition party, Tymoshenko's BYuT received an impressive 30 percent of the vote, and in October 2007 it seemed likely that Tymoshenko would again assume the post of prime minister.

Ukraine is the largest country in Europe after Russia, occupying 603,700 square kilometers (233,090 square miles). The country is divided into twenty-five oblasts (provinces) plus the autonomous republic of Crimea. The major industrial centers are all located in the eastern part of the country, and include Kharkiv, Dnipropetrovs'k, Donets'k, Luhans'k, Zaporizhzhia, and Kryvyi Rih. Mykolaiv, Kherson, and Odesa are port cities; Sevastopol' is the home of the Black Sea Fleet; and formerly Hapsburg L'viv is Ukraine's westernmost city. Ukraine shares borders with eight other nation-states: the Russian Federation, Belarus, Poland, Slovakia, Hungary, Romania, Moldova, and Bulgaria. According to the 2001 census, Ukraine's population is around 47 million, a decline of more than 6 percent since the 1989 census. This ongoing population decrease is the result of low birth rates (according to one study, between 1989 and 1996 the birth rate fell an incredible 31.6 percent [Steshenko 1997:17]), high mortality, and out-migration. The ethnic makeup of the permanent inhabitants of Ukraine includes mainly those who consider themselves Ukrainian (78 percent); of these, 44 percent speak Ukrainian, and 30 percent Russian (Wolczuk

2000:673). Seventeen percent of the population self-identifies as ethnically Russian and is Russian-speaking. Although 0.9 percent of the population identified as Jewish in the 1989 census, this percentage had declined to 0.2 percent by 2001. Other groups represented in Ukraine include Belarusians, Moldovans, Bulgarians, Poles, Hungarians, Romanians, Greeks, Roma, Crimean Tatars, and Armenians, as well as significant numbers of immigrants from Afghanistan, China, Vietnam, and other countries.[5] Immigration into Ukraine, however, has been confined mainly to ethnic Ukrainians who have been residing in the near abroad (especially Russia) (90 percent of immigrants in 1993); returning ethnic deportees such as Crimean Tatars; and asylum seekers from war-torn areas such as Azerbaijan, the Transnistria, and Chechnya (Frejka, Okólski, and Sword 1999).

The population of Ukraine is extremely mobile, and internal migration, migration between Ukraine and the successor states of the former Soviet Union, and international migration are common. Economic hardship has motivated migration and emigration of Ukrainians to Western Europe and North America, causing a "brain drain" of scientists, skilled workers, and others. Temporary migration is also common, since there are relatively lax border controls between Ukraine and neighboring countries (i.e., Russia, Poland, the Czech Republic, and the Slovak Republic), and many Ukrainians travel to these countries for temporary work and for trading. In 2001, the National Institute of Ukrainian-Russian Relations estimated that three hundred thousand Ukrainians were working in Russia alone (Libanova 2001). Although traveling for work to countries that are members of the European Union (starting with neighboring Poland) is becoming more difficult, it is still common. During 2005, I visited a small town in Western Ukraine and was told that at least half the town's residents were currently working abroad. Men typically held construction jobs in Russia, and women were employed as caregivers for children and the elderly in Italy and Portugal.

Since Ukrainian independence, the residents of Ukraine have been struggling to forge a national identity.[6] During the Soviet era, ambiguities in national identity, ethnicity, and language use could be subsumed under collective membership in the broader category of the "Soviet people." Today, the erosion of cultural and linguistic barriers between Ukrainians and Russians poses a formidable challenge to fashioning a seamless Ukrainian national identity. Regional divides have threatened the national idea even further, as the country is comprised of four areas (north, south, east, and west) with distinct histories and complicated linguistic and cultural differences. Tensions between the highly Russified and industrialized East (including the mining center of Donets'k and the steel and chemical-producing center of Dnipropetrovs'k) and the historical Hapsburg region of Galicia (including L'viv, Ternopil', and Ivano-Frankivs'k) are often emphasized in popular and scholarly discussions, and these tensions frequently are framed in terms of "two Ukraines" (Riabchuk 1992). Regional tensions became even more apparent during the contested 2004 presidential election and the Orange Revolution, with Western and Central Ukraine showing strong support for Viktor Yushchenko and his political party Our Ukraine, and much of Eastern and Southern Ukraine backing Viktor Yanukovych and the Party of Regions. But supporters of the Orange (Yushchenko) and Blue (Yanukovych) camps during the 2004 presidential elections were not always neatly divided along regional lines, and the events of the Orange Revolution served as a unifying factor for many, resulting in a certain ambiguous community of protestors from different ethnic, class, religious, and linguistic backgrounds. Regional divisions did come to a head when members of the Yanukovych camp met and proposed a referendum on the federalization of Ukraine. The specter of federalism dissipated when Yushchenko and Yanukovych reached a compromise in early 2005, but for a time the threat of the country's splitting into "two Ukraines" seemed real to many. However, Ukraine's internal ethnic, linguistic, and religious diversity, as well as variation in local and regional histories, make for more complex negotiations of identity than the frame of "two Ukraines" allows.

It is in this complicated context that political and cultural elites have sought out national symbols to unite the people of Ukraine. The goals of such articulations are manifold: to simultaneously imbue the citizenry with a unifying historical consciousness and submerge internal divisions in the "nation," to replace the previous supra-national Soviet community, and to nurture the aspirations of Ukrainians to reconnect with a European identity (Wolczuk 2000). The search for national symbols is manifest in many venues, including the changing cityscape of Kyiv, where architectural renovations tangibly reflect the combination of historicizing and modernizing projects that the ruling elite in Ukraine have articulated in recent years.[7] Kyiv's Independence Square is a particularly good example of how Ukrainians are looking to both the past and the future for unifying symbols. On the one hand, several new monuments erected since 2000 seem to freeze time in the mythical Ukrainian past. These include the Oranta-Berehynia (a Ukrainian Earth Mother), whose angel-like figure towers above other recently erected representations of Ukrainian folkloric figures: a Cossack with his trusty horse, saber, and kobza (similar to the lute, the favorite instrument of the Cossacks), and the legendary founders of Kyiv—the brothers Kyi, Schek and Khoryv, and their sister Lybid'. Today, these three monuments stand where a huge statue of Lenin once presided over the square during the Soviet era, thus replacing the designer of early Soviet nationalities policies with representations of the ancient Slavic/Ukrainian past. On the opposite side of the square is an elaborate arch graced with a statue of the Archangel Michael, the longtime patron saint of Kyiv (since 1108) and also the symbol of the Zaporozhian Cossacks. The icons of folk culture that have mushroomed on Independence Square are fairly neutral symbols from the distant past that are unlikely to raise the ire of Russified Ukrainians. Contentious historical themes from the Soviet era are notably absent, and the statues function in ways similar to Tseretelli's monumental fairy-tale scenes in Moscow described by Bruce Grant (2001): they promote visions of a romanticized folk culture and a "simpler time," and thus have a tranquilizing effect.

Figure 6. Builders erect a statue of Lybid', one of the mythical founders of Kyiv, on Independence Square, 2001. In the background is the Oranta-Berehynia monument. Photo by Victor Pobedinski, courtesy of UNIAN.

Competing with these folkloric, nationalizing images, however, are new modernist structures, such as a submerged shopping mall under the square, mirrored domes and concave structures doubling as skylights for the mall, and a hodge-podge of abstract fountains. These new, modern structures work in tandem with the (equally new) nationalizing statues to project simultaneously a romanticized Ukrainian past, and a hopeful European future. Such structures evoke a sense of moving "toward Europe," a narrative promoted by former president Kuchma in his "European Choice" program, and an ideology Yushchenko has upheld via projects for "Eurointegration."[8] Architecturally, the culmination of this effort lies one block away from Independence Square. There, European Square proudly hosts a center for arts and culture, previously the city's Lenin Museum, now called the Ukrainian House. Here, Ukrainian history and culture—as embodied in the Ukrainian House—are nestled firmly in Europe—as embodied in European Square. The current focus on the "universalist culture of Europe" serves to de-center and mask the widespread uncertainty and disagreement about the essence of Ukrainian identity (Wolczuk 2000:689), without directly engaging the specter of Soviet Ukraine or of Russia.

The apparently successful wedding of Ukrainianization and Europeanization between these stone and glass structures, however, belies the tensions that these symbolic imaginings have produced for everyday citizens. By no means do all Ukrainian citizens identify themselves as Europeans; nor do they agree on the criteria for taking up such an identity. The regime's attempts to blot out the Soviet period in Ukraine have not been successful; many Ukrainians identify with Soviet ideals and practices, and they cultivate both real and imagined ties with Russia and Russians (indeed, 17 percent of Ukraine's permanent residents identify as ethnically Russian). Thus, despite the current administration's ideology of "Eurointegration," many Ukrainian citizens remain unconvinced. They struggle with the meanings and legacies of the Soviet past, and they negotiate their personal and collective identities vis-à-vis murky European and Russian "Others." Given the symbolic and real space they occupy between Europe and Russia, and a Soviet past and unknown (European? Slavic-oriented?) future, many people in Ukraine feel like part of a middle ground, to quote Mykola Riabchuk (2002)—"for the most part invisible, mute, uncertain, undecided, ideologically ambivalent and ambiguous." These ambiguities result in a certain "amorphousness of the nation" that is both exalted and ridiculed by cultural critics in Ukraine. Yury Andrukhovych, a popular Ukrainian writer, has proposed only half-jokingly that, "according to various sociological polls, [half the Ukrainians] have no certain answer to any question. Do you approve or disapprove? Like or dislike? Want or don't want? Do you live or simply survive? Do you exist at all? Remain undecided" (Riabchuk 2002).

As Ukrainians became swept up in the events of the 2004 Orange Revolution, it appeared as if the people *had* decided. Nearly half Kyiv's population participated in the political protests, and, countrywide, one in five residents participated either locally or in Kyiv (Kuzio 2005). Yushchenko's victory was hailed as the triumph of democracy in a state that seemed to have sunk into a quagmire of corruption, crony capitalism, and a muzzled public media since Ukrainian independence in 1991. But reform has been slow, and the administration has been plagued by infighting and allegations of corruption and nepotism. Economic reform and social spending have been flash points of disagreement between Yushchenko and other political elites, debates that can be traced back to perestroika and the early years of Ukraine's independence. Reforms in social and labor policy, and particularly those policies affecting women such as the "working mother contract" (Rotkirch and Temkina 1997), have been important motivators for women to become involved in NGO activism. Women have taken up leadership roles in NGOs both to secure their rights and those of other vulnerable groups, but also to eke out a living in the context of a tight labor market for women.

Holes and Loopholes in the Working Mother Contract

A French woman is walking down the street. On one arm is her husband; on the other arm her lover. Behind her, her servant carries her hat boxes; in front of her a chauffeur drives her Renault.

An American woman is walking down the street. On one arm is her husband; on the other arm her boss. Behind her walks her secretary taking notes; in front of her a chauffeur drives her Cadillac.

A Soviet woman is walking down the street. On one arm is her baby daughter Svetka; on the other arm her mesh shopping bag (Rus. *setka*). Behind her stumbles her drunken husband Ivan; in front of her is the GosPlan (state plan).[9]

—Joke told by Zoia, 1999

In 2000, the Ukrainian economy showed signs of growth for the first time since independence. According to one Ukrainian source, between July 2000 and July 2001 salaries rose 37.2 percent, to an average monthly salary of 327.31 UAH, or $61.[10] If in 2000 the GDP per capita (PPP US$) was $3,816, by 2003 it had risen to $5,491.[11] This general growth trend continued in subsequent years, with an estimated 4.8 percent growth in real GDP in 2002, 9.4 percent in 2003, and 12.4 percent in 2004. It was expected that President Yushchenko, an economist and former head of the National Bank of Ukraine, would oversee continued growth in the Ukrainian economy, but the economy showed renewed signs of trouble during his first year in office in 2005. The growth trend slowed dramatically during that year, with an increase of real GDP of only about 3 percent. Analysts attribute this slowdown to the economic policies introduced by the new presidential administration, which included a dramatic increase in social spending and public wages. These policies, which were championed by the then prime minister Yulia Tymoshenko, were designed to extend increased support to the poor. Opponents of Tymoshenko and this increased social spending frame these policies as "neo-socialist" and decry Tymoshenko's "populist" redistribution strategies as antithetical to "growth and prosperity" (People's Union Our Ukraine 2006). (Some Western scholars are also suspicious; Andrew Wilson (2005a) has called Tymoshenko "the East European Evita, friend of the poor.") Ostensibly because of falling macroeconomic indicators during the first half of 2005, attributed not only to social spending increases but also to other of Tymoshenko's economic policies, she and other members of the government were dismissed by Yushchenko in September 2005. (Many speculate that the ouster was actually motivated more by personal differences and political maneuvering.)

Social welfare reform has had especially far-reaching impacts on the lives of women, who were the beneficiaries of a range of entitlements during the Soviet period. Soviet women entered into a working mother contract with the socialist state, through which they were offered various types of assistance (paid child care leave and subsidies) that allowed them to fulfill their productive and reproductive obligations. The withdrawal of these benefits in practice (even as protective legislation is still on the books) has made women very vulnerable on the labor markets of many former socialist states (Bridger, Kay, and Pinnick 1996; Bridger and Pine 1998). I often tried to imagine myself in the position of my informants, an exercise of the imagination that became somewhat easier after I got married and had a child. Still, it was difficult to fathom the dramatic life changes these women had experienced in the last few years, and harder still to predict how I might react in similar circumstances. What would I do if I lost my job and suddenly my skills were obsolete in a transformed political economy? What if, like Svetlana, I was responsible for one or more children, had just lost my life savings, and could not rely on anyone else for support? What opportunities would I seek out? More important, what opportunities would be available for me? In the absence of economic capital, what social and cultural capital would I possess, and how would I use it? Would it be enough to survive? How could I produce more? In more abstract terms, how would I find the strength to cope when a system I believed in—or at least knew how to operate in—collapsed, and my worldview was devalued? These are some of the challenges my informants, and millions of others in Ukraine and other postsocialist states, have faced during the past decade and a half.

Many analysts see the negative trends for women that have developed in postsocialist Ukraine and other formerly Soviet countries as a natural product of the Soviet government's botched attempts to address the "woman question."[12] Although some early Soviet thinkers did question traditional gender roles, and also challenged the idea that men and women possess different personalities, characteristics, and abilities based on their biology, the early Soviet project to emancipate women failed in many respects. The Soviet government theoretically granted women equal participation in the labor force, and placed emphasis on women's economic equality with men, but women were not relieved of their burdens of domestic chores, or their "female" responsibilities in the family as wives and mothers. This disjuncture resulted in a "double (or quadruple?) burden" for women, who were expected to work full-time (part-time work was only rarely an option); engage in the activities of organizations such as the Komsomol (the Communist Youth League), trade unions, and the Communist Party; manage their households by performing almost all the shopping, cooking, cleaning, and laundering (often by hand); and act as the primary caregivers for children and other family members.[13] Women were thus expected to combine paid employment, political activism, housework, and motherhood. On the other hand, the Soviet system made real improvements in the lives of many, such as providing free educational opportunities to practically all women.

Despite rhetoric on equality between men and women in the workplace, in the Soviet Union women were concentrated in low-paid, low-skilled, and often manual work, and they earned considerably less than men (Lapidus 1978:161–197).[14] On the other hand, the Soviet state did provide generous maternity benefits to women workers, such as extensive paid leave, free birth clinics, and on-site nursing facilities or breaks for nursing children at home during the workday. These benefits for working mothers helped ease the burden for many. This arrangement, dubbed the "working mother contract" by Russian sociologist Anna Temkina (Rotkirch and Temkina 1997), was the basis of identity formation for Soviet women, who articulated their personal identities both to the institution of the home, and to the collective of the workplace and other activities in the public sphere. In the context of the new market economy in postsocialist states, many women long for these extensive maternity and other workplace benefits.

On paper at least, many of the Soviet-era entitlements for working mothers are still in place. Current Ukrainian legislation retains a Soviet-era dual emphasis on benefits for working women and on women's reproductive roles, and includes extensive provisions for pregnant women and those with children. In fact, the current Labor Code of Ukraine actually came into force in 1972 and simply underwent changes and additions after Ukrainian independence in 1991 (Akhaladze et al. 1999:111). In today's free market context, this focus on women's roles as reproducers and mothers is potentially problematic, because emphasis is placed on the protection of motherhood rather than women's rights more broadly, and women's issues are inevitably placed within a context of "family problems" (Zhurzhenko 1998:3).[15] Ironically, the extensive provisions made for women workers in Ukrainian legislation may actually work *against* women, constituting a form of "positive discrimination" (Einhorn 1993:35). Because women are given so many workplace benefits (which employers must provide, whether they are state enterprises or private businesses), employers view women as a potential liability and as unreliable and expendable workers. Most important, perhaps, the laws governing women's labor in Ukraine do not address the more pressing problem of women's general declining status in the labor sphere, and extensive laws governing women's labor rights are of little use to women if they cannot secure paid employment in the first place. Moreover, labor laws are rarely enforced.

For these reasons, the "reorganization" of enterprises that resulted from market reforms has been especially hard on women: of those who lost their jobs as a result of reorganization in Ukraine after perestroika and independence, 80 percent were women (Zhurzhenko 2001c:183). By contrast, in the Soviet Union women constituted 51 percent of the workforce in the late 1980s. In 2002, women still made up two-thirds of Ukraine's unemployed (Kravchuk 2002:27). Today, in Ukraine, women form the majority in service industries (between 1995 and 2002, 55 percent of women workers were in services) (UNDP 2004:230), especially in positions that carry little prestige and are considered "women's work." For example, women dominate in spheres such as secretarial work (81 percent) (Romaniuk 1998:48), health care (82 percent), low-level buying and selling (76.6 percent), education (75.2 percent), and culture (70.2 percent), and only 5 percent of women in these "pink-collar" professions occupy managerial positions (Dovzhenko 1998:198). Men, on the other hand, dominate in defense, industry, agriculture, transport, and construction. Irina Averianova has found that, although women make up 53 percent of the faculty of institutions of higher education in Ukraine, "women are still disproportionately bunched together on the lowest levels of the academic hierarchy" (1998:31).

Women's access to the new world of private business is also limited—in Ukraine, women occupy only 21 percent of administrative posts in small businesses, and just 13 percent in large businesses (Koval', Mel'nyk, and Hodovanets' 1999). Tatiana Zhurzhenko has noted that "women's entrepreneurship in Ukraine turns out to be inserted into the ideology of 'women's destiny,' using traditionalist values and historical myths for the 'revival of Ukrainian statehood'" (2001b:42). When Zhurzhenko attended the first all-Ukrainian conference on "Women and Entrepreneurship" in 1997, she heard it stated "that the 'objective of women's entrepreneurship is benevolence and the revival of the intellectual and technological potential of the nation.'" She warns that, "the mechanisms of discrimination, existing at the level of political discourse, which assign women entrepreneurs a special 'moral' function in fact thrust them into marginal, low-income niches" (2001b:42). Furthermore, Zhurzhenko notes:

> Women entrepreneurs in Ukrainian society inevitably end up in a situation of dual resistance. They are forced to realize their initiatives under the conditions of risk, the absence of legal guarantees and during the political and economic instability of the transitional economy. It is necessary for them to resist not only the bureaucratic system which blocks their initiative as entrepreneurs, but also the patriarchal stereotypes and the practice of discrimination in the male business environment. (Zhurzhenko 2001b:41)

Given this dual resistance, many women, not surprisingly, are reluctant to start or participate in business endeavors. Both women and men in Ukraine report that they feel incapable of going into business, but women feel even more incompetent than men. In one survey, for example, when asked the question, "Do you feel competent to engage in business activities?" 26 percent of men respondents, and 13 percent of women, answered yes (Komykh 2001:209). Women who do engage in business tend to go into typically "female" spheres (food service, health care, handicrafts, fashion, etc.), which seem to them less risky and more "natural."

Many in Ukraine perform jobs in the shadow economy that offer no social security benefits after retirement. Of all workers in this situation, 80 percent are women (Romaniuk 1998:50). Salaries also reflect a marked gender inequality; in the total economy, a woman's average salary constitutes only 53 percent of a man's (UNDP 2005:304). In 2003, the estimated earned income (PPP $US) for men was $7,329, whereas women only earned an estimated $3,891 (UNDP 2005:300). Depending on the sector, women's salaries range between 45 and 70 percent of men's (for comparison, however, Polish and American women also earn just 61 percent of men's average salaries) (Dudwick, Srinivasan, and Braithwaite 2002). Despite a situation where women frequently enjoy higher levels of professional and educational training than men, women usually occupy less prestigious, less remunerative posts (Akhaladze et al. 1999:137). In no sector of the economy do women's earnings exceed men's, even in health care where the majority of workers are women. Sex discrimination in hiring practices is widespread, as is age discrimination (Human Rights Watch 2003). Some newspapers carry preposterous advertisements for employment opportunities, ads specifying height, weight, age, and other requirements for women applicants.[16]

Given the constraints they face in the current labor market, naturally many women have sought out somewhat "nontraditional" employment (official and unofficial). More women are leaving the country to work than men, who enjoy somewhat better job security and higher wages. These women engage in low-paying menial jobs in host countries that local women might shun. The growing problem of prostitution in Ukraine and Russia is gaining attention, especially the thriving international trade in the trafficking of women and children (Denisova 2004; Hughes and Denisova 2004). Ukrainian women, desperate for work, are attracted to notices advertising employment in foreign countries, jobs, for example, for bartenders, waitresses, and dancers. When women arrive in those countries—including countries in central and western Europe, as well as Israel and Turkey—they find that they have been deceived about the nature of the job and are forced to work in local sex industries. The women's passports are stolen, and they become slaves to international trafficking rings operated by Mafias of various stripes. According to Ukraine's Interior Ministry, as many as four hundred thousand Ukrainian women have left the country pursuing such work in the last decade (International Organization for Migration 2001).

Another survival strategy many women adopt involves "speculating," the informal selling of goods on the street. The avenues of Kyiv and other cities are lined with vendors—the overwhelming majority of them women—who sell everything from vegetables, beer, and dried fish to hair ornaments, flowers, imported clothing, and household pets. Women with a penchant for crafts and sewing utilize their creative talents by making and selling items such as colorful house slippers, shower caps, potholders, and sweaters. A step up, perhaps, from "speculating" is "shuttle trading." "Shuttle traders"—*chelnoki* in Russian, from the Russian word *chelnok,* "the part of a tool that makes rapid, regularly repeated motions to and fro" (Zhurzhenko 1999:244)—travel back and forth between Ukrainian towns and cities to locales in Turkey, China, Poland, Russia, and Belarus on "shopping tours," where they buy goods in bulk (e.g., clothing, handbags, and shoes) for resale at the Ukrainian markets. Some shuttle traders double as resellers of market wares, but others sell the goods wholesale to other traders or to retail shops which then resell them at higher prices. Zhurzhenko has noted that, although shuttle trading is a valuable temporary form of self-employment for women, it ultimately contributes to women's unemployment, since the cheap foreign goods brought into the country by *chelnoki* undercut the price of goods produced in Ukraine's light manufacturing sector, an industry heavily dominated by women (1999:245).

Some individuals have found it possible to engage in trade at a more prestigious level by becoming entry-level distributors for foreign firms such as Oriflame (a cosmetics company), Avon, and Amway. Manufacturers of cosmetics, cleaning products, and cookware operate on a consignment principle and allow selected associates to eventually graduate to managerial positions. Depending on one's selling finesse, such distributor positions can provide associates with a reliable and significant source of extra income. During my fieldwork in the late 1990s many women I knew were compelled to juggle multiple jobs to support themselves and their families. For instance, a friend of mine, Lena, a thirty-two-year-old single doctor who helped sustain her elderly parents with whom she lived, worked full-time at one government clinic for Chernobyl victims, part-time at another state-run clinic, and also as a distributor for two foreign firms in Kyiv. With the recent improvement in the Ukrainian economy, the work lives of many women I know have become less harried. Lena took an office job at an advertising firm, rented an apartment, and finally enjoyed some free time. Despite these advances, long-term solutions to labor inequalities are not visible on the horizon. Although a new equal rights and opportunities law was adopted by Ukraine's Parliament in September 2005, little appears to have changed for the women of Ukraine. Issues relating to women's rights are low-prestige items in the political marketplace and so have not been addressed seriously in political discussions.

Goddesses and Government

An ad was running on one of the state television channels encouraging people (specifically women, and even more specifically, mothers) to vote in the upcoming presidential election. It shows a young pregnant woman eating junk food and vegging out in front of the television. Then we see an image of her baby in vitro, bobbing around in amniotic fluid. A child's voice says, "*Mamo! Proholosui za moie zhyttia*" (Mama! Vote for my future). (Fieldnotes, November 2, 1999, Kyiv)

"Mama," I look in mummy's warm eyes, in which it seems the entire blueness of my native land's skies is reflected, and I ask: "What does Berehynia mean?"

"Berehynia, my dearest little son," she replies, "is our home. Everything in it, all
we have, everything we saved from our parents and grandfathers, all that we hold
dear and consecrated—our household things, children, songs, accord and argument,
a kind word, all the memories of this home—all that, now you'll know, is Berehynia."
(Vasyl' Skurativs'kyi, *Berehynia*, 1987)

Women's vulnerable situation in the labor force is paralleled and exacerbated
by a reassertion of patriarchy in the political sphere and women's ongoing marginalization from the political process. Ever since Gorbachev began asking
what should be done "to make it possible for women to return to their purely
womanly mission" (1987:117), women in Ukraine, as in other former Soviet
states, have been the subjects of re-nationalizing and re-traditionalizing projects. Rukh, the pro-reform Popular Movement for Restructuring in Ukraine
that played a key role in achieving Ukrainian national sovereignty, pursued a
conservative agenda with regard to women. At Rukh's founding Congress in
1989, only 8.8 percent of the 1,109 delegates were women, and only 3 women,
along with 45 men, were elected to central leadership positions. At the second
Congress, only 2 women won leadership posts. Rukh's charter did not offer a
plan to strengthen and protect women's rights; instead, it proposed that reforms
should allow women to "return to their maternal role in order to facilitate the
revival of the traditional Ukrainian family" (Hrycak 2000:5). Since the early
1990s, representatives of other major political parties have espoused similar
views. As Marian Rubchak notes, during Ukraine's first parliamentary hearing
on women's issues in 1995, Oleksandr Moroz—socialist politician and former
speaker of the Parliament—presented an "appeal for measures that would facilitate the performance of women in their contemporary roles as mothers and
full participants in the public sector" (2001:158).[17] Moroz "noted that what the
country needed most were 'enlightened' [male?] leaders who would 'create the
necessary conditions for allowing women to be women'" (Rubchak 2001:158).

A crucial element in the re-traditionalizing of Ukrainian society and women's
roles has been the revival of the myth of the Berehynia, a pagan goddess from
ancient Slavic mythology. Conceptualized simultaneously as a hearth mother,
an earth goddess, and a domestic Madonna, the Berehynia is understood as
the guardian of both the family and the nation. Although the origins of the
Berehynia are somewhat unclear, chroniclers have indicated that the *berehyni*
were the most ancient of divinities among the Slavs. First conceptualized as
river, lake, and forest nymphs, *berehyni* were early incarnations of the hunt-
ing and fertility goddesses. Eventually the goddesses were "domesticated" and
became associated with particular clans or extended families (Hubbs 1988:14–
15). Material evidence suggests that the cult of the Berehynia was widespread
in pre-Christian Ukraine. The Berehynia has been portrayed in ancient stone
and ceramic figurines, and later in metal; she is also shown in folk arts such as
painted Easter eggs, textiles, ritualistic texts, and in embroidered ritual towels. According to the late Solomea Pavlychko, in recent times the figure of the
Berehynia became widely popular after ethnographer Vasyl' Skurativs'kyi pub-

lished a popular book by that title in 1988. In his book, Skurativs'kyi glorified Ukrainian rural culture and encouraged its preservation. Pavlychko described the idea of the Berehynia:

> Berehynia is the main symbol of this rural culture, the home hearth itself, the peasant house with all its attributes, towels and pillows with embroidery, hand-made rustic furniture, rituals of the rural holidays, folk costumes, etc. A woman singing folk songs, sewing a folk blouse, teaching the same to her daughter and granddaughter is the centre of this idyllic world of the lost and adored past. (Pavlychko 1992:91)

The revival of this rural culture—which is equated with the entire national culture as such—noted Pavlychko, "means restoring its peasant patriarchical structures" (1992:92). In other words, the revival of the Berehynia, and the re-romanticization of so-called traditional gender roles, is part of what Anastasia Posadskaya (1994) has called the "renaissance of patriarchy" after socialism's fall.

The Berehynia has become a major symbol of womanhood and motherhood in independent Ukraine, and politicians routinely evoke the Berehynia in discussions relating to women. President Yushchenko, for example, closed his March 8, 2005, speech commemorating International Women's Day with an imprecation for a "thankful Ukraine to respect the Berehynias of our worthy Cossack nation."[18] Today, depictions of the Berehynia appear on calendars, posters, advertisements, and other media, and in 2001 President Kuchma unveiled a huge monument on Independence Square of a woman dressed in robes and raising her hands to the heavens. She literally presides over the capital city, towering above the square on a pedestal more than 60 meters high. The statue, which Kuchma dubbed the Oranta-Berehynia, fuses the image of the ancient Slavic goddess with that of Oranta, the Praying Virgin of the Eastern Orthodox. As Rubchak (2005) notes, "A pagan matriarch, or domestic Madonna, [has] been conjoined with the Virgin Mary to form an even more compelling symbol of Ukrainian womanhood." A flowing shawl is wrapped loosely around her arms and is swept up by the breeze, giving her the appearance of having wings. Holding aloft a spring of snowball berry (*kalyna*), a traditional symbol of rebirth and immortality, the Oranta-Berehynia is a powerful icon of national revival and generational continuity. Although the statue—and the Berehynia myth—resonate with many in Ukraine, this physical representation of the rediscovery of "traditional woman" is ridiculed by some locals, who deridingly call the monument *Batmansha* (She-Batman) or "the chick on a stick."

During Ukraine's 2004 Orange Revolution, Yuliia Tymoshenko, then forty-four years old, stirred the Ukrainian public to protest while she stood near the famous monument, with her hair done up in her now trademark matriarchal plait, a veritable Berehynia herself. Tymoshenko was practically the only highly visible woman involved in the events of the Orange Revolution, apart from the pop singer Ruslana Lyzhychko (who was later elected to Parliament in March 2006) and two political wives—Kateryna Chumachenko (the wife of President

Figure 7. Cranes begin to raise the statue of the Oranta-Berehynia on Independence Square in celebration of the tenth anniversary of Ukrainian independence, August 2001. Photo by Alexander Sinitsa, courtesy of UNIAN.

Yushchenko) and Liudmila Yanukovych. Chumachenko kept a low profile, and Ms. Yanukovych became an embarrassment to the Blue (Party of Regions) camp when she made ridiculous allegations that protestors were being "drugged" on tainted oranges and provided with felt boots (Rus. *valenki*) from the United States. Tymoshenko's radical and unwavering leadership during the protest actions endeared her to many supporters of the Orange Revolution, who amiably referred to her alternatively as the "goddess," "princess," or "heart" of the revolution; the Ukrainian Joan of Arc; Lady Yu; and, simply, "Yul'ka." (It is hard to imagine anyone referring to President Viktor Yushchenko as "Vitia.") Marian Rubchak (2005) has pointed out the similarities between Tymoshenko's image and that of the mythical Marianne of the French Revolution; indeed, a caricature emerged during the Orange Revolution with Tymoshenko as the bare-breasted Marianne depicted in Eugene Delacroix's famous painting *Liberty Guiding the People*. Tymoshenko was a decisive leader during the Orange

Figure 8. The Oranta-Berehynia towers over Independence Square in front of a shopping mall and the hotel Ukraina. Photo by author.

Revolution, when she encouraged protestors to seize airports and railway stations and personally led the storming of the Parliament. Tymoshenko's brave and dangerous acts received extensive media coverage, but one of the most widely reproduced and photogenic images of the revolution was the moment when Tymoshenko placed a carnation in a militia man's shield, a gesture denoting peace and perhaps motherliness, and thus seen as an appropriate one for this woman revolutionary. Tymoshenko also appealed to her own "womanly" characteristics to explain her brave actions during the Orange Revolution. When asked if she found inspiration in figures such as Catherine the Great, Tymoshenko replied: "Women carry a crown not on the head, but in the heart. They do politics with more soul, especially when such a woman has to deal with danger" (Gnauck 2005).

Although appropriating the Berehynia as a symbol of Ukrainian womanhood may have helped Tymoshenko propel herself into the seat of Ukrainian Prime Minister in 2005, the revival of the idea of woman as protectress of the nation has not translated into political empowerment for the majority of Ukraine's women. With the exception of Tymoshenko and a few others (such as Rayisa Bohatyr'ova, who in 2006 became head of the largest faction in Parliament at the time, the Party of Regions faction), very few women in Ukraine hold positions of real political power. In fact, during the first fifteen years of Ukrainian independence only a handful of women have belonged to the country's party elite.[19] Politics is widely perceived as a "dirty business" not appropriate for women, who are charged rather with upholding culture and morals; the brawls and shouting matches that sometimes break out on the floor of the Parliament are often televised, adding fuel to the perception that politics is violent and politicians uncouth. The Ukrainian public seems unsure how to interpret women in politics, and women politicians are characterized in the mass media and in popular discourse in ways that alternately emphasize their "femininity" and mothering qualities or their "abnormal" aggressiveness, which is seen as a male trait. As Oksana Sknar noted, women politicians, in order to succeed, must develop a "dual" image by successfully wielding traits considered to be masculine and feminine (2001:204). Tymoshenko is representative of this trend. She is often called a "firebrand nationalist" in the local and foreign press, and her "combative, emotional style" is frequently commented upon. She has also been called "the only man in Ukrainian politics." Tymoshenko is described as tough, power-hungry, headstrong, a passionate radical, and a populist. Throughout her political career she has been smeared as the "iron princess," the "gas princess" (during the late 1990s Tymoshenko served as vice prime minister for the fuel and energy sector in the Cabinet of Ministers), and a range of other epithets. On the other hand, Tymoshenko's glamorous appearance softens her image and begs to be commented upon. She dresses expensively in designer wear, and her fashion statements often attract more attention from the public and the press than her political ventures. Tymoshenko posed for a photo shoot and interview for the Ukrainian *Elle* magazine during 2005 (not surprisingly, the author of the article heroically uncovered Tymoshenko's "beauty secrets"),

Figure 9. Yuliia Tymo-
shenko. Copyright ©
Alexander Prokopenko,
www.tymoshenko.
com.ua.

and in 2005 she also appeared (fully clothed) on the cover of the Polish *Playboy*. Two journalists said that the session of Parliament during which Tymoshenko was voted in as prime minister in February 2005 reminded them of the Oscar ceremonies (Danylenko and Nazarov 2005). Tymoshenko's photogenic image has earned her much coverage in the Western press, and her trademark hairstyle has been in demand since the Orange Revolution.[20] Andrew Wilson speculates that the political movement she has spearheaded since 2002, the Bloc of Yuliia Tymoshenko, was intentionally given the acronym BYuT because it is easily modified into BYuTy (beauty) (2005b:18). After being fired as prime minister and effectively forced to jettison the Orange imagery, Tymoshenko (and BYuT) adopted the symbol of a red heart for her 2006 parliamentary campaign, imagery unmistakably "feminine." The symbol invokes Tymoshenko's role as the "heart of the revolution," thus asserting that she has not abandoned the ideals of the Orange Revolution, even though she was (during 2005, at least) ousted from the Yushchenko camp. Tymoshenko has been the butt of satire in Ukraine for years, and the Russian press has been equally merciless. Bizarrely, in 2005 a

Russian deputy, Aleksei Mitrofanov of the Liberal Democratic Party (LDPR), made a pornographic movie called "Yuliia" in which the lead characters resemble Tymoshenko (braid and all) and Georgia's president Saakashvili, who was also swept into office via a "revolution" (his was rose-colored).

As Tymoshenko's vivid example demonstrates, because so few women are in politics, women politicians are constantly under close scrutiny. Scandals involving women politicians receive extensive media coverage, fueling the argument that "proper" women do not belong in politics. Nataliia Vitrenko, formerly head of the Progressive Socialist Party, is a case in point. During the past decade, the Ukrainian media has delighted in reporting on scandals involving Vitrenko that underline her ruthlessly confrontational (read: unladylike) nature and lack of couth. In 1998, Vitrenko made headlines when, during a session of Parliament, she was involved in a fistfight with several male MPs and even used her high-heeled shoe to beat an opponent on the head. During her campaign tour for the presidential election in October 1999, Vitrenko was injured when a homemade bomb was thrown at her. Vitrenko is popularly referred to as the "witch of Konotop," after the site (Konotop) of her first electoral victory ("The Witch of Konotop" is the title of a popular 1836 story by the writer Hryhorii Kvitka-Osnovianenko in which the wicked witch of the north tries to trick the southern Cossacks). But even Vitrenko, who completely ignored traditional "women's issues" (i.e., child care and maternity leave) in her political campaign, referred to her role as a mother to explain her focus on labor and education issues (Popson and Righter 2000:3)—this despite the fact that she had given herself the title of Ukraine's "one true Marxist."

Describing press coverage of Ukraine's women politicians, Orysia Kulick noted that "there seems to be a tendency to hyperbolize their roles in Ukrainian political life. These women operate in a political climate characterized as a 'theater of the absurd' in which language and imagery are overly stylized and characters larger than life" (2005:12). Public attention is often drawn to personality, dress, and behavior, leaving political issues in the background. Even though they cater to public expectations of traditional gender roles when accounting for their interest in politics, women politicians nevertheless are often regarded as breaching accepted gender norms and transgressing gendered expectations of behavior—they do not act like "mothers"; nor do they act like "ladies." These overblown and negative perceptions of women politicians make it more difficult for women to be elected to office, effectively depoliticizing women's issues. Furthermore, women are shut out of "big politics" by a lack of access to the economic, social, and cultural capital necessary to propel oneself into the political realm in contemporary Ukraine. Politics in Ukraine (as elsewhere) is big business, and the seats of Parliament are crowded with the wealthy elite of Ukraine's business sector. One of Tymoshenko's stated goals as prime minister was to decouple politics and business (and her strategies for re-privatizing state assets presumably accounted in part for her ouster), but thus far little has been done on this score. Tymoshenko herself, who emerged in the mid-1990s via the energy sector as one of Ukraine's richest people, is sometimes referred to as "the only female oligarch." She was investigated and jailed (though never convicted) for several weeks in 2001, ostensibly on suspicion of money laundering, though her accusers likely had political motives.

Although Soviet politics was populated with more women, women politicians were not very influential. In the Ukrainian Soviet Socialist Republic, a high percentage of women in positions of political power was guaranteed through quotas, and women deputies constituted at least 50 percent of local Soviets (Councils) and 30 percent of the republican Supreme Soviet. In the Soviet Union, however, relatively few women advanced in the Communist Party, and those who did were usually given tasks associated with maternal and child welfare, low-prestige issues assumed to be most relevant to their interests. In the last Supreme Soviet of Ukraine, women held 36 percent of the seats, and 50 percent of the seats of municipal councils, but the number of women in political positions plummeted during the 1990 election, which saw a steep decline of women's representation in the Verkhovna Rada to just 3 percent. Free elections after Ukrainian independence in 1994 produced a slight increase, with women constituting 5 percent of parliamentarians. Women's representation rose to 8 percent in the 1998 elections.[21] In the 2002 parliamentary elections, however, the percentage of women deputies elected declined again to 5 percent. In a promising trend, the percentage of women representatives at the local (less powerful) level did rise to 50 percent in 2002. The percentage of women in the Verkhovna Rada climbed slightly in the 2006 parliamentary elections, up to 8.7 percent (thirty-nine women parliamentarians). Women's representation in Parliament declined in early elections in 2007, to around 7 percent. Whereas women constitute about 68 percent of the labor force in government service overall, the share of women in high-ranking civil service positions is only 15 percent (UNDP 2003:29). Proposals to reimplement the Soviet-era quota for women (at 30 or 35 percent) in the Verkhovna Rada have been debated by parliamentarians but have not been approved.

As in the Soviet era, women parliamentarians are frequently appointed to low-profile parliamentary committees dealing with family issues rather than to committees that oversee the distribution of important resources or deal with high-profile political issues. In 2003, three of the nineteen women parliamentarians sat on the Motherhood and Childhood Protection Parliamentary Committee, and only two women were appointed as committee chairpersons. In 2002, the political scientist Taras Kuzio (2002) noted that of Ukraine's 130 registered political parties, only 5 were devoted to women's issues. The only widely visible women's party to participate in the 2002 parliamentary elections was Women for the Future (Zhinky za Maibutne), whose emblem was a dove over a nest encircled with the Women for the Future logo. The party was headed by Valentyna Dovzhenko, former head of the State Committee for Family and Youth Affairs, and a close ally of former President Kuchma and his wife, Liudmyla. Because of Dovzhenko's connections to the embattled Kuchma administration, the legitimacy and integrity of Women for the Future has been questioned by much of the electorate—it is widely perceived as a "fake" party set up by Kuchma and various oligarchs. In 2002 the party, which espoused an agenda concerned with women's health, domestic violence, and other issues (but based its campaign largely on distributing humanitarian aid to the needy), failed to hurdle the 4 percent voting barrier and thus secured no seats in Parliament (the party received just 2.1 percent of the vote).

In the 2006 parliamentary elections, two small parties (Women for the Future, and Solidarity of Women of Ukraine) represented women's issues, and both were incorporated into larger blocs that did not clear the 3 percent threshold (the threshold was lowered from 4 percent to 3 percent between 2002 and 2006). The only major political parties besides Tymoshenko's BYuT associated with women politicians were the Viche ("Public Meeting") Party, a pro–small business party funded by the oligarch Viktor Pinchuk and led by the businesswoman Inna Bogoslovska, and Nataliia Vitrenko's "People's Opposition Bloc" (which incorporated the Progressive Socialist Party). Neither cleared the 3 percent hurdle, and Andrew Wilson notes that both parties had "virtual platforms" that were either nebulous or closely resembled those of another, more popular party. He thus characterizes Viche and the Vitrenko bloc as "virtual parties" designed to draw votes away from other parties (Hofmann 2006). It does not bode well for women that two of three visible women politicians in the 2006 elections were merely figureheads of virtual parties. The situation worsened in the 2007 early parliamentary elections. Although three parties were headed by women politicians, none of the parties included gender equality or women's issues in their platforms. A new party was formed under the leadership of woman politician Liudmyla Suprun (the Election bloc of Liudmyla Suprun-Ukrainian Regional Asset), but it failed to clear the 3 percent threshold. BYuT was the only woman-led party to secure seats in Parliament.

Overall, the Ukrainian government has made little progress in improving the status of women. There was no official state structure in Soviet Ukraine devoted to women's rights issues. In 1990, a Permanent Commission on the Status of Women, Family, Motherhood, and Childhood was formed (actually not so permanent, as the commission was dissolved in 1994), but it did not raise issues of gender equality, and its work was focused on child welfare and women in their capacity as mothers. To help enhance women's roles outside the family, during the 1990s several National Action Plans were approved by the Cabinet of Ministers of Ukraine in response to the recommendations made by the Fourth World Conference on Women in Beijing and the action program adopted by the Fifth Session of the UN General Assembly in Vienna. These programs were inadequately funded and staffed, and issues related to women's equal rights continue to be couched in maternalist language and segregated into the realm of children and the family (Hrycak 2005:78). In fact, overt reference to "women" disappeared when the Presidential Committee on the Status of Women and Children was dissolved in 1995 and replaced by the Ministry of Ukraine on Family and Youth, although the ministry's contemporary heir, the Ministry of Ukraine for Family, Youth, and Sport does deal with issues of women's equal rights.[22]

In 2002, in response to women's lack of visibility in "big politics," the continuing decrease in the number of women elected to political office, and the failure of the government to address women's issues in general, a coalition of women politicians, NGO leaders, and others formed the Civil Parliament of Women of Ukraine. The Civil Parliament was organized to duplicate the Ukrainian Parliament—matching its 450 seats and having the same committees —in order to exert pressure on the government. The Civil Parliament was also envisioned as a forum in which to train future women cadres for political office. Major figures included Kateryna Vashchuk, then of the Agrarian Party and an MP, and Liudmyla Suprun of the People's Democratic Party. My activist friend, Sofiia, was involved in founding the Civil Parliament but withdrew her support when, as she put it, "it devolved into a forum for women politicians to advance their own business interests." Subsequently, the Civil Parliament of Women of Ukraine does not appear to have had much influence over the political process.

This is the context in which Ukrainian women have turned to NGOs as a site of participation in the public sphere and an avenue for articulating their rights and needs as women, mothers, and Ukrainian citizens. Further, in the context of ongoing economic crisis, many women have taken up NGO leadership positions as a form of alternate employment and a way to develop skills. As women have sought out these opportunities, parts of the NGO sector (the realm of youth, children, and "social issues") have indeed developed a "women's face." This does not mean, however, that women's rights issues are being addressed by most NGOs—on the contrary, NGOs with an agenda focused specifically on women constitute less than 1 percent of all NGOs in the post-Soviet milieu (Hrycak 2002:75) and just 4.1 percent of NGOs in Ukraine (Sydorenko 2001:54). Groups that do have a women's platform tend to concentrate on national culture and the patriotic upbringing of children, or on women as mothers. On the other hand, it has been noted that more than half the women who turn to women's NGOs as a source of assistance and advice have elicited help to protect their personal, work, or family rights (Hrycak 2001:157). This would indicate that the "third sector" of NGOs is a potential site for the empowerment of post-Soviet women, who so far have had little success entering the spheres of politics or business. This fact has not been lost on transnational development organizations seeking to address issues of women's equality. International interventions into the Ukrainian "woman question" via the NGO sphere have met with some success but have also produced unexpected effects, which we explore in the next chapter.

Pedestals

My friend Lidiia and I are strolling along Khreshchatyk, people-watching and stopping to listen to street musicians. We reach the Maidan and decide to rest a while before continuing on to a concert at the Philharmonic. We perch ourselves on the marble edge of a fountain. Visitors to the city are milling around the square, stopping to snap photos of picturesque objects, including

Figure 10. Workers complete the torso of the Motherland monument during the late 1970s. Photo in author's possession.

Figure 11. The Motherland monument competes with the bell tower of the nearby twelfth-century Pechers'ka Lavra (Monastery of the Caves) as the tallest structures in Kyiv. Photo by author.

a section of "Orange graffiti" from the days of the revolution, now preserved under glass on a support column in front of the Central Post Office. Squinting into the bright sun, I crane my neck upward to peer at the Oranta-Berehynia. It is hard to make out the details, soaring as she does 60 meters in the air. I have already taken a few pictures of the statue but none are satisfying—my camera cannot zoom in close enough to get a good shot. Lidiia notices me gazing up and turns to see the Berehynia, too, shielding her eyes from the sun. "It's hard to see her way up there on that pedestal," she says. "She floats up there like an angel in the clouds but who can tell what she's all about?" I wonder if she is reflecting on her own situation. As if reading my mind, Lidiia continues, "They are trying to make goddesses of Ukrainian women, they tell us we have important roles to play, that we're crucial for shaping Ukraine's future. But what good does that do? She isn't flesh and blood, is she? It's all just words." I ask

Lidiia if the Berehynia isn't preferable to the other huge monument portraying a woman in the city—the Soviet monument to the Motherland erected in 1980 on the banks of the Dnipro River? The shiny steel monument, holding a sword and shield and bearing a stern facial expression, towers more than 100 meters and competes with the nearby bell tower of the twelfth-century Pechers'ka Lavra (Monastery of the Caves) as one of the tallest structures in the city. We cannot help but chuckle as we picture the gargantuan statue, hated by many and yet somehow integral to the cityscape. With her muscular form and strict demeanor, the Motherland seems to demand something totally different from women—strength, brute force, and a surrendering of femininity. It is time for us to go, and as we stand and turn our backs to the Berehynia, Lidiia asks: "Why do we have to be a steel heroine or a distant goddess? Why can't we just be women?"

2 Ukrainian NGO-graphy

When I step off the minibus taxi, Maryna is there waiting for me. She looks tired, and I am grateful that she found the time to meet with me. She had already called twice this morning to postpone the interview for a few hours, so I did not know whether I would see her. It is a crisp fall day in 1999, but the late afternoon sun warms our backs as we navigate our way across several busy crosswalks toward the complex of former day care facilities where Maryna rents three rooms as quarters for her organization, Lily of the Valley. The blocks of grey and cream-colored buildings all look the same, which is why Maryna met me at the bus stop to lead the way.

During a previous interview, Maryna told me about her former career as a biology researcher. She was earning an advanced degree in the early 1990s when her daughter, Olenka, then in her early teens, was diagnosed with cancer. Maryna took a leave of absence from her work and studies while Olenka had surgery and underwent treatment. Just as she was ready to resume her research, the Soviet regime fell, and Maryna's boss advised her to "just give up." She did. She regrets her choice at times—she was a good scientist—but she finds NGO work very satisfying and feels she has found her niche. It is only she and Olenka, as Olenka's father left Maryna when she was pregnant; they had married young, and he was not yet cut out for family life. She says it is easier to do her activist work without having to wait on a man. She doesn't have to "cook for or coddle anyone," she tells me, and she has her daughter, who is now a university student, to help out with the housework.

Maryna became the director of Lily of the Valley in the mid-1990s. She joined the group in conjunction with her daughter's illness—Lily is a mutual-aid association for children suffering Chernobyl-related cancers, and their families. Responsibility for nearly all aspects of Lily's activities falls to Maryna, no small task in an organization with a membership of 350 people. Some women members of the organization (mothers of children who are or have been sick) volunteer to help around the office, but Maryna feels guilty asking them to do much since they do not get paid and have families to take care of. I have never seen any children here, but Maryna shows me a scrapbook with pictures and newspaper clippings that highlight some of the NGO's recent activities. Lily was originally founded to provide members with humanitarian aid in the form of medicines; medical treatment; medical trips abroad for free care in Cuba and France, for example; food, clothing, and money; as well as entertainment such as trips to the circus and theater. Under Maryna's direction, Lily still retains its earlier functions, but she has introduced some changes that she hopes will increase the organization's resources. She received a grant the previous year to create a resource center (also registered as an NGO, called "Mist" [Bridge]) for disability rights organizations, which includes a computer database of Ukraine's disability-related NGOs. This means that Lily (via Mist) received two much-needed computers.

As we approach the office, Maryna fills me in on her day. She got tied up at an exhibition of Kyiv's government social service departments and service NGOs, an event she characterizes as "a total waste of time." I ask her why—wasn't it a good opportunity for Kyivans to become acquainted with social services and the work NGOs are doing, if they ever need to access these services? Maryna chuckles: "It wasn't open to the public! It was just for show [*pokazukha*], to 'educate' city officials about social services. We had all received funding from the city government, so we had to showcase our work for them. Everyone already knew one another, so we just stood around and talked the whole time." She had dropped in on a roundtable organized to discuss disability issues. "I walked in and started laughing because all the participants were women. There wasn't a single man! We joked that it wasn't a roundtable; it was a *mams'kyi klub*, a *babs'kyi klub* [a mamas' club, a broads' club]."

During our interview I ask Maryna to tell me the ins and outs of NGO work. It is all I can do to keep up with Maryna and her vivid descriptions of activist life. We talk about tax laws, customs laws, funding sources, and competition between NGOs for information and resources. As Maryna offers examples to illustrate the difficulties of receiving humanitarian aid from abroad, discusses the local tax regulations that work to discourage business from giving charitable donations as tax write-offs, and tells of her fellow activists who were lured into lucrative deals with transnational corporations to act as tax-free funnels of manufactured goods (and are now serving prison terms), it becomes clear that one must be knowledgeable, savvy, and very careful to survive in Ukraine's NGO world. I want to know what Maryna's plan is for Lily. She says she needs to provide Lily with cash flow, but she also has to arrange some income for herself. Right now she is an unsalaried "volunteer." She notes that NGOs are beginning to receive financial aid from international organizations that want to create small business structures to help organizations become "self-sustaining" and less reliant on donor and state support. But she is not sure if this would work for Lily. She does not feel prepared to go into business, and she is uncomfortable asking her organization's members, especially sick children, to help her in this venture.

As a way to address her own financial woes, Maryna is becoming increasingly involved in the activities of foreign donor organizations. She has attended a gamut of seminars ("trainings") on topics such as fund-raising, public relations, and grant writing that were facilitated by so-called trainers, paid employees of donor organizations. Maryna was hired to run a few trainings herself, and she ended up developing her own cycle of seminars for NGO activists dealing with disability issues. She tells me that she recently applied to be a paid "trainer of trainers" for an international donor organization; if she is hired for this position, she will travel extensively around the country leading seminars for others who want to become paid trainers. She admits, "I seem to have found a solution for myself, but I can't say it will benefit my organization."

When we leave the office it is already dark, and Maryna walks me back to the bus stop. I tell her that I will try to find my way to Lily's office on my own next time. The minibus taxi isn't crowded, and I have a row of seats all to myself. As the minibus bounces over the city streets, I take out my notebook and look over my scribbled notes. My head is spinning with all the details of NGO organizing that Maryna so effortlessly reeled off. I write down a few phrases to summarize my thoughts on our conversation: Keen eye for opportunity. Diversification. Flexibility. Networking. Upward mobility.

The NGO-graphy of Postsocialism

Lily of the Valley was part of the late- and post-Soviet NGO boom in states such as Ukraine. As Maryna herself once told me, in the years just prior to and after the collapse of the Soviet Union, "NGOs grew like mushrooms after the rain." Many of the first "public associations of citizens" (*hromads'ki ob'iednannia*) were groups created in the months and years following perestroika and Ukrainian independence as means to help members cope with the turbulent social and economic changes they faced in their daily lives. Many such groups were formed by and for members of categories who faced specific disadvantages, including persons with disabilities and serious illnesses, veterans of the Afghanistan war, members of minority ethnic groups (such as Crimean Tatars and Roma), and large families. Unable to rely on the state for their survival in postsocialism, these groups formed mutual aid associations through which they shared resources and advice in efforts to improve their lives collectively. The numbers of civic and charitable organizations have risen steadily during the last decade.[1] Registered civic organizations (*hromads'ki orhanizatsiyi*) in Ukraine more than doubled between 1997 (14,148) and 2001 (29,918) (Sydorenko 2001:54). By 2006, there were more than 40,000 registered civic and charitable organizations.[2] In 1996, the majority of civic organizations (hereafter, NGOs) were devoted to problems of veterans and the disabled (14.6 percent), but by 1999 the number of NGOs dedicated to issues of health and sports had risen to form the majority (16.1 percent). Other common types of organizations include professional and cultural associations, minority rights groups, youth and children's associations, and NGOs dealing with ecological issues.

The range of groups registered as NGOs is truly vast. In 2003 I attended an event in Kyiv called "Kyiv Civic Organization Day" where NGO activists set up booths and tables to showcase their organizations, described their work to passers-by, and handed out printed materials and freebies. I picked up brochures from groups as diverse as the All-Ukrainian Workers' Union, the All-Ukrainian Coalition of Ecological NGOs, the "Elite Gymnasium 'Euro-land,'" the International Charitable Fund of Engineers, the Kyiv Association of Political Prisoners and Victims of Repression, the International Charitable Foundation "Otchyi Dim" (Father's House, for homeless children), the All-Ukrainian

Association of Entrepreneurs, the Kyiv Civic Organization "Amazonky" (for women with cancer), Mama-86 (an All-Ukrainian Environmental NGO), the All-Ukrainian Association of Lifeguards, and the Charitable Organization "Edelweiss Plus," dedicated to tourism development. Like Edelweiss Plus, more than a few of the NGOs seemed like thinly veiled businesses.

Women's groups make up a small percentage of Ukrainian NGOs (4.1 percent), but the number of women's NGOs doubled between 1997 and 2001 (Sydorenko 2001:53). As of 2001 there were approximately twelve hundred women's organizations in Ukraine, but growth seems to be slowing. In one survey of two hundred women's NGOs, 34.3 percent indicated a founding date before 1997, 63.2 percent were founded between 1997 and 1999, and just 2.5 percent were founded in 2000 (Sydorenko 2001:54). Of NGOs whose leaders and members consider themselves "women's groups," sociologist Alexandra Hrycak estimates that only roughly two dozen seek to improve women's status as a group rather than focusing on women in relation to children and the family (2006:74). Examples of the former include self-identifying feminist organizations, and those for women entrepreneurs and women in certain professions such as law and journalism.

Although the NGO boom is certainly partially a response to greater freedom of association and the need to address social problems and advocate for citizens' rights, it is also a product of the enormous resources that Western countries—particularly the United States—have devoted toward "civil society building" in the region. The Clinton administration allocated millions of dollars to projects designed to place limits on states, decentralize political power, and increase civic participation in Ukraine, a project that the George W. Bush administration continued. The U.S. government extended financial backing to numerous groups (such as Pora, the youth organization called "It's Time") that were key players in mobilizing the populace for the Orange Revolution, and, in 2005, $174 million was budgeted by all U.S. government agencies for assistance programs in Ukraine. Roughly one-fourth of this was directed to democracy programs, of which civil society development is a key component.[3] A range of institutions based in the United States, Canada, and the European Union have undertaken civil society development initiatives, including USAID, Freedom House, Counterpart Alliance for Partnership (CAP), the Soros Foundation's Open Society Institute and the International Renaissance Foundation, Technical Aid to the Commonwealth of Independent States (TACIS), the Eurasia Foundation, the United Nations Development Programme (UNDP), the Charles Stewart Mott Foundation, the National Endowment for Democracy-USA, the National Democratic Institute for International Affairs, the Canadian International Development Agency, and the NIS-US Women's Consortium. The *Guide to Foreign Funding Sources Available for Ukrainian Non-Profits*, published by the Innovation and Development Centre in Kyiv (2000b), lists sixty-eight foreign donor organizations, and this list is not comprehensive.

NGOs have been the bread and butter of international civil society building initiatives in Eastern Europe; William Fisher has called them the "favored

Figure 12. Kyiv Civic Organization Day, 2003. Photo by author.

child" of development (1997:442). Historically, an array of institutions have been understood as part of civil society, including schools, churches, interest groups, and even businesses—any institution, in short, that provides a forum for some type of "basic collective solidarity in a moral community" (Hann 1996:4). Increasingly, however, the international community—policy makers, granting agencies, and others with an interest in facilitating the "growth" of civil society—has tended to conflate civil society with NGOs, to the exclusion of other institutions. This narrow vision of civil society often leads politicians, granting agencies, and even some scholars to equate the "strength" of a given country's civil society with the number of NGOs. Why have international development organizations focused their efforts on civil society and NGOs in recent years?

Many anthropologists see this trend as a response to the failed modernization-oriented development efforts initiated in 1949, when President Truman introduced his "bold new program for making the benefits of our scientific advances and industrial progress available for the improvement and growth of underdeveloped areas."[4] The era of "development" was ushered in, and Truman was keen to distance the project from old-style imperialism, pitching it instead in terms of economic growth and modernity. Development historically has been measured in terms of economic growth, with the assumption that "even if not everyone benefits directly from growth, the 'trickle-down effect' will ensure that the riches of those at the top of the economic scale will eventually benefit the rest of society through increased production and thus employment" (Gardner and Lewis 1996:6–7). The trickle-down effect has failed to deliver, and critics of the development industry argue that development has worked mostly to the benefit of donor countries rather than beneficiary countries. According to Wolfgang Sachs, in 1960 the northern countries (which have historically been donors) were twenty times richer than the southern countries (historically recipients), and in 1980 the former were forty-six times richer (1999:3). A challenge to modernization discourse has arisen via the "basic needs" movement, whose proponents draw on neo-Marxist theory and dependency theory in which capitalism is interpreted as an inherently inegalitarian system. In the basic needs paradigm, stress is placed on the importance of combating poverty rather than focusing on modernization and industrialization. A basic needs agenda targets vulnerable groups such as small farmers and women-headed households for aid.

These critiques of "trickle down" have influenced contemporary development strategies, which have become more focused on a "bottom up from the grassroots" approach to change. Stimulating democratic-style "participation" among citizens, supporting NGOs as watchdogs for citizens vis-à-vis the state, and kindling "people power" in general have been especially important foci for development initiatives in postsocialist states such as Ukraine and Russia. In the postsocialist context, a "healthy civil society," in the minds of many Western politicians and scholars, is central to processes of democratization. Representatives of international development programs often tout a tripartite scheme of separate civil society, state, and market spheres (Cohen and Arato 1992) and thus encourage citizens' groups to develop "partnerships" with institutions of the state and the market (Hemment 2000). In this vision, as Chris Hann has argued, civil society is cast "in the role of David against the Goliath of the modern state, epitomised by the bureaucratic apparatus of state socialism" (1996:6). Based on such understandings, international foundations that promote civil society building in Eastern Europe see the development of civil society as a way to decentralize political power and increase civic participation in formerly socialist countries from the "bottom up."

It is generally assumed that civil society as such did not exist in the Soviet Union, since there was practically no place for citizens to convene and discuss public matters outside the watchful eye of the state. Countering this view, a number of scholars have argued that, in fact, the Soviet bloc had the ultimate civil society (Buck-Morss 2002) or at least a viable one characterized by a range of informal interpersonal practices that contributed to social cohesion and distinctive citizenship regimes.[5] Assuming that civil society as such was absent in the Soviet Union disregards the importance of Soviet-era networks that enabled citizens to come by scarce goods, obtain documents, enjoy special privileges, and generally sidestep or undermine state restrictions. These networks, one could argue, formed the basis of a "proto"-civil society. As David Abramson has written:

> Soviet life was not entirely devoid of the kind of relationships that make civil society work. To believe that it was lacking is also to take Soviet ideology, or the way it has often been represented, at face value. We know that there was a thriving underground economy, or market. We know that Soviet citizens relied on large networks of relatives, friends, colleagues, and friends of all of these categories of acquaintances to do what needed to be done—gain access to rare goods and services. The main difference has to do with the scale of civil society. (Abramson 1999b:8–9)

Additionally, discounting the socialities produced through Soviet social organizations (for instance, the Young Pioneers, the Komsomol, trade unions, common interest clubs, work collectives, and housing arrangements) ignores the important forms of political and social consciousness that such groups engendered, and the ways in which Soviet education and socialization processes prepared people to engage in social justice struggles in the postsocialist period. My informants stressed, for example, that their Komsomol activities had provided them with the organizational skills and knowledge necessary to deal with contemporary bureaucracies. However, the Western civil society models that have been uncritically transplanted to Eastern Europe by political actors and donors do not leave much room for different ways of thinking about civil society, or for recognizing and valuing the pertinent expertise that former Komsomol and Party activists might possess.

Many of these civil society building and NGO development efforts have centered on teaching and training people to become successful NGO cadres. International donor organizations provide local NGOs with project grants and impart technical assistance such as seminars on leadership, fund-raising, grant writing, working with mass media, and others. Some donor organizations also seek to foster coalition building between different groups and provide networking opportunities to NGO leaders. And, as Maryna admitted, "it is no secret that NGOs' goals are motivated by the priorities of donors." My informants who were tapping into foreign grant sources for their NGO work found themselves scrambling to keep up with donors' changing priorities, and to reconcile the "hot topics" with their own mission statements. Although many had successfully developed and carried out important projects (computer courses for youth, a database of NGOs, a series of seminars, a consciousness-raising video), sources of funding were often fleeting and donor exit frequently resulted in the abandonment of projects. That so much aid was directed toward technical assistance in the form of seminars, lectures, and meetings means that many NGO leaders have become employees of international foundations as trainers and even trainers of trainers. Activists who were involved in various NGO coalitions and in the work of international foundations often complained that so much of their time was occupied with "just talk" or "games." Technical assistance seems to have taken on a life of its own, and a veritable industry of

NGO management has grown up around the NGO sector. Institutions such as the Innovation and Development Centre (a nonprofit group encompassing both a civic organization and a charitable foundation) and the Gurt ("Cluster") Resource Center maintain databases, publish journals and handbooks for NGO activists, organize seminars, and offer for-fee services such as project assessment, "trainings," and event management. These institutions receive funding from international bodies, including, among others, the Charles Stewart Mott Foundation and the Renaissance Foundation.

Although many NGOs in Ukraine are highly regarded for the important advocacy and consciousness-raising work they do, average citizens in Ukraine tend to be somewhat suspicions of civic organizations. NGOs are often perceived as fictitious fronts for money laundering, and I heard numerous reports of bogus organizations that were supposedly registered with the exclusive purpose of procuring funds rather than advancing a social cause.[6] I have met many individuals who distance themselves from the work of NGOs, which they perceive as corrupt. This suspicion is even harbored by NGO activists themselves, who are apt to accuse other groups and activists of untoward behavior. Because funding and training so often come from foreign or transnational organizations, locals frequently assume that outsiders are being taken advantage of by cunning Ukrainian go-getters. NGO cadres who "live off grants" are sometimes denigrated as "grant-eaters" (*hrantoyidy*), since they seem to consume one grant after another.[7] Because the NGO sector is saturated with terminology and practices unfamiliar to many, those outside the sphere may see it as mysterious and suspect. One handbook for NGO activists includes a glossary with creative translations of words and concepts such as "vision" (*kontseptual'ne bachennia*, or conceptual view), "endowment funds" (*rehuliarni investytsiyi zadlia pidtrymky diial'nosti orhanizatsiyi*), and "charitable purpose" (*blahodiina meta*), among others (Counterpart Creative Center 2002). Some of the activists I knew initiated discussions of "civil society," "the third sector," "fund-raising," "grant writing," and "business etiquette," using a transnational NGO phraseology that would be unfamiliar to most people. They used awkward-sounding Russified and Ukrainianized English words such as *konsul'tant, partysypaturnyi, volontery* (volunteers), and *demokratizatsiia*. A break for coffee was even referred to by some activists as *kava breik,* a phrase they learned from attending seminars and trainings. The lexicon employed by NGO activists differed markedly from that utilized by acquaintances and friends who were not part of this scene, most of whom had no idea what the phrase "civil society" referred to. Many had never heard of "gender," a term for which there is no straightforward Russian or Ukrainian equivalent (although the words *gender* [pronounced with a hard "g"] and *hender* are being introduced into common language).[8]

In recent years, anthropologists have critically assessed the professionalization of NGO work and the "managed" quality that civil society has accrued in postsocialist Eastern Europe. Anthropologists studying NGOs and civil society processes in the region have questioned the romanticism of the "grassroots," exposed the less than altruistic motives of many NGO activists, critiqued donors' practices, questioned the clear-cut distinction between public and private spheres that much civil society theory assumes, and disputed the assumption that civil society necessarily constitutes a non-state, non-market sphere.[9] One aspect of transnational donor interventions that has been less remarked upon includes the social and economic dislocation of particular types of NGOs and activists that often occurs as a result of civil society development interventions. The prioritizing of certain agendas over others by donors effects an evaluation and sorting of NGOs, which then have uneven access to the resources offered by international donor organizations. This has certainly been true for different types of women's NGOs in Ukraine, and for the individual organizations in my study. Civil society building programs thus have the potential to stimulate processes of differentiation among social activists, a consequence of international development initiatives that has been little explored. Differentiation also occurs as the result of strategies for self-improvement and self-reflection that are introduced to women in Ukraine via NGO leadership and women's rights training programs. As activists begin to inhabit the new NGO world and rethink themselves as women and citizens, they develop new criteria with which to evaluate themselves and others. To grasp how the Ukrainian "third sector" has become an important site for the differentiation of post-Soviet citizens, and to contextualize the little histories of the NGO activists I studied in Kyiv, it is necessary first to trace the history of women and NGO development.

"This is up to women, of course": NGO Histories ("Herstories")

For centuries a Ukrainian woman was the guardian [Berehynia] of the home hearth, took care of the customs of the ancestors, national language, morality, ethos, education, culture, [and] participated in the struggle for the high ideals of Ukrainian statehood.

—from the 1990 statute of Soiuz Ukrainok
(Ukrainian Women's Association)

Ukraine has a long history of social activism among women extending back into the pre-Soviet period.[10] As inhabitants of lands that were continuously divided between one regime or another, "Ukrainians almost never had a state capable and willing to support even rudimentary welfare programs, [and] Ukrainian communities devised a whole network of community cultural, economic, educational, and social organizations to address those needs" (Bohachevsky-Chomiak 1994:21).[11] Historically, women were especially active in establishing community-oriented organizations that engaged in practical work, such as aiding the elderly, the sick, and children. This was particularly true in Western Ukraine, which was part of the Austro-Hungarian Empire until the First World War, at which time Western Ukraine became part of Poland, Romania, and Czechoslovakia until finally being incorporated into the

Soviet Union during the Second World War. Women's groups in that region in the late nineteenth century could be characterized as organizations with a "patriotic" orientation emphasizing family, self-sacrifice, and national tradition (Bohachevsky-Chomiak 1988:97). Some of these groups were quite large; one Ukrainian women's organization called Zhinocha Hromada (Women's Community) had eighteen branches until it was disbanded after the Bolshevik Revolution (Stites 1978:227). Another group, Soiuz Ukrainok (Ukrainian Women's Association), was originally founded in the then Polish city of L'viv in 1917, and included more than fifty thousand members. These traditions of local volunteerism and community activism were squelched by the Soviet regime, since any organizational activities not sanctioned by the Party were deemed subversive. This was especially true for the non-Soviet women's organizations such as Soiuz Ukrainok, whose agendas were interpreted as nationalist.

After the Bolsheviks came to power, a Women's Section of the Communist Party, Zhenotdel (Zhinviddil in Ukrainian), was established to coordinate work with women Party members. But it was abolished in 1930, and Stalin promptly declared that Soviet women had been liberated from all forms of oppression. Although historical information on the Ukrainian zhinviddily is sketchy, by all accounts they were never very large or active (Bohachevsky-Chomiak 1988: 292). Richard Stites notes that villagers resisted the work of zhinviddily in rural areas of Ukraine, and that provincial zhinviddily offices also suffered from shortages of funds and personnel deficiencies (1978:339). A common perception among rural folk was that the zhinviddily reflected the aspirations of the Muscovite center, not local priorities. Language barriers were also an issue, since Russian-speaking women frequently were used for propaganda work in the Ukrainian villages (Bohachevsky-Chomiak 1988:293). Reportedly, "at the beginning of collectivization women organizers in the Ukraine had to dispel the rumors which said that in the new kolkhozes [collective farms] the young women would be 'shared' by the men and the old ones boiled down for soap" (Stites 1978:339). During the 1920s, some elite women known as the *obshchestvenitsi* (*obshchestvo* is the Russian word for "society") engaged in philanthropic and activist work as a way to "make themselves useful," since, much to the chagrin of representatives of the new socialist state, they did not take up paid employment. These women, often wives of industrial managers and other elite cadres, took part in the activities of the Zhenotdel, volunteered in children's crèches, and lent assistance to workers at their husbands' factories. The "social work" that women undertook was largely unremunerated, and thus social activism was seen as the choice women made who elected not to engage in wage labor—in other words, it was viewed as their hobby.

With the dissolution of the Zhenotdel, women were prevented from developing other channels to advance women's issues, which were funneled to lower-tier structures that focused on encouraging higher birth rates and offering services to children. During World War II, Soviet women were mobilized to provide assistance to war orphans and wounded veterans in antifascist committees that became the basis of the Zhensovet (Women's Soviet), a Union-wide structure centered in Moscow with local Zhensovety in all fifteen Soviet republics. Hrycak notes that these structures operated "primarily as transmission belts for official policies that perpetuated norms that held women primarily accountable for family responsibilities" (2005:70). Women were active in officially sanctioned youth and children's groups such as the Young Pioneers, the Komsomol, and a range of clubs, and they made up a considerable membership of official Party groups based in the workplace. But they were less visible in the Party leadership and in positions of political power, despite quotas guaranteeing women a certain percentage of seats in local and republic-level government.

In 1987, Gorbachev, as part of his reform program, revived the Zhensovety (Zhinochi rady, Women's Councils, in Ukrainian) with the goal of helping working women better fulfill their "womanly mission" as wives and mothers. The Zhinochi rady were attached to workplaces and were never very popular, even though it was decreed that every woman in a major work collective was required to join. The leaders of the Women's Councils—seen by most as a token, rubber-stamp organization—were regarded as Party functionaries uninterested in the real problems of working women. The Women's Council never addressed existent questions of women's equality, and it petered out when the Soviet Union disintegrated. The structure was subsequently revived as the Spilka Zhinok Ukrainy (Confederation of Women of Ukraine), the only women's organization in Ukraine born out of the Soviet system. Spilka Zhinok did adopt a women's rights orientation, and its leader, Mariia Orlyk, articulated its major goals: achieving equality for women and men, protecting women's interests in the conditions of the market, and fostering the creation of women's small businesses (Smoliar 2000a:25). Subsequently, today Spilka Zhinok supports cooperatives, joint ventures, and a Society of Ukrainian Businesswomen. The organization's preoccupation with economic questions (and thus women's adaptation to new market conditions) is in step with the tradition of state socialism from which Spilka Zhinok emerged, and this focus has engendered suspicion toward the group on the part of women who seek to make a clean break with socialist thought and practice.

Soiuz Ukrainok (The Ukrainian Women's Association) was reestablished in L'viv in 1990, and the conscious reference to the pre-Soviet organization has served to legitimate the new women's movement in Ukraine as a patriotic activity (Bohachevsky-Chomiak 2000:33). The group has not pursued a stated women's rights agenda, and in 1990 the president of Soiuz Ukrainok in L'viv, Oksana Sapeliak, declared that, "before she and her Association sisters start liberating women, they must first liberate the nation" (Rubchak 1996:317). The various chapters of Soiuz Ukrainok (which exist countrywide) have concerned themselves primarily with the well-being of children and orphans, and have striven to "take care of the formation of national consciousness, to engage women in public activities and to elevate the spirituality of Ukrainian women" (Pavlychko 1992:91). Like many women's organizations in Ukraine, Soiuz Ukrainok has a maternalist character (women's roles as mothers are stressed) and emphasizes the roles women play in preserving and shaping national culture. However, on the practical level, members of Soiuz Ukrainok actively engage in humanitarian work for children, the disabled, and the elderly, support the activities of women entrepreneurs, and take part in political affairs by cooperating with various political parties and sponsoring candidates during parliamentary elections.

Zhinocha Hromada (Women's Community), also named after a previous women's association in Ukraine that was disbanded by the Soviets, was formed as the women's section of Rukh in early 1990. The Hromada split off to pursue its own women-centered agenda in 1992. The early founders of the Zhinocha Hromada were less concerned with women's rights than with national liberation, and some of these activists expressed their conviction that "women should be politically active only during the present state of unrest in the country but in the future, when the goals are fulfilled and Ukraine is independent, women should return home to fulfill their primary maternal obligations" (Pavlychko 1992:93). As with Soiuz Ukrainok, the group's initial agenda privileged national emancipation over women's liberation. Today the group focuses on women's equal rights, raising women's national and political awareness, and getting women elected to political office. The leadership and membership of Zhinocha Hromada contains a large number of women scientists, and the group's work often focuses on issues of women's and children's health. Zhinocha Hromada frequently holds international conferences on women's rights and health issues and publishes the conference proceedings. These three organizations—Spilka Zhinok, Soiuz Ukrainok, and Zhinocha Hromada—are the largest women's groups in Ukraine, and the most well known. They are all-Ukrainian organizations with many local branches. They are headed by what my informants called "political wives" (the wives of prominent politicians), and are thus associated with the Ukrainian political elite. These activist women belong to different political factions, which has stymied the creation of a women's coalition. None of the leaders in my study was affiliated with these large, powerful women's groups, but some referred to them frequently to distinguish themselves from the political wives who, they said, "are supported by the backs of their husbands."

During the late 1980s and early 1990s several other important women's organizations were established in Ukraine, including the Organization of Soldiers' Mothers of Ukraine (OSMU), an offshoot of the Committee of Soldiers' Mothers in Moscow. The OSMU was formed in 1990 by mothers of military conscripts to call the Soviet government to account for the poor conditions in the armed forces, and to draw attention to the hazing of new conscripts and the untimely deaths of soldiers during peacetime. The organization has a political character and coordinates its efforts with other organizations. The group was successful in pushing through legislation regulating the conscripting of Ukrainian soldiers to serve in other republics, and it was involved in efforts to dismantle the Soviet army and create an independent army for Ukraine (Smoliar 2000b:15). My acquaintances in Ukraine have high regard for the

Soldiers' Mothers. One friend who sought advice for a young disabled veteran regarding his rights to a pension found the OSMU's leadership to be very approachable, knowledgeable, efficient, and dedicated to issues of soldiers' rights. In 1992, some members of this group broke away to form Mothers and Sisters for Soldiers of Ukraine; this organization has been concerned with raising national consciousness among servicemen and among Ukrainian youth and children more generally.

Many women's groups have organized around ecological issues, demanding more stringent standards for industry and seeking to garner medical assistance for ill children. The most well-known ecologically oriented women's organization in Ukraine is Mama-86, a group founded in 1990 by mothers whose children were born around the time of the 1986 Chernobyl accident. The organization continues to focus its efforts on providing medical assistance to women and children who suffer Chernobyl-related illnesses, lobbying for reform of Ukraine's burdensome energy policy, pushing for a cleaner water supply, and promoting general environmental consciousness. Mama-86 is a highly visible group, and its representatives frequently appear in the Ukrainian mass media to discuss ecological problems and avenues for reform.

Like Mama-86, many of the women's groups that began to form in Ukraine during perestroika were mainly concerned with women in their capacity as mothers. Ukrainian women have rarely organized on the basis of political agendas concerned specifically with women's rights in general (as opposed to mothers' rights). Rather, they have most often organized as wives and mothers to protect the rights of their children, or as specific groups of women (e.g., disabled women, elderly women). Mothers themselves have also been targets of women's activism, as many groups demand state protection or assistance for various categories of needy mothers, including mothers of disabled children, single mothers, mothers of large families, and soldiers' mothers. The centrality of motherhood, nurturing, and care giving for women's subjectivities is taken as a given by many activists and their constituencies, who believe that women can best serve society and their families by executing their "natural-given" duties as wives and mothers. These groups do not seek to challenge the existing gender order, and many see a return to the Ukrainian tradition of a strong family and equal (but separate) roles for men and women as a solution to contemporary social crises (Hrycak 2006:75). Such mandates have been bolstered in the post-Soviet years by a Ukrainian nationalist discourse that lifts women up as "mothers of the nation." In many respects this is a pronatalist agenda, one that emphasizes women's roles and responsibilities as mothers, nurturers, and culture bearers. Indeed, when my husband (a Ukrainian) and I married in Rivne oblast' (district) in 1999, as part of the scripted ceremony the Justice of the Peace charged us with the mission of "birthing many children for our Ukrainian state."

Several of the groups in my study focused on the needs of mothers, children, and youth, including the NGOs led by Svetlana and Vira, Maryna, and Ivana. It was interesting to track how my relationships with these women changed over the years after I married and had a child, and was thus expected to have a better understanding of their concerns as wives and mothers. Svetlana and Vira threw a wedding party for me just after I had married, and from that moment our conversations took on a whole new dimension. We shared funny wedding stories (Vira ate too many pickles at her wedding and developed an allergy, Svetlana's parents bought so much wine for her wedding that they drank it for the next six months, and the women doubled over with laughter when I described trudging to the outhouse in my wedding dress); the women also began to talk more about their family lives. The change was even more marked after I had a son in 2001. When I returned to Kyiv in 2002, Svetlana and Vira were very excited to meet my "little Cossack," and I think it is no coincidence that, after I became a mother, Svetlana's youngest daughter mailed me a drawing of her mother, herself, and her two siblings that she titled "My Family." In their eyes, I finally had one.

The close symbolic association between NGO activities, women, motherhood, and the national idea is represented in concrete terms on the cover of one glossy directory of Kyiv's civic and charitable organizations, which sports on its cover a compelling image of the Berehynia, a photograph of the statue on Independence Square (Innovation and Development Centre 2001). The centrality of motherhood and the restoration of Ukrainian tradition to women's social activism are also reflected in the large numbers of women's organizations that call themselves "Berehynia" or utilize Berehynia symbolism. At the "Kyiv Civic Organization Day" event in 2003 I collected printed material from all the women's NGOs represented and spoke with many of the NGO leaders. At least two of these groups were called Berehynia—the Makariv Rural Women's Association Berehynia and the charitable fund Kyiv Berehynia. The Makariv group's symbol is two hands cradling the earth and a couple of leaves, and the Kyiv Berehynia brochure depicts a woman in a traditional Ukrainian embroidered blouse reading to a young boy. Perusing a directory of women's NGOs, I found that a group called Berehynia exists in practically every city and region of Ukraine, and frequently more than one. In line with this maternalist focus, several other groups at the NGO fair utilized the Madonna and Child in their organizational symbolism, including a charitable organization called the Kyiv Mother's Movement and a women's center and newspaper from the city of Cherkasy. The most high-profile women's organizations with booths at the event were Mama-86 and La Strada-Ukraine, an NGO working to combat trafficking in women. Aside from this latter group, few organizations had a stated women's rights or feminist orientation.

The "women's face" of caring and service-oriented NGOs in Ukraine is a result of several factors—local nationalistic, patriarchal discourses about women's roles, and the structural constraints that shape women's lives in the post-Soviet milieu. Like Svetlana, Vira, Maryna, and others in my study, many women have taken up NGO leadership roles as a form of alternative employment in a tight labor market. Although my informants were usually classified as volunteers in non-salaried positions, they were often able to budget creatively and carve out some kind of recompense for their work and time. Those activists who became trainers for international NGOs were quite well paid ($75 for a day-long session in the late 1990s), though this work was time-consuming and required frequent travel. Women activists I knew were motivated by the idea that women are particularly suited for advocacy and caring work. At the same time, they certainly recognized that women were going into the NGO sphere while men predominated in business and politics.

On the one hand, tropes describing "women's nature" and maternal instincts were used by some activists to explain why so many NGO leaders in Ukraine were women. Ivana, for example, often referred to women's public roles as an extension of their familial roles:

> These problems that we address, they are more connected to the emotional sphere, and women are better at solving such problems. A man is more rational, he wants to address everything pragmatically. But a woman knows how to talk to a person, to have a psychological effect. She uses more emotional methods. Men think that these social problems—drug abuse, alcoholism, and so on—will solve themselves, or that they are the purview of specialists. But women turn the fight against such problems into a kind of dedication, like I have. My husband thinks it is all nonsense. . . . You have to ask the girls questions and then listen to them. It takes a lot of patience to hear out girls with these kinds of problems, and to give them advice. And this is up to women, of course. It's usually up to mothers.

At the same time, Ivana also recognized that NGOs were one of the only public spaces open to women in conditions of post-Soviet economic crisis. She understood that sex discrimination in hiring was partly to blame and that activist work was becoming a women's sphere precisely because it was not prestigious:

> Many women work in social organizations, and men either go without work or find themselves [work] that is considered more "masculine," in *serious* institutions, enterprises, and so on [my emphasis]. More women than men are unemployed. These are mostly women educated as engineers who became the army of the unemployed when all of our enterprises in Ukraine closed down. Now I meet a lot of women who I used to work with at a [state] enterprise. Now they work at the bazaars. They were fairly highly qualified economists and mechanical engineers. Other women found themselves a way out of this situation, and they went into social work. It is sad . . . I don't want to say it is sad that they do social work, but that . . . the rights of women here are violated.

Despite her flowery narratives about women being suited for work dealing with the "emotional sphere," Ivana saw that women's inequality on the job market was pushing them into the "third sector" as volunteer social workers. The common perception that women are sympathetic caregivers means that they have been left to pick up the pieces doing advocacy and relief work while representatives of state institutions have remained relatively disinterested in the plight of disadvantaged populations, withdrawing their efforts to focus on markets and globalization. This trend has become institutionalized: during the 1990s the buildings that once housed state-run day care centers (now defunct because of low birth rates and a lack of funds) were being offered by the state to new civic organizations—many of which are designed to protect the interests of children and families—as subsidized premises. This represents a clear shift of responsibility for social welfare from the state to NGOs, especially the caring-focused NGOs that women tend to run. Meanwhile, women continue to make up the majority of the unemployed, face glass ceilings in nearly every profession, are poorly represented in the new business sphere, and have a weak political voice. Despite the establishment of many new women's NGOs, some of which have the backing of political elites, a discourse of "women's rights" has not been established firmly in Ukraine, and most women certainly have not situated their activism within a feminist paradigm.

The lack of connection with ideas of feminism felt by many women in formerly socialist countries has been well documented.[12] The term "feminism" conjures up negative connotations in many post-Soviet countries, as it is associated with loss of femininity, a hatred for men, lesbianism, and a desire for total independence. As Nancy Ries has noted, for Russia, "Feminists are supposedly part of a movement against *nature* itself, presumably desiring to turn women into men and men into women, something seen as being as illogical, absurd, brutal, and ruinous as the worst follies of the communist world-remaking project" (1994:245). Many also associate feminism with a rejection of the family, and may correlate contemporary feminism with the failed state feminism of the Soviet Union. As in other former Soviet countries, gender studies and women's studies have emerged from the initiatives of a few academics, not via a mass women's movement (Chukhym and Skoryk 2000; Zhurzhenko 2001a: 504). Centers for these studies have been founded in Kyiv, L'viv, Odesa, Sumy, and Kharkiv, where scholars are working out approaches to gender theory and local histories through historical and sociological research. Some of these include the Kyiv Center for Gender Studies, the Kyiv Center for Women's Studies, the Kharkiv Center for Gender Studies, the Odesa Scientific Center for Women's Studies, the Sumy Center for Women's Studies, and the L'viv Research Center "Woman and Society." Since 1997, the Kharkiv Center for Gender Studies has sponsored a Summer School in Gender Studies, held in Foros, on the Black Sea coast. These efforts, thus far, have not engendered a widespread feminist consciousness in the country, and self-identified feminists, without doubt, comprise the smallest number of women activists in Ukraine.[13]

Empowering (a Few of) Ukraine's Women

Given the inequalities women in Ukraine face, numerous international NGOs (several of them based in the U.S.) have targeted Ukrainian women for assistance since the early 1990s.[14] The major sources of funding for programs focusing on women and women's NGOs have been the "civil society" programs of the Open Society Institute, USAID, UNDP, and Technical Aid to the Commonwealth of Independent States (TACIS). The agenda of these donors is to facilitate women's empowerment and strengthen the capabilities of women's NGOs. The programs they sponsor are designed to help women develop leadership skills, foster reeducation and job placement opportunities, prepare women for political office, and address problems such as domestic violence and the international sex trade. They provide several types of assistance: grants for the implementation of women-focused projects, programs to facilitate transnational and local NGO networks, and "trainings" for NGO activists and other women interested in acquiring leadership skills. Each of these donor organizations has funded a range of specific initiatives, some of which have been contracted to other groups.

The unexpected and sometimes even potentially detrimental effects of well-intentioned donor aid on women's movements and the work of women's NGOs in Eastern Europe have received considerable attention from scholars in recent years.[15] It is no secret that donor organizations often base priorities and development agendas on understandings of gender relations and women's roles that diverge from those held by many of the women the interventions are designed to help. "Feminism-by-design" (Ghodsee 2005), or "foundation feminism" (Hrycak 2006), are terms scholars have used to describe gender assistance programs based on Western feminist ideas that fail to address local women's perceived needs. Such interventions in the region have led some women's groups to abandon or modify their original mandates as they pursue funding opportunities based on the priorities of foreign donors. Counter to the stated goals of many programs designed to strengthen women's initiatives and facilitate local coalition building, the infusion of resources into women's NGO development frequently has resulted in the empowerment of an elite cadre of NGO leaders, experts, and trainers without a concomitant strengthening of the "grassroots." On the other hand, programs promoting "women in leadership" and others have resulted in upward mobility for some activists, who have developed skills and networks they can use to enter into important roles in the public sphere, and into rewarding careers. Processes of differentiation are thus an integral part of the NGO development industry, as the mandates of various NGOs are evaluated relative to how well they square with the donors' priorities and visions for development and "empowerment."

In Ukraine, programs implemented by transnational advocacy groups to support women and NGO development have had mixed effects. Frequently international interventions have decreased local control over women's NGOs and agendas, making local groups dependent on international donors. Although such support has resulted in the establishment of programs for women's economic empowerment, anti-trafficking initiatives, and other projects, competition for foreign funding sometimes has caused local groups to split further apart rather than form coalitions and undertake joint projects. Thus, the interventions of Western women's rights organizations have strengthened international coalition building but have actually weakened local coalitions between women's groups. Moreover, Alexandra Hrycak has found that, in Ukraine, "only a handful of the hundreds of [women's] organizations that have formed since independence have benefited from foreign training or encouragement"

(2006:78). In the case of women's groups, this has much to do with donors' evaluations of local organizations' mandates.

For the most part, donor organizations in Ukraine have devalued the maternalist orientation of the majority of women's groups, which normally have not received much Western funding or had access to trainings and other resources. Donors appear to have a working assumption that a motherist or mothers' rights platform is incompatible with a women's rights platform. This view overlooks the political potential of maternalist claims, and the fact that social activism centered on motherhood and a "feminine consciousness" allows women to extend their influence beyond the private life of their families into the economic and political spheres—organizations for Soldiers' Mothers are a good example of this possibility (Caiazza 2002). Nevertheless, the orientation of maternalist organizations and their focus on women as mothers and wives is rejected by most foreign donor organizations and their local, Ukrainian representatives in favor of a mandate that more directly engages issues of women's rights (as donor organizations see them). In this context, as Hrycak (2006) argues, the primary beneficiaries of many civil society development initiatives targeting women have been a self-selected group of educated women who share donors' models of activism and Western feminism, and are hostile to the discourses of reviving "tradition" that have motivated much of women's social activism in the country. Far from bolstering the work of local and all-Ukrainian women's NGOs, Hrycak has found, development programs have actually drained resources from them. She notes that several of the former leaders of Soiuz Ukrainok and Zhinocha Hromada left these organizations and founded their own organizations with a feminist mandate in order to better suit donors' priorities. Hrycak refers to these remade activists as "hybrid feminists," women whose dedication to feminist ideas are doubted by other NGO leaders, and who eventually abandoned civic work to become full-time salaried employees of foreign donor organizations (Hrycak 2006:89).

Some of Hrycak's findings were confirmed by a conversation I had with Ivana during 1999, when she discussed the difficulties she had experienced establishing contacts with one of the transnational women's advocacy organizations in Kyiv. She initially read about the organization in a women's magazine, but the contact information was incorrect and Ivana spent several weeks tracking down the right phone number. Finally, she said:

> I visited the NIS-US Women's Consortium and became familiar with their programs. But . . . in those organizations, unfortunately, they do not allow outsiders (Rus. *chuzhie*) in right away. One must be very careful with them; it is a really closed circle of personal relationships. For the most part it is people of the circle (Rus. *vse svoi liudi*). It is [a group of] girlfriends, brothers, sisters, and so on. They don't need outsiders.

Ivana went on to describe how she gradually became an insider by proving her character and by being generally useful and accommodating to the administration:

For a long while I had to prove that I am an absolutely normal person, and that they didn't have to fear any shenanigans out of me. [I had to prove that] I am totally open and that I help those people who ask for it. That it is possible to work with me. And until I was able to establish friendly contacts with them—by visiting them often at first, and by asking to participate in those seminars and so on—getting into that organization required me to beat my forehead against a wall for a long time.

Eventually Ivana became a paid trainer for the organization, and she said that gaining recognition through the Consortium had allowed her to become a part of city, national, and international NGO development networks. Ivana's experience illustrates how an insider clique of activists has formed around Western funding agencies, making it difficult for "outsiders" to break in. Valerie Sperling (1999) found the same situation to be true in Russia, where competition for access to NGO resources posed barriers to networking among groups and activists. Leaders that did manage to become part of such exclusive cadres enjoyed a range of privileges, but the creation of an elite cadre of NGO activists around Western funding efforts may subvert donors' stated goal of "promoting democracy" by supporting a flourishing NGO sector, since participation in some NGO networks is open only to a select few.

Will the Market Set Them Free?

Not all development interventions into the Ukrainian "third sector" are designed to target women and women's NGOs, of course. But given local conditions—especially those of a transforming economy and the reassertion of patriarchal attitudes toward women's roles—NGO development aid sometimes ends up affecting women and women's groups in unanticipated ways. Programs designed to stimulate "social enterprise" are a case in point. During 1999, Counterpart International, Inc., a global partnership organization headquartered in the U.S., introduced social enterprise (Rus. *obshchestvenyi biznes*) to NGOs in Ukraine via a training and granting program that lasted until 2002.[16] I have found that social enterprise as it has unfolded in Ukraine is an NGO development strategy implicitly directed toward women. It is thus important to assess the potential of social enterprise initiatives to empower women in Ukraine's emerging civil society and market economy. Two of the women in my study—Maryna and Myroslava (the director of an umbrella organization for NGOs serving women with disabilities)—had experience with social enterprise. I also interviewed another activist in Kyiv (Svetlana Mishchenko, not to be confused with Svetlana of Our House) more extensively about her experiences with social business.[17] Additionally, during 2002 I interviewed several Ukrainian employees of Counterpart Alliance for Partnership (CAP), the organization most instrumental in introducing the concept of social enterprise to Ukrainian NGOs. Counterpart's social enterprise program ended in Ukraine in 2002, but the social enterprise program has been replicated in Belarus and also in Bulgaria as the "Bulgaria Pilot Community Fund and Social Enterprise program" (Alter 2002:i). A close examination of the Ukrainian case may shed light on prospects for the failure or success of the social enterprise model of NGO development throughout the region.

In recent years, social entrepreneurship has been promoted worldwide by organizations such as Ashoka (a global organization that funds individual social entrepreneurs as Ashoka Fellows), USAID, and Virtue Ventures (a management consulting firm that specializes in helping nonprofits develop business expertise and encouraging for-profits to integrate social goals into their business practices) (Alter 2001, 2002). Very little has been written on social entrepreneurship in the Eastern European context; exceptions include Alter (2002) and Kenny (2002). Others who have referred to "social entrepreneurs" in the former Soviet bloc have used the concept in a very general fashion to refer to key social actors or creative leaders, who might include individuals (intellectuals, religious figures), committees, NGOs, and the state itself (Najafizadeh and Mennerick 2003), or persons and groups who "explore new organizational forms as ongoing sources of innovation" (Bach and Stark 2002:3).

This "catalytic leadership" understanding of social entrepreneurship diverges from the ideas on social enterprise that emerged in the context of perceived crises in the welfare states of Europe, Australia, Canada, and the U.S. Social enterprise surfaced in these regions in the 1990s as a strategy to shift some of the burden for welfare provision from states to nonprofit agencies while empowering individuals and communities to generate sustainable social and economic development. As Gray, Healy, and Crofts note, "In general, the direction of social enterprise initiatives is towards practices which extend the options available to service users [i.e., welfare recipients] for both social and economic participation, based on the notion that government should, at most, facilitate rather than provide such options" (2003:144). Some critics see the social entrepreneurship movement as a neoliberal attack on the welfare state, one that ignores macroeconomic constraints and, by attributing "welfare dependency" to individuals' own "lack," threatens to replace social justice with social control (Cook, Dodds, and Mitchell 2003:67–68).

Social entrepreneurship is usually conceptualized as initiatives that are either for-profit yet pursue some socially beneficial goals ("businesses with a conscience") or nonprofits that lay down business structures in order to generate a funding base and free themselves from dependence on and obligation to donors. Also included are "affirmative businesses" that provide employment opportunities to disadvantaged groups such as the physically, mentally, economically, and educationally challenged. This is the dominant form social enterprises have taken in Western Europe, where they are often described as "social firms." Social enterprise, which straddles the sectors of nonprofits and business, is a "fused discourse" drawing on "ideas of engagement and self-determination located in the activist framework" and "the individualistic idea of self-determination in the market framework, where competition and leadership are important, and where individuals, left to their own resources, become resilient" (Kenny 2002:296). Alan Fowler has noted that social entrepreneurship "links the morality and objective of public benefit to characteristics commonly attributed to entrepreneurs in the private sector," such as "risk-taking, self-confidence, self-motivation . . . with keen attention to an economic 'bottom line'" (2000: 645). Generally, social enterprise is an idea infused with can-do notions of self-reliance, sustainability, innovation, creativity, risk taking, organizing, and leadership (Mort, Weerawardena, and Carnegie 2003). Socially engaged scholars in Western Europe, the U.S., and Australia have critiqued the "fused discourse" of social enterprise; nevertheless, the model has been exported to Eastern European countries such as Ukraine by international development organizations.

Why might donors perceive postsocialist states as a natural testing ground for aid programs to facilitate the development of social enterprise? First, the promotion of social enterprise strategies in the region is part of the wider approach of "transitology," an analytical and policy-oriented paradigm that has tended to conceive postsocialist transformations as a progression toward a natural, known, and specific end (i.e., from centralized socialist economies toward market-based, Western-style democracies) (Verdery 1996:228). Although motivated partly by the problematic teleological ideology of "transition," international development organizations such as Counterpart also recognize that welfare reform in postsocialist states has left many categories of citizens in dire straits, and that local NGOs are obligated to address these needs. In this context, social enterprise is valued as a strategy to empower these service-providing NGOs to generate their own operating capital to promote "sustainability." This is perceived as especially pressing in a context where many local NGOs are in a funding crisis, competition for sponsorship runs high, donor exit is always immanent, and NGO-state relations are often fraught with tension. Representatives of state institutions may see NGOs as a threat, and are often intent on keeping a tight rein on their activities, especially those perceived as potentially profitable.

With its focus on NGOs, social enterprise as promoted in Ukraine fits hand in glove with the international community's emphasis on civil society development initiatives in Eastern Europe since the mid-1990s. Indeed, the social enterprise initiative in Ukraine was spearheaded by Counterpart Alliance for Partnership (CAP), a civil society program designed to cultivate "social partnerships" between NGOs and local governments. As a strategy to build partnerships between nonprofit (civil society) and business (market) structures, social enterprise emerges from the "third sector" model of civil society development that has been promoted in the region by many international donor organizations. This model privileges the need for a strong civil society, with minimal state interference, yet with strong "cross-sector partnerships" across the spheres of state, market, and civil society (Hemment 1998). It has been part and parcel of democratization projects implemented in the region.

Although social enterprise in the Eastern European context may be critiqued as issuing from the flawed model of transition, it actually has a historical precedent in the region. In the Soviet Union, in a sense, social enterprise already existed, since enterprises in the socialist economies of Eastern Europe pursued both economic and social objectives. State-run firms carried a certain burden of social service provision, such as operating kindergartens and shops, offering medical care, providing extensive family leave, and so on. In the Soviet Union, workers' cooperatives (artels) were developed specifically to employ persons with disabilities, and many enterprises were required to hire a certain number of disabled persons as a percentage of the workforce. Thus, the fusion of social service provision and business structures that social enterprise entails is not entirely new to the region. In this regard, social enterprise departs from earlier interventions in the region that posited the Soviet Union as a tabula rasa and discounted or devalued local forms of knowledge. Similarly new is that technology transfer here is not unidirectional, in contrast to many other development programs in the region.[18] In this regard, social enterprise, though a somewhat fraught development strategy when applied in the postsocialist context, represents a more innovative and dialogical development encounter compared to previous programs.

How has social enterprise played out in Ukraine? In 1999, CAP implemented a pilot program to provide recoverable grants (i.e., interest-free loans) to NGO leaders interested in establishing a social enterprise. The program ran into problems from the start owing to what one CAP employee, Serhiy, called the "low level of applicants' business skills." Only previous CAP grantees were invited to enter the grant competition; five of these applicants were selected to undertake business plan training in preparation for the final selection. According to Serhiy, the submitted business plans were unacceptable, and CAP recognized the need to provide more extensive business training before awarding any recoverable grants. Thus, forty-five NGO leaders who had previously enjoyed Counterpart support received business training (Serhiy explained that the cost to train five versus forty-five persons would be approximately the same), and four of these were awarded recoverable grants of $1,000 to start a small business.

A Counterpart-sponsored publication titled *Case Studies* (Alter 2002) includes detailed information on the four NGOs and their leaders (all of them women) that received these grants. Mercy Charitable Foundation (Mercy) is a Christian faith-based organization with several programs to support vulnerable populations in the city of Zhytomyr, especially low-income families and substance abusers. In 2000, Mercy opened a café (the café catered to paying customers and provided free meals to the hungry) that became a permanent funding source. Among Mercy's other successes, it is noted that, "of Mercy's $10,000 annual operating budget, 100 percent is generated from earned income," and that, in successfully navigating a range of bureaucratic and legislative hurdles, Mercy's leadership "influenced public policy and legislation for future social enterprises" (Alter 2002:18). The successes of the Alisa Society for the Disabled appear equally impressive. In 2001, the organization provided jobs to more than seven hundred persons with disabilities, by establishing six business enterprises and providing job training and placement opportunities for the disabled since 1997. The organization became less dependent on donor support (25 percent of operating costs are self-generated) and improved public perceptions about the ability of disabled persons to perform in the workplace (Alter 2002:28). Other organizations highlighted in *Case Studies* include the Peace Beauty Culture Association, an organization promoting Ukrainian national culture that started a fashion business in 2001, and Ariadna, an NGO in Kharkiv that provides educational opportunities for schoolchildren in the areas of business and computers. In 2000, Ariadna's leadership established a pay-for-service International Education Center for Youth to help generate revenue to sustain its activities.

Case Studies also details the difficulties involved in launching social enterprise in post-Soviet Ukraine, problems that include dealing with convoluted, corrupt, even violent bureaucracies; undercapitalization (inadequate financing); and balancing the intermingled demands of business and social mission. The problems faced by the Ukrainian recipients of CAP's social enterprise grants reveal some of the difficulties inherent in importing a capitalist model of business to a postsocialist society. But they are also symptoms of (mis)applying Western ideologies about NGOs, civil societies, markets, and states to development endeavors in formerly socialist countries. The most salient (and potentially problematic) ideas embedded in the social enterprise strategy include the treatment of the radical free market as a natural solution to citizens' problems, and a neoliberal vision of minimal state support for social service provision. These framings dismiss certain important legacies of state socialism, particularly the hostile post-Soviet business climate, local definitions of citizenship and citizens' needs and entitlements, and local gender formations. Overlooking such legacies may hurt Ukrainian NGO activists in the long run, and women especially.

For those trained in classical civil society rhetoric, the combination of NGO and business structures entailed in the social enterprise strategy may strike an odd note. Convention dictates that nongovernmental organizations are necessarily not for profit, and there are laws to this effect in Ukraine. However, in recent years scholars, policy makers, and development organizations have privileged a model of society (often described as a "partnership") that emphasizes the linkages between institutions of the market, the state, and civil society (particularly NGOs).[19] The social enterprise model of development draws on this integrated approach to society, making it—in the eyes of donors—an attractive way to kill several birds with one stone. As noted by William Fisher in his seminal critique of NGO practices worldwide, proponents of NGOs believe that NGOs have the potential to "efficiently transfer training and skills that assist individuals and communities to compete in markets" (1997:444). The social enterprise program is an extension of this goal. Further, as Janine Wedel has stressed, since the early 1990s a key goal for Western donors has been to help foster "stronger, more highly developed business sectors as a prerequisite to the development of a market economy and democracy" (1998:165). In collapsing the elusive ideals of civil society, capitalism, and democracy into the social entrepreneurship project, Western aid agencies reveal their conviction that, to quote Gerald Creed, "the capitalist market itself [is] an instrument of civil society, granting individuals, through their market behavior, an influence on the state" (1991:4). NGOs are also conceptualized as democratizing institutions that, as part of a growing civil society, can engage with the state. According to this logic, what better way to empower the postsocialist citizenry than to provide additional free market fuel to NGOs, thus doubling people's chances to exert influence on corrupt states?

Problems arise, however, when this Western-grown model of social enterprise is applied to states such as Ukraine with transforming economies. Most citizens, NGO leaders included, have little or no experience in business. Although there was some opportunity for private business in the state socialist economy of the former Soviet Union, it was very limited, and most private enterprise was carried out underground on the "black market," or what was negatively termed "speculation." In the postsocialist context, business sometimes continues to carry these negative connotations and can be a very dangerous prospect indeed. The July 9, 2004, murder in Moscow of the editor of the Russian version of *Forbes* magazine, Pavel Khlebnikov, is just one example of the violence surrounding business in the former Soviet Union. In post-Soviet states, any type of business venture is often perceived as dangerous and "corrupt," in a context where Mafia organizations control market structures through "violent entrepreneurship" (Volkov 2002). Furthermore, privatization is not perceived positively by all Ukrainians, many of whom yearn for the stability and economic security that the socialist system provided. In one sociological study respondents were asked, "What is your attitude to the development of private business (entrepreneurship) in Ukraine?" To this question, only 24.1 percent of respondents stated that they "completely approve," and 13.6 percent said they "completely disapprove" (Panina and Golovakha 1999:24).

Would-be entrepreneurs in Ukraine face a range of daunting structural constraints. A recent Crossroads report noted that "regulations covering business activities in Ukraine are excessive, ambiguous, and sometimes contradictory, leaving entrepreneurs, business owners, and managers at the mercy of government officials and their inconsistent interpretations of these rules," and that "the intersection among criminal, business, and political worlds as a feature of corruption in Ukraine is pivotal" (Mychajlyszyn 2004:9). The country is notorious for its crippling tax laws; in Kyiv the rumor (probably unfounded) circulated that, were a business to actually pay all the required taxes, it would owe the state 110 percent of its earnings. One USAID study found that, when questioned about the obstacles to business development in Ukraine, 43 percent of respondents cited "tax laws" as the major obstacle (Koval', Mel'nyk, and Hodovanets' 1999). One also wonders how the Mafia and corrupt local officials—who often demand "protection payments" from small business owners—might treat the small enterprises founded in conjunction with humanitarian organizations. This is the uncertain and dangerous context in which NGO leaders are being encouraged to take up business ventures.

Even more problematic, legislation to facilitate social enterprise (i.e., to allow for partnerships between businesses and nonprofits) is not in place in Ukraine. When I asked him in 2002 about the legal climate for social enterprise, Serhiy told me:

> I can tell you that in Ukraine there is no law that regulates social entrepreneurship. So legally there is no such concept as social entrepreneurship. What we are doing with this program, we are making this to be a tradition, and to be recognized at all levels. And the NGOs who start up their businesses, they have to adhere to the common laws that exist for general enterprises and businesses.

This lack leaves social entrepreneurs vulnerable to the whims of corrupt officials, who see NGOs and social enterprises as a threat to their hold over local resources. According to *Case Studies*, Mercy's director, Natalya Prokhorenko, was harassed by local authorities, who believed her social enterprise to be a tax shelter or a black-market business; she was obliged to cooperate with a "private entrepreneur" in order to preserve Mercy's nonprofit status, and she was unable to secure loans from Ukrainian banks (Alter 2002:15–17). Activists I spoke with were always worried about keeping proper accounts; corrupt officials, they told me, could "throw our accountants in jail at the drop of a hat." On many levels, entrepreneurs such as Prokhorenko are operating outside the laws (which are ambiguous and inconsistently applied), putting them in a precarious situation. Because the laws governing social enterprise in Ukraine are so murky, and since business is generally perceived negatively, NGO activists may view social entrepreneurship as a Trojan horse. Research on the Russian case has shown that activists are suspicious of "the requirements of Western aid organizations for community organizations to be run in a 'business-like' fashion," fearing that this means that nonprofits will be ripe for "take-over as for-profit businesses" (Kenny 2002:297).

Even those NGO leaders who had founded social enterprises were unclear how to describe the arrangement. I had the opportunity to interview Svetlana Mishchenko (hereafter Svetlana M.), the director of Alisa Society for the Disabled during the summer of 2002. Since 1997, with Svetlana M.'s guidance, the Alisa Society has established six social enterprises: an office supply store, a café, a trading company, an architecture firm, an advertising agency, and a sports facility. Although she emphasized the useful business skills she had acquired as a CAP social enterprise grantee, Svetlana M. refused to call herself a "businesswoman," since, she said, "charitable work and business cannot fully intersect." She emphasized that Ukrainian laws forbid NGOs from carrying out business ventures; rather, they can only "found" enterprises that will then be run independently. She underlined the state's negative attitude toward NGO enterprises run by and for the disabled, and described the bureaucratic morass involved in pursuing social entrepreneurship—obtaining permission to engage in business, opening a bank account, and dealing with various government offices. She explained, "Our state is afraid that invalids are going to steal some huge piece of profits." Svetlana M. also emphasized the "nerves" that dealing with a business could cost, especially when negotiating bureaucratic issues such as taxes, land, water rights, and so on. Svetlana M. said that she valued the social entrepreneurship strategy for allowing her to avoid the "shame" of being dependent on "aid" (Rus. *pomoshch'*). But she also stated that the businesses she had established alongside her NGO provided only around 25 percent of her operating costs, and that most operating funds came from the state (especially the Kyiv City Administration and the Fund for the Social Protection of Invalids) and from grants. At the same time, Svetlana M. valued social entrepreneurship for providing the Alisa Society with a "predictable, stable, source of funding," since grants and state assistance were inconsistent from one year to the next. However, she said that the most important benefit of the social enterprises she established was not the funds they generated but the role they served in placing disabled persons in jobs. In order to enjoy a range of state benefits (primarily tax exemptions) extended to "enterprises for the disabled" (Ukr. *invalids'ke pid-pryiemstvo;* Rus. *invalidskii biznes*), 50 percent of the employees of these firms must be disabled.

On the one hand, Svetlana M.'s story reveals the slippage that may occur when the NGO-business "partnership" model is applied to the postsocialist milieu. Despite the various challenges Svetlana M. described, however, she was very positive about the social enterprise model. Indeed, of the NGO activists in Kyiv with whom I discussed social enterprise, Svetlana M. was the most enthusiastic, and she considered herself a successful social entrepreneur. She had become acquainted with many of her most valued colleagues while attending Counterpart events around social enterprise. Svetlana M. assessed Counterpart and its social enterprise program only in positive terms.

Despite this activist's positive evaluation, and notwithstanding the opportunities that social entrepreneurship has provided for a handful of activists and some others in Ukraine, the constraints I have examined here make the strategy's widespread success in the country unlikely. The hostile business environment and bureaucratic stonewalling are not the only obstacles. Social enterprise assumes a neoliberal vision of social service provision that is out of step with local conceptions of citizenship and citizen entitlement. This general dismissal of citizens' claims on various types of state assistance promises to have especially dramatic impacts on women. As the main caretakers of families, women today are forced to shoulder the burden of social responsibilities previously managed by the state (Zhurzhenko 2001b:37). The logics of social enterprise and similar programs reinforce this burden through their implicit dismissal of citizens' claims on state assistance and support, and the stress they place on "self-sufficiency" and "independence from donors." As Kristen Ghodsee has pointed out for Bulgaria, outfitting women to participate in the new free market economy (here as social entrepreneurs) conveniently convinces them that it is their "duty" to provide the services (child care, health care, care for the elderly) for their families that the state previously took care of (2004:747–748). This in turn allows states (which are beholden to institutions such as the International Monetary Fund [IMF]) to cut back social services even further, and also allows transnational investors to avoid offering adequate workplace benefits. Even worse, women business owners in Ukraine automatically become ineligible for most types of government social assistance (Zhurzhenko 2004:40).

After socialism, NGOs—especially charitable, caring-focused NGOs, many of them led by women—have also taken on some of the functions of the socialist state. Promoters of social enterprise are asking women NGO leaders to continue their "existing roles as safety nets (to mitigate the new social problems of emerging market economies) and as safety valves (to give voice to social groups underrepresented in the newly competitive polities)" (Bach and Stark 2002:3), *and* to become businesswomen to ensure the self-sustainability of their NGOs. This is a triple burden that few NGO activists are prepared to shoulder. While women are compelled to juggle their familial, social, and market responsibilities, men dominate in private business, largely unencumbered by the expectation to engage in "philanthropic business." When social enterprise is presented as an avenue for social service provision, the burden of maintaining the social safety net is shifted from the state to women, who are positioned as caregivers in Ukrainian society. What might be the long-term effects of social entrepreneurship for women, who thus far seem to be the most active consumers and agents of social enterprise?

When the interventions of social enterprise intersect with local gender formations, ambiguous consequences are produced. On the one hand, social enterprise has given women in Ukraine a unique opportunity to attend seminars in business administration, and to acquire a range of important skills. In a situation where women are poorly represented in private business, social enterprise may provide much-needed opportunities for small business development and economic empowerment. The situation, however, is complicated when social enterprise intersects with local ideas concerning "women and business" that move along the lines of a traditional gender ideology that places men in the "public" (read: business, providing) sphere and women in the "private" (read: domestic, caregiving) sphere. Women in business (and politics or any "public" realm, for that matter) are often perceived as "bad mothers," "bad wives," and "bad homemakers," and women occupying any relatively high post in commercial or political structures are often frowned upon.

Additionally, by buttressing the social service "caring" functions of NGOs, roles associated especially with women, social enterprise may reinforce essentialist discourses about gender in the postsocialist context. When we discussed the prospects of business careers for women in Ukraine, Maryna, for example, said that she felt it was "natural" for women to base their initial business ventures on "women's work," such as knitting or sewing. Later, she said, women might branch out into other spheres. Similar statements were made by Myroslava, who had worked as a trainer for the NIS-US Women's Consortium. As part of the Women's Economic Empowerment (WEE) program in Ukraine, seminars were offered to women on the topics of "women's business" and "family business." Myroslava had led such seminars, and when I asked what types of "small businesses" women were likely to establish, she cited typically "womanly" (Ukr. *zhinochi*) undertakings, such as embroidery and cheese making. The danger here is that women's business endeavors are being ghettoized via local gender ideologies into the marginal, devalued service sector, a trend that international foundations promoting social enterprise and women's economic empowerment have not successfully addressed.

More research needs to be done to assess whether women and men are equally likely to succeed at social enterprise, given these added constraints women face. It is encouraging that all four of the grantees selected by CAP to receive recoverable grants for social enterprise were women. On the other hand, unless efforts are made to engage the concept of gender—to engage local stereotypes about the proper "spheres" for women in business—women's small business endeavors may be relegated to low-prestige spheres. Similar trends have been noted across postsocialist countries, for example, in Bosnia-Herzegovina (Walsh 1998) and in Central Asia (Gapova 2000). Ironically, by neglecting to adequately address the perceived "natural" division of labor between the sexes, aid programs may fail to challenge the inherently patriarchal character of the very institutions of market society that they are promoting. It is disturbing that these inequalities replicate those found at the administrative levels of the social enterprise conceptual scheme internationally. Gray, Healy, and Crofts note that, in the Australian context, "many of the most vocal advocates [of social entrepreneurship] are male, yet it is largely women who staff the services sector and informal caring networks" (2003:152). They warn that "sensitivity to gender dynamics is needed if social enterprise is to avoid becoming yet another vehicle through which a small group of dominant male 'visionaries' impose their worldview on the primarily female world of service provision."

We must also be concerned about the potential long-term effects of empowerment strategies for women that emphasize women's roles as caregivers and matrons of the market, yet fail to address women's declining influence in the halls of government and "meaningful" politics. In other words, might development programs that privilege the role of women in the market and in providing social services undermine their potential to engage in the overall political process? In her paper, "State Men, Market Women," Mihaela Miroiu describes the current situation in much of Eastern Europe as one in which "men have successfully appropriated the state, while women were simply delivered to the market" (2004:1). She stresses the pressing need for women's voices to be heard in the political process, through real and meaningful political representation. This need is certainly urgent in Ukraine. In shoring up women's roles as civil society actors and businesspeople, the social enterprise program may threaten to exacerbate the "state men, market women" phenomenon. Alternatively, might the program—by supporting their important roles in NGO and business structures—enable women eventually to climb back up the political ladder? Is it possible that women who become proficient in business will be better prepared to successfully engage in the political process? Could social enterprise—which seeks to combine women's strengths in NGO organizing with new opportunities for competing in the tough new market economy—be postsocialist women's pathway to political power? These are important questions that deserve thorough consideration in future studies as social enterprise continues to play out in postsocialist states like Ukraine. It is clear that, by trying to better understand the alternate models of citizenship and gender employed by local activists—but not necessarily treating such models uncritically—

international development organizations could better equip postsocialist citizens, especially women, to meet the challenges they continue to face.

We must also question the "democratizing" potential of the social enterprise initiative, since the program and the opportunities it offers have been extended to certain categories of citizens unequally. Only former CAP grantees that had successfully carried out previous grant projects were invited to apply for the "recoverable grants" to start a small business, and it is possible that an elite cadre of NGO activists-turned businesspeople is forming around such programs. Despite the origins of social entrepreneurship as a strategy to facilitate the provision of social services, in Ukraine the tactic threatens to marginalize the very categories of citizens that need these services the most. My interviews with NGO activists revealed that small business ventures are not viable strategies for all types of NGOs. Those NGOs that were excluded from social entrepreneurship opportunities were often the ones serving the most marginalized of postsocialist citizens—sick children, the elderly, large families, and others. These are citizens who were accustomed to a medium of social protection under state socialism, and who expect the same entitlements today. By failing to consider these expectations, transnational initiatives such as the social enterprise program may sideline these groups even further, thus contributing (wittingly or not) to postsocialist processes of differentiation.

Of *kava breiks* and Consortia:
Leadership *treininh* for Women

Another of the primary transnational groups promoting NGO development in Ukraine at the time of my research during the late 1990s was the NIS-US Women's Consortium, the group Ivana began to work for as a paid trainer. The Consortium, which received financial support from USAID and the Eurasia Foundation (a Soros-backed organization supporting the development of democratic and free market institutions in the region), was founded in 1992 by Winrock International, a private nonprofit organization in the United States.[20] As USAID's main contractor on women's rights issues, Winrock, in 1996, was awarded a grant to develop the NIS-US Women's Consortium, in a program aimed at increasing the participation of women in democracy building by providing instructional and technical assistance to women's groups and enhancing the leadership skills of women activists. This was to be done via a strategy commonly undertaken by donor organizations seeking to strengthen civil society: facilitating "partnerships" or "counterparts" between local and foreign NGOs (Hrycak 2006:79).[21] The Consortium's statement of principles included fostering "participatory decision making," achieving equality for women in all cultures, respecting a diversity of opinions and methods of operation, focusing on women's rights and women's economic development, and fostering a self-help attitude among women.[22] Most of my informants who were involved in transnational NGO initiatives had participated in Consortium training programs for women activists on women in leadership, women's human rights, conflict resolution, and fund-raising. In some cases, after receiving a grant to develop a specific woman-focused project, activists were required to attend these trainings. Trainings were often led by paid local trainers who had been instructed in the Consortium's methodologies.

As activists progress in the trainings offered by transnational NGO development organizations, they are expected to develop not only valuable skills in fund-raising, bookkeeping, business planning, and working with mass media but also to emerge from these seminars as changed people. Trainings are designed to offer participants a new way of thinking about themselves, the world around them, the past, and the future. They are equipped with new criteria with which to evaluate their own personal and social worth, and the worth of others. Frequently this entails confronting the ghosts of the Soviet past and reflecting upon the probable "damage" the socialist system has wrought on oneself and others. Trainings are supposed to enable participants to develop the qualities that donor organizations deem necessary for citizens' empowerment: positive thinking, self-reliance, initiative, individuality, and a positive self-image. Indeed, USAID has defined empowerment as "getting people to believe in themselves, to rely less on government to guide their daily lives, and to take control of their destiny through economic opportunities and political choice."[23] Trainings and other interventions carried out by international donor organizations are presented in terms of modernization and progress; Maryna, for instance, credited Counterpart with "bringing Ukrainian NGOs out of the Stone Age." In 2000, a representative of the NIS-US Women's Consortium described to me the organization's training seminars for women leaders:

> What I have noticed about these trainings is the power of creating a framework and atmosphere during the training that ensures that each woman feels respected, valued, and heard. This is radical for the former Soviet Union! The trainers establish rules at the beginning of the training. I don't know them all but they include: be on time; speak briefly and not too often; be positive (don't criticize); speak one at a time; personify (don't say "everyone knows or believes" but instead "I think").

The representative's assertion that "this is radical for the former Soviet Union!" underlines the intended democratizing and modernizing effects of the training seminars.

In interviews with activists who had been through these trainings, some of them having become trainers themselves, I learned that they had begun to differentiate themselves from activists they deemed "Soviet," "backward," or "passive." As a rule, these latter "types" were NGO activists whose agendas were devalued by international donor organizations and representatives of the Ukrainian state, and who did not have ready access to the trainings and other resources offered by donor organizations. In this way, the interventions of foreign donor organizations into the sphere of women's NGOs have produced a kind of double differentiation. First, certain types of organizations are promoted over others: NGOs whose mandates are in line with the neoliberal and feminist-oriented philosophies espoused by donors are privileged, whereas others—for example, those that make "socialist-era" claims for more support from the state or have a maternalist orientation—are devalued. Further, select NGO activists are equipped with criteria and language with which to differentiate themselves from other activists, and this lends them the social and cultural capital to springboard themselves from NGO work to other careers. Together, these processes of differentiation have had the ultimate effect of further marginalizing already vulnerable women (leaders of maternalist, entitlement-oriented organizations like Our House, such as Svetlana and Vira) while enabling other women to advance in their careers (like Ivana).

In March 1998, I received a phone call from an acquaintance named Sonia. Sonia worked at a research institute, and I had met her a month earlier at a conference on the health and social effects of Chernobyl. Originally trained as a high school history teacher, Sonia worked at the institute as a secretary of sorts, running errands for senior scientists and typing documents and articles on one of the institute's outdated computers. Sonia was calling to invite me to a "training" seminar at the center, but she gave me few details. The seminar would be on "women in leadership" (Ukr. *zhinoche liderstvo,* the word *liderstvo* clearly a Ukrainianized version of the English word "leadership"). Sonia's boss, Halyna Oleksandrivna, who was a key member of a major women's organization, had instructed her to round up a group of people to attend. The seminar could not take place unless there were at least twelve participants. Sonia told me to show up at 10:00 AM the next morning, which happened to be March 8, International Women's Day.

Upon arriving at the institute, I found Sonia, who ushered me into the room where the training was to take place. The room was usually used as a laboratory, but the tables that normally stood in the center had been removed, and chairs had been placed in a semicircle facing one wall. Several other women had already arrived and were chatting. Halyna Oleksandrivna seemed to know everyone present, and she introduced me to several women. A few more stragglers began to filter into the room, and we arranged ourselves in the semi-circle. There were about ten women in the group, including Sonia, her mother, Halyna Oleksandrivna, and myself. By the time we began it was almost 10:30. A tall woman with short red hair and gold-rimmed glasses took her place beside a flip chart in front of us. She welcomed us to the *treininh,* introduced herself as Nina, and began to tell us, the *partysypanty* (another borrowed term from English) about the training program. Nina stressed that men were welcome to attend the trainings, but I noticed that our group was made up entirely of women.[24] We learned from Nina that these seminars had been prepared by members of the Consortium based on the experience of trainers in Ukraine, Croatia, Russia, the United States, and Great Britain, and were founded on the philosophy of nonviolence (*nenasyl'stvo*). The seminars, which had been conducted in Ukraine since 1995, were designed to heighten participants' leadership skills and teach them how to work effectively in small groups. Nina outlined how women's organizations could become members of the Consortium, namely, by submitting a letter of interest detailing the organization's activities, a copy of the organization's by-laws, two letters of recommendation from active members of the Consortium, and a completed questionnaire.

Nina opened the flip chart and stated that we would create a list of rules that our group would be expected to follow. She began the list with the following rules:

1. Be on time. ["You have already violated this one," Nina told us.]
2. Be positive in your thoughts and comments.
3. Do not criticize yourself or others.
4. Listen to others; do not interrupt.
5. Do not speak for too long or too often.
6. Only one person may speak at a time.
7. When volunteers are called for, nominate yourself only.
8. Each person has the right to withdraw from any activity.

Nina asked us to confirm that we would honor these rules and asked if anyone would like to add to the list. No one did. She then requested that participants agree upon a signal which would indicate that someone was breaking the rules. The suggestion was made to raise one's hand with the index finger pointing upward. Everyone agreed. Nina then began to lead us through a series of exercises—large group discussions, small group discussions, role playing, brainstorming, and drawing—all designed to foster cooperative decision making and conflict resolution.

To help participants become acquainted with one another, Nina proposed an activity in which each of us would imitate an animal we would like to be and then explain why we chose that animal. Though we felt somewhat silly performing this exercise, it got people laughing and created a relaxed atmosphere. In another activity designed to build self-confidence, each participant had to finish the sentence "I am proud . . ." by citing something about themselves that made them feel proud. I said, "I am proud that I am able to get along with many different types of people." The other women, in turn, each said that she was proud of her family, her children, her mother and their good relationship, her husband, her marriage, and so on. Nina pointed out that I (an American) was the only participant to refer to a personal quality rather than to a relationship. This, she said, was a "flaw" in the "mentality" of Ukrainian women, who "must learn to find pride within themselves, and not only through other people." Thus, a key "lesson" of development initiatives in post-Soviet societies came to the fore: people's (especially women's) sense of self is too relational; instead, individualism and self-sufficiency need to be cultivated.

For another activity, we were each given a picture of what appeared to be a coat of arms, divided into six sections. We were then told to fill in each section with drawings corresponding to the following items:

1. two things you do well
2. your greatest accomplishment in life
3. the part of the home most ideal for your soul

4. three people who have influenced you the most
5. three words you would like to hear about yourself
6. how you would spend this year, if you knew it would be your last

We each showed, and explained, our drawings to the group. Regarding item 2, most of the women referred to their successful marriage or their children as their greatest accomplishment in life. Most indicated, in response to item 6, that they would spend the last year of their lives patching up strained relationships and spending more time with family and friends.

"Leaders and Leadership" was a brainstorming exercise to offer examples of "leaders," "leadership," "spheres where leadership takes place," "spheres where women strive to be leaders," and "spheres where women have significant leadership roles." For "Styles of Leadership," we were asked to evaluate different approaches to leadership, primarily contrasting authoritarian styles of leadership with more democratic approaches. Nina then led us in a discussion on the nature of conflicts, listing their possible sources (differences in opinion, differing values, etc.). She also outlined typical conflictual behaviors: communication problems, the need to control the discussion, defensively impeding ideas, and failing to listen. Some people, we were told, deal with conflicts by avoiding problems and running away; others react competitively; some respond by adapting; and still others are cooperative. We were, of course, encouraged to behave cooperatively when faced with conflicts.

Another activity asked that participants volunteer to present their own conflicts to the group for discussion. Three women volunteered, and we separated into three groups, each using various techniques, which Nina explained, to help the volunteer resolve her conflict. We were instructed to listen attentively and ask questions so that the person could expand on the problem, describe what she is feeling and thinking, and why. The conflicts largely involved arguments with colleagues, spouses, and family members, most notably daughters-in-law.

At the end of the *treininh*, participants gathered in a circle and told one another what they had gained from the session. We then got into a huddle and stacked our right hands one on top of the other, in the style of a basketball team. After thanking Nina for her direction, and one another for a rewarding experience, Nina distributed questionnaires so that participants could evaluate the *treininh*. We were then invited to enjoy a late lunch. Young men from Halyna Oleksandrivna's laboratory carried in the tables, and I helped Sonia and other young women workers arrange plates of open-faced sandwiches, salads, appetizers, and bottles of wine and vodka. Workers from other laboratories in the institute trickled in to join our party, including men, among them Halyna Oleksandrivna's supervisor. The men seized upon the occasion of International Women's Day to toast the women and convey their praises. The men, most of them senior officials in the center, made sure everyone had a full glass and enough to eat. Finally, in good Ukrainian tradition, after several shots of vodka or glasses of wine, everyone burst into song.

"Don't talk that way"

Although the training I attended was unlikely to have much impact on women's organizing efforts (most attendees were not affiliated with NGOs but rather were friends of Halyna Oleksandrivna), it did significantly influence individual women. When I met Iryna, one of the participants, more than a year later, I found that she had become a paid trainer for the Consortium. Several of the participants later told me that attending the training session on women and leadership had taught them a lot about resolving conflicts and that they had "learned a lot about themselves." They felt more self-confident after the session and experienced a boost in self-esteem. Overall, it appears that training programs offered by the Consortium and other NGO advocacy organizations are valued by women NGO activists: one study of women's NGOs found that the majority of organizations list participation in training programs as a top priority (Suslova and Karbovs'ka 2002). The authors speculate that this can be interpreted as an indication of "aspiring to self-development" and the desire to gain knowledge and skills, but respondents were not asked directly for their motivations in seeking out opportunities for training.

Although the handbook for Consortium trainers (NIS-US Women's Consortium 1997) that I later consulted included guidelines for introducing the concepts of "gender," "gender roles," "feminism," and "women, money, and possibilities," Nina did not mention these issues during the training session. She focused instead on conflict resolution and fostering leadership skills, avoiding the more loaded concepts such as gender and feminism, and even women in business. This indicates that the more "radical" ideas about gender roles and feminism remained unpalatable for some Ukrainian women. A reticence to adopt "gender theory," which proposes that gender roles are socially constructed, is, of course, not unique to Ukrainian or postsocialist women. Many women in the United States would also reject gender theory. Second wave feminism in the U.S., which began around 1965, was focused on "practical" problems of women's civil rights, the right to work, equal pay for equal work, and institutionalized misogyny (DuPlessis and Snitow 1998:3–12). Like the Ukrainian women I knew, many second wave feminists, academics included, struggle to accept the new gender theory that challenges sex-role stereotypes.

As elsewhere, Ukrainian women's difficulties in accepting the notion of socially constructed gender roles are compounded by the pervasiveness of local gender constructions that assign men and women specific roles in the family and society. These constructions have become sharpened in the post-independence period of nation building in Ukraine, as seen in the revival of the Berehynia and other symbols aligning women with the home, hearth, and nation. In some regard, perhaps, the Consortium-sponsored "Women in Leadership" seminars did not have the intended effect, since many local activists could easily associate their NGO leadership roles more with nation building than with advancing women's rights. On the other hand, even if gender theory holds little resonance for most people, "gender" is a term one hears more and more in Ukraine—it has entered the lexicon of political parties, state documents, and the titles of increasing numbers of women's groups. But, as Natalia Kutova notes, in this usage it is usually ignored "that the notion of 'gender' is defined as a social construct, which unlike biological sex, is not a natural phenomenon, but is produced by different political, cultural and other social means" (2003:4). In other words, in Ukraine, the word "gender" often simply replaces "women" or "sex" and thus becomes a token phrase emptied of its theoretical content.

The aspect of the training that I found most interesting, however, was the heavy emphasis placed on cultivating individualism in participants. Clearly, a major goal of the seminar was to inculcate a sense of individuality and self-sufficiency in post-Soviet people, through exercises such as "I am Proud," which was designed to inspire women to talk about themselves positively and focus primarily on their individualized, bounded self (Mauss 1938) without reference to their relationships with significant others. Participants were encouraged to engage in self-reflection and to work on themselves to develop their sense of "I." The power of these seminars to teach women to assert themselves as individuals was brought home to me in a telephone conversation I had with Ivana during the fall of 1999. Ivana took her participation in my study very seriously, and she liked me to call her often so that she could tell me about her NGO activities on a regular basis. When I called her after a two-week hiatus, she expressed her displeasure that I had "gotten lost" for so long. I apologized and made some self-debasing comment like "I didn't want to bother you; I know you are very busy and you probably don't sit around waiting for me to call you." My comment miffed Ivana, who replied, "That's the . . . Ukrainian mentality. 'Not waiting for my phone calls.' Don't talk that way. It's called *opravdyvat'sia* (Rus.), to justify oneself for every action. And I, on the contrary, search for people who . . . are more self-confident. And suddenly Sarah, you . . . good grief (Rus. *na tebe*)!" This exchange was fascinating, because Ivana, drawing on ideas about women's leadership and positive self-image, criticized me (an American) for my low self-esteem and "Ukrainian mentality."

Ivana was working against the more relational, inter-articulated type of personhood that presumably was inculcated in Soviet citizens, one that often is labeled "passive" in popular and scholarly discourse. For example, prominent Ukrainian sociologists have written that "a traditional national feature" is "to find social support in family and friends first and foremost," and they link this with the idea that "almost all Ukrainian citizens believe that outer conditions are responsible for their life" (Panina and Golovakha 1999:156–157). Similarly, the authors characterize Ukrainians as exhibiting a "passive expectation of a good time [i.e., better times]" (Panina and Golovakha 1999:145). The idea of the *seredniak*, or "middle person," also has been used in the popular imagination to characterize how the Soviet system inculcated citizens to be at once anonymous and passive subjects, and yet also part of the productive fabric (Petryna 2002:155).

Ivana was also critical of the "Soviet psyche," and it was precisely the Consortium's focus on individual integrity and leadership skills that she found most compelling. When conducting her own trainings, she had become attuned to spotting participants who "still clung to the Soviet mind-set," as she put it. Once over the telephone she described difficulties she had experienced that day while conducting a seminar for vocational education teachers in Kyiv. She criticized the educators for their "Soviet conduct," telling me that they were "unable to speak for themselves" and "didn't know how to listen to others." She was frustrated with individuals who "could not personalize their opinions, but rather said, 'Everyone thinks that . . .' instead of 'I believe that. . . .'" Another activist and trainer, Myroslava, told me very directly that the training sessions were intended to undo socialist legacies by teaching women to value themselves as individuals, rather than relationally with their husbands, children, and other significant persons:

> We give them exercises on self-confidence and teach them to value themselves. We ask them to finish this phrase: "I am proud of my personal characteristics and my achievements . . ." How difficult it is for a woman to say, "I am proud of myself!" She will talk about her husband, about her children, about her environment. But about herself . . .! A woman cannot even understand that she has her own merits. And these sessions change a woman. Her self worth . . . It is the "inferiority syndrome" [*menshevartist'*] that the communist system instilled in us. . . .
>
> A woman begins to understand that the postcommunist system dominates in her and that it is necessary to fight it and establish oneself as an individual, as a leader of the organization. And if the leader of the organization will . . . value her own merits adequately, then the members of her organization will also stand tall and will have the same high regard for themselves [and realize]that they are valuable members of their society.

In seeking to overturn the perceived suppression of individualism in Soviet Ukraine, these leadership training programs—and trainers' assessments of them—overlook the fact that the entitlement and dignity of the individual was actually central to Soviet ideology, as exemplified in the work of Krupskaia, Iaroslavsky, and others. Although it is often assumed that the Soviet state sought to squelch individualism, there was a native socialist project to cultivate the individual through the development of *lichnost'*, a Russian term that connotes both *person* ("the expression of the unique set of qualities of a given individual") and the *individual* ("each human being as a subject of action in everyday life and as a carrier of individuality") (Kharkhordin 1999: 189–191). (The Ukrainian term is *osobystist'*.) The cultivation of the self, however, was to be undertaken in the collective to create, in the words of Lunacharsky, a "granular" or collectivist individual. In the 1960s, an official line on *individual'nost'* (Rus. individuality) emerged, and the Soviet state was to pay particular attention to citizens' "unique features of the set of human capacities," to ensure that "people should have vocations and positions precisely in accord with their individuality" (Kharkhordin 1999:339). Thus, in the official discourse at least, the individual was still squarely centered within the collective, since primary emphasis was placed on his or her position in production.

The work of fashioning *lichnost'* was undertaken by encouraging individuals to engage in "work on oneself," as well as through public confessions, disciplinary measures, and mutual surveillance among citizens.

The effects of these official programs for self-making in the Soviet Union were mixed. It has been argued that many Soviet citizens became split, dissimulated subjects, comprised of a hidden, intimate self that was only displayed to one's family or close friends, and an official, public self (Kharkhordin 1999). Soviet citizens, it also is noted, sought to cultivate and display individuality through fashion (the *styliagi*—stylishly dressed persons), and through consumption (of rock music and prestigious deficit items, for example) in an economy of shortage. Such trends point to an unintended effect of campaigns of *lichnost'* development in the Soviet Union—they frequently produced guarded (and non-"granular") individuals who placed little trust in consociates or institutions. As has been well documented, the Soviet system also produced social groupings whose members considered themselves to be outside the system—Soviet "dropouts," in effect (Shlapentokh 1989; Yurchak 2006). Despite these complexities, many Ukrainians and observers of Ukraine assume that the socialist system of education and ideology work fashioned people to be more dependent on their consociates for formulating their sense of self than in Western, capitalistic societies. This inter-related type of personhood is usually perceived to be more passive and in need of correction in the new, post-Soviet, capitalist milieu. The training sessions that activists such as Myroslava and Ivana had led for the Consortium were all designed—at least in part—to undo this "communist" legacy of collectivization of the person. Of course, international development organizations are not the only entities promoting a focus on the individual and his or her potential in the postsocialist world. The Ukrainian state has also actively promoted an ethos of individualism and the worth of the individual self, as a way of introducing a model of active citizenship.

One example of this effort could be seen in 1999 in creative montages that the private television station 1 + 1 ran between programs. The channel's slogan was "1 + 1, *ty ne odyn*" (Ukr. "1 + 1, you are not alone"). The channel featured short profiles of various "ordinary" people, often children. These spots might include a photo montage of a child, and then a video clip and a voiceover of the child talking about herself. All over the screen the letter "Ia" (Я) was overlaid, which means "I" in both Ukrainian and Russian. These short biographies sent the message that each individual was an asset, and had worth, even if there was nothing "extraordinary" about the person's life. The spots included feel-good messages about what is important in life—family, everyday pleasures, hard work, and dedication to an ideal. Although rooted in ideas about individual worth and self-initiative, this campaign also went along with the "you are not alone" slogan to give people the sense that they were part of the larger community of the Ukrainian nation. The "I" campaign drew on multiple, contradictory narratives (the worth of the individual, the importance of socialities ["you are not alone"]), and a nationalizing campaign. It revealed the complex negotiations of self and society occurring in the new Ukraine at the levels of the person, the family, and the nation-state, and the attention paid to the minute details of individual lives presumably carried an anti-Soviet message.

This resembles the work done by international NGO development initiatives. However, development interventions based on critiques of the Soviet system and Soviet ways of doing things were complicated and made incomplete by the fact that almost all activists, regardless of their position within or outside the Western-oriented NGO networks, grappled with their own Soviet pasts. Many activists had participated—and held leadership roles—in Soviet organizations such as the Komsomol, the Communist Party, and trade unions.[25] In light of the roles they had recently taken up to reform society, many of them found it necessary to justify past actions they had taken as Soviet activists. Despite the efforts of international foundations to inculcate a particular type of democratizing, modernizing consciousness in NGO activists, my informants were resisting such an abrupt and total sea change in worldview. Although they saw themselves as "progressive" people responsible for creating positive social change in independent Ukraine, many informants who had been Soviet *aktyvistky* (activists) refused to discount this aspect of their lives; on the contrary, some repeatedly highlighted how Soviet ideals and training had prepared them for their current NGO work. Ivana, for example, cited Soviet-era political slogans to explain her participation in the Consortium's trainings. She said, "They say one must study his whole life in order to achieve something," a reference to Lenin's oft-quoted admonition to "study, study, and study some more" (Rus., *uchit'sia, uchit'sia, i eshchyo raz uchit'sia*). When telling me how much she had moved around during her student years, she joked, "My address is the Soviet Union," a refrain from a popular Soviet-era song, which included the line, "My address is not a house or a street, my address is the Soviet Union."[26] Ivana also located the roots of her social activism in her former role as a Komsomol leader in school. She had served as her school's *Komsorg* (Komsomol Organizer) for four years, which, she said, for her, had been a "very heavy burden of social work."[27] Ivana proposed that, "probably, even then I realized it was my calling, to work with people, to lead, and to impart knowledge." Several informants made such assessments, thus establishing continuity between their Soviet and post-Soviet activism.

On the other hand, many went to great lengths to distance themselves from their "communist pasts" and told me repeatedly that they were ashamed of this aspect of their personal history. None of my informants, except Sofiia, had been members of the Communist Party, and most were quick to point this out. Those who had been very active in the Komsomol stressed the positive aspects of this organization for Soviet youth: the Komsomol provided young people with opportunities for socializing, traveling, learning important survival skills, developing leadership abilities, and so on. Some activists, however, emphasized that participation in the Komsomol was practically mandatory, as if to say, "I'm not the only one who was in the Komsomol—we all were" or "I had no choice but to join the Komsomol." These negotiations show the indebtedness

Figure 13. "Always ready, or, a pioneer girl's salute." Kyiv, Kontrakt Square, 1966. Photo by Yury Sayenko.

NGO activists felt to the Soviet legacy, even as they were being encouraged to leave it behind. This aspect of these women's identities as social activists was frequently overlooked in transnational NGO development and women's rights initiatives.

Not all women activists enjoyed the opportunity to attend training seminars and network with representatives of international donor groups and other NGO leaders in the country. The interventions of foreign donor groups—which encourage women to take up narratives of self-reliance and positive self-image, and offer them various types of training and other resources—have led to the personal empowerment of a select group of women NGO activists, some of whom have become employees of donor organizations, and others (like Ivana) have propelled themselves into more lucrative and powerful careers. Differentiation processes wherein a select group of activists are funneled through NGO development training have tended to produce small groups of empowered elites. And the effects of transnational NGO development initiatives are even more far reaching. Not only do NGO development programs empower individual leaders and equip them with new forms of social and cultural capital; they also introduce activists to new models of citizenship. As we see in the mission statements of international donors and the narratives of activists like Ivana and Maryna, this citizenship model is based on ideas of self-reliance, individual initiative, and the development of new market forms that combine advocacy work with profit motives (social enterprise). The mandates of these international development organizations (recall the USAID statement on citizens' empowerment, which emphasizes "getting people to believe in themselves, to rely less on government to guide their daily lives, and to take control of their destiny through economic opportunities and political choice") dovetail with those of the Ukrainian state—to streamline social welfare and make people more independent of state support. This includes the differentiation of categories of citizens (and NGOs) and their claims to recognition and redistribution during Ukraine's market "transition." Activists who envision citizenship differently are marginalized from transnational NGO development networks. The ideologies of individualization and privatization promoted by transnational NGO development organizations, which devalue relational types of self-understanding and the articulation of entitlements, thus have produced unexpected results for women in NGO leadership. So far, these interventions have not resulted in sustained sociopolitical change for Ukraine's women. Furthermore, some types of organizations and their leaders have been "weeded out," as they are denied access to funds and training provided by international donors.

This is not to discount the important work that transnational organizations such as the NIS-US Women's Consortium have carried out in Ukraine and other post-Soviet countries. Indeed, the funding and know-how that these organizations provide have helped support important and much-needed local ventures like women's crisis centers, business incubators, anti-trafficking initiatives, and gender studies centers. My focus here has been to document ethnographically some of the unexpected and probably unintentional effects of interventions such as leadership seminars, which equip women with new ways of thinking about themselves and their roles as women and NGO leaders. These largely involve processes of individualization and work on the self, exercises some women found useful and transformative. Although their experience with Western foundations allows some women NGO activists to develop social and cultural capital—which they may then translate into economic capital by becoming trainers or moving into other careers—such opportunities are closed to many NGO activists who lack access to these resources, which effects and perpetuates differentiating processes within the NGO sector.

> Self-esteem
> Self-attainment
> Self-abasement
> Self-understanding
> Perfection itself
> Egoism—if it's by yourself
> For yourself, of yourself . . .
> It's self-love
> It's pride.
> Self-admiration
> No, it's not an achievement,
> No, it's not progress
> And it's not the path to harmony.

—Poem written by Zoia, 1991

January 27, 2000
Dear Sarah!

I was very pleased to receive your Christmas card. Best wishes to you also for Christmas, the New Year, and the new millennium! I wasn't able to answer your letter right away because I was on a ten-day business trip around Ukraine. I was accepted into the trainers' school for those who prepare trainers for NGO leadership all over the country. So I will be doing a lot of traveling during the first half of this year. We have good news—we got a grant to carry out computer courses and psychology sessions for teenage girls with disabilities, and for women who are bringing up disabled children. This means my colleagues will finally get a small salary, which is great! People are tired of working without money. Tomorrow we have a big annual membership meeting to discuss our organization's work over the last year. There's a lot to do—tying up loose ends and making accounts. My daughter isn't feeling too well, and she's going in for some tests next week. Besides that, not much has changed for us. My colleagues send you a big Hello.

Write me soon,
Maryna

Edited Field Notes, July 2, 2002

It was great to spend the afternoon with Maryna. She was just as I remembered her—she exuded professionalism and competence, and gave sensitive and thoughtful answers to all my questions. Many of them she anticipated before I even had a chance to ask. She has such a keen sense of what issues a foreign researcher might find interesting, and gives wonderfully detailed accounts of the minutiae of NGO organizing. She doesn't like to talk about herself very much, but she does enjoy talking about her work. It's clear there are certain qualities she admires and seeks to embody; definitely top among them are hard work, seriousness, and a sense of purpose.

Maryna is planning to leave Lily of the Valley—she says she has "grown out of the children's theme" (Rus. *detskaia tema*)—and she has gotten more involved in advocacy for disabled adults, especially women. Also, Maryna feels like the Chernobyl theme has run its course: "The Chernobyl movement is falling apart, and the government is losing interest. Chernobyl victims keep advocating for a higher disability pension, but the perception is that *Chernobyltsi* are being spoiled by the state." She said that [the then] prime minister Yushchenko "favors politics without entitlements" (Rus. *l'goty*), so "it's been hard to get support for groups that are socially defenseless."

Even though she's leaving Lily of the Valley, Maryna is hanging on to Mist (Bridge), the resource center she founded for disability rights organizations. I was surprised to learn that she's gotten involved in two "social businesses" during the last year. When I asked her about social enterprise back in 1999, she seemed reluctant to venture into the business sphere. Today she characterized her recent ventures into social business as "partnerships with existing businesses" initiated by young businessmen she trusts, and emphasized that she doesn't get involved in the business aspect of things. From what I've learned so far about social enterprise, it is a hybrid NGO-business form that is being promoted by international organizations like Counterpart and Winrock that offers NGOs a funding base and extends businesses some tax breaks. Maryna's social enterprise activities have gone through Mist, which has received considerable grant support from international NGO development organizations, and through which she and her colleagues continue to publish newsletters for disability and women's rights organizations. I was hoping to tap into Mist's database of disability rights NGOs for my new project on the Ukrainian disability rights movement, but Maryna told me today that the computer crashed last year and all the data were lost. She didn't seem too upset about it, and said that no one had used the database in a long time.

Most of Maryna's time lately has been dedicated to a new, ambitious endeavor—she is involved in the work of a large coalition of disability rights NGOs as the coordinator for women's affairs. Through this work she has gotten to know the representatives of all the major disability advocacy groups in the country, and has given presentations before Prime Minister Yushchenko,

President Kuchma, and other high-level officials. She is organizing leadership training camps for disabled women that will take place this fall, and her office phone was ringing off the hook during our conversation today. The camps are a huge undertaking, she said, and the participants were handpicked: "We chose women who aren't likely to cause conflicts. We wanted to offer this training to those who are really willing and really need it." Maryna was very proud of some recent publications she coordinated—she said she adapted the "trainings" of the Consortium and Counterpart to "our Ukrainian conditions" and to the needs of disability rights activists, and this work has received a lot of recognition. Maryna seems to have gotten even more involved in the world of trainings for NGO leaders. And much of her work with the NGO coalition focuses on creating and disseminating information in the form of newsletters, bulletins, booklets, and NGO guides. Through her work with Lily of the Valley and the NGO coalition she also has been involved in drafting and lobbying for legislation to better protect the rights of the disabled, including Chernobyl children. During the years of our acquaintance she seems really to have launched herself into politics, especially with her recent work on gender and disability issues.

Maryna said she is not putting too much stock into getting support for the "women and disability theme" from international NGOs, because "funding for women's issues is drying up." She characterized Winrock as a pretty "weak" organization, and reminded me that the main office of Counterpart is closing up, leaving behind only the Counterpart Creative Center, a Ukrainian NGO-support wing of the larger organization.[28] The NIS-US Consortium has been all but defunct since 2001. She said that another donor organization is planning a new focus on women in business for the next couple of years, but she doesn't know if she can tap into those resources.

I see Maryna as a good example of the upward mobility that NGO work can provide. She has really springboarded herself to a professionalized, elite career in NGO work. Much of her success has been facilitated by international organizations—the trainings she's developed, the grants she's received for her various organizations, and the publications she's written. She has been going in many different directions in her NGO career; her ability to stretch is impressive, and she has positioned herself to take advantage of a range of opportunities that intersect the local and international. Even though she's working with women's issues now, it is really hard to say what kind of gender consciousness she has. It sort of seems more like a grant topic to pursue than a political consciousness. Even though her primary motivation may not really be women's rights (though this is debatable), she is doing very important work, since almost no attention has been paid to the needs of women with disabilities. No matter what brought her here, Maryna seems to have found her niche. It may be tempting to devalue the twists and turns of her NGO work as crass careerism. But she's done a lot of good. She worked closely with one of Kyiv's cancer treatment facilities to improve services for children with cancer; she helped thirty-five families with Chernobyl children acquire apartments from the state; she was a member of the team that successfully drafted legislation and lobbied the government to assign several hundred of Kyiv's children Chernobyl victim status. Women with disabilities in Ukraine sorely need advocates, and Maryna seems like the perfect person to take on this task (because of some of her own health problems she also has "invalid" status herself). Despite the reservations one might have about many aspects of NGO development as it's playing out in Ukraine, I'm frankly humbled by women like Maryna, who have been able to create a vision and muster the energy to pursue social change. If they can make a career out of it in the process, who is to blame them for seizing this opportunity?

3 Claims and Class

Do you want to know me?
Then don't ask me
About the dacha, about the car
Don't talk to me
About imported goods, rugs
And fashionable *"ekstrasensi"*[1]
And how much I'm worth
And which books I'm stuffed full of
And the sorts of friends I have . . .
All of that—is not me
You can't know me that way.
Is it possible to appraise something
Based on a shadow, a coincidental reflection,
Can you get to know a phenomenon, an essence?
Eyes?
But eyes are open only in the presence of a friend.
Soul?
You'll open it with the key of kindness.
Then you will know me . . .

—Poem written by Zoia, 1991

Middle-Class Fantasies

February 2, 1999

Vania is to pick up Svetlana, Vira, and me at the designated meeting place—the trolleybus stop nearest to Svetlana's apartment. It's 9:30 AM. We stomp our feet on the frozen snow to ward off numbness and tug our coat collars tighter to stave off the icy wind and blowing snow. Vania finally pulls up in his car. The burgundy Opel, a fairly new sedan, looks promising, but it soon becomes clear that this trip will be a slow one. Every few miles the car dies and Vania gets out to tinker with something under the hood, willing the engine back to life so we can travel on. Vania is a member of Our House (and a father of five children) who recently lost his job, Svetlana informed me earlier, so she calls him up whenever she and Vira need a driver for their NGO affairs, and they pay him a small sum for his trouble and for gas. I'm tagging along with the women as they scour the city for discount food items to include in food baskets they are putting together for distribution to the members of their organization.

If we find a good price, we will purchase what we can fit in the car today and then return tomorrow for the rest.

As we drive around to different bazaars and warehouses searching for discounts on bulk quantities of cooking oil, sugar, and *hrechka* (buckwheat groats), with frequent stops for engine tinkering, Svetlana and Vira begin an elaborate verbal exchange about their "dreams and wishes." They seem to go to another place as they imagine themselves in different life circumstances—lives released from denial and liberated from worries about how to put the next meal on the table. These dream narratives are fascinating windows to the lives that these women live; they are testaments to their poverty, the desires it engenders, and the dreams it snuffs out.

We turn the corner from Shevchenko Boulevard onto Khreshchatyk (a giant statue of Lenin to our left), and my friends conjure an image of a "women's club" they would like to start. If they had a women's club, the moms in their organization could gather every so often to enjoy female fellowship and relax from their home life and domestic chores. "Yes," Svetlana offers, "We'll have soft and luxurious couches to rest our weary bones." "Oh sure," adds Vira, jokingly, "The women can lounge on the couches and drink tea with lemon." In a more serious tone, Svetlana explains that many of the women in their organization (including themselves) suffer from a lack of female companionship, since most "mothers of many children" are homemakers and cannot leave the home and their children very often. She tells me: "Sometimes I think I should have been a psychologist or gone into psychiatry. Because I sit there so often and listen to women—we give them a chance to get everything off their chests. They can talk to us because we are in the same situation as they."

The women's fixation with the lemon continues throughout our quest around the city for discount foodstuffs. While we wander through a warehouse hoping to find wholesale cereals, Vira leaves the rest of us as she goes on a search for "one little lemon, so we can have tea with lemon later." She runs up to all the makeshift fruit stands around the warehouse in pursuit of the elusive lemon. She finally finds the right lemon at the right price and buys it, triumphantly carrying it to show our small collective. She cradles the lemon until we reach the car, her little symbol of the indulgences of life that she and Svetlana are so rarely able to enjoy.

Later we're stopped at a corner while Vania again looks quizzically under the car's hood. We spot a fish store across the street, and Svetlana says, wistfully, "Oh, if I could have some fish right now . . . How I love fish. I haven't had fish in such a long time." She and Vira launch into a long discussion about the prices of different fish in Kyiv's markets—even though they rarely buy it, they know the prices down to the kopeck, where to get the freshest and tastiest fish, and which individual sellers are likely to have the best deals. They can tell I am impressed, and Vira explains: "Even though I can't buy fish I just can't resist looking it over at the market. Because I always think that someday—" Svetlana cuts her off to switch the conversation to canned fish, another item she says she can rarely allow herself. They talk about the consistency of different kinds of fish, the presence or absence of big bones, the amount of oil in the can, the taste, and how various types of canned fish are best prepared. Open-face sandwiches with butter, parsley, and a tiny slice of lemon? Salads with mayonnaise, boiled eggs, and pickles? Mixed with bread and fried into patties? I try to figure out what kinds of fish they are talking about—I cannot identify most of the varieties in English, much less in Russian or Ukrainian. Anything beyond salmon and sardines is lost on me. What could *skumbriia* possibly be? Is that mackerel, pike, or something else? And *kil'ky*? Are those the tiny ones in tomato sauce? My vocabulary is not adequate to continue this conversation (though we do enjoy some laughs trying), but the women try to console me: "That's just how we feel about some of the imported foods. One of my friends ate a can of Whiskas once—only later did he realize it was cat food!" (I had heard this story many times in Ukraine.) This turns the conversation to different foreign foods the women have tried. One of the boys in their organization had a home stay visit to France and returned with Camembert cheese. "That stuff is awful," Vira offers. "It tastes like someone left it out on the balcony in the hot sun too long." But the women love the word "Camembert" and keep pronouncing it with a throaty French accent (Camembert ... Caaaaamembert ... Camembeeerrrrt) until we are all rolling with laughter.

After our shopping trip, I invite Svetlana and Vira to my apartment to continue our chat and finally enjoy that tea with lemon. They are surprised to see the ancient Soviet refrigerator ("Siberia") that came with my rented apartment. "That thing sounds like a car motor," Svetlana observes, and adds: "So I'm not the only one who still has one of those energy-sucking dinosaurs." As I prepare a snack, I try to keep Vira from seeing that I already have four or five lemons languishing in the bottom drawer of the refrigerator. Svetlana reflects on her own poverty: "If you ask me what my children and I live on, I can't tell you because I don't know myself. Our expenses greatly outweigh our income." Her teenage son has aged out of the system of social welfare, so her family no longer qualifies as a "large" one. This means that all three of her children have lost their right to collect a monthly allowance of 70 UAH ($20). Svetlana's son receives a 9 UAH stipend ($2.60) as a student at a state university, her eldest daughter gets child support from her father (6.40 UAH, or $1.90), and Svetlana's youngest daughter receives 6.40 UAH as the child of a single mother. Svetlana sews house slippers from scrap material and sells them for 2.50 UAH ($.70) a pair to make extra money. This is the extent of her family budget, and Vira once told me, in secret, that "Svetlana's children go around hungry."

Svetlana again begins to articulate her middle-class fantasies: "My dream is to have a big kitchen with a huge refrigerator that is never empty. And a couch right beside the refrigerator. I would be able to relax there and open the refrigerator and take out anything I want at anytime and just eat it, without having to worry about dividing it into four parts [for me and my kids]. Because there will always be more." She continues: "And I dream about walking up and down the aisles of the Besarabs'kyi Market and being able to buy anything and everything I want." Svetlana takes a spoon and dunks a round slice of lemon to the bottom of her teacup, squashing the lemon to release the tangy juice: "All I want is a normal life."

Calculations of Class

As I spent more and more time with activists such as Svetlana and Vira, talking to them about their lives and their NGO activities, and accompanying them around the city to meetings and events and on shopping trips, I thought a lot about issues of class. Some of my acquaintances in the city would look askance at me when I told them I had been spending time with *bahotoditni* (large families) and *pensionery* (pensioners/retirees): "What could you possibly have in common with them?" The lifestyles of some of the activists I knew were so different from those of my friends who were moving into the Ukrainian middle class. These were younger people: some had studied abroad; most had knowledge of foreign languages. They were either working for foreign firms or had started their own small businesses. By 2002 and 2003, many of my friends were buying newly built or renovated apartments and modest foreign cars, and taking vacations to exotic places like South Africa, Egypt, and the United States. They had bank accounts, credit cards, and leisure time. Meanwhile, social activists like Svetlana, Vira, Sofiia, and others remained socially vulnerable, despite the long hours they devoted to raise public awareness, lobby government officials, and procure humanitarian assistance.

The literature on postsocialism has had strikingly little to say about class. Certainly important work has been undertaken to explore the myriad affects of marketization and privatization on different aspects of personal and communal life.[2] But these processes have most often been examined through the lens of consumption or labor, without an explicit focus on the intricacies of new forms of class differentiation in the post-Soviet world.[3] This is curious given the history of the region and the importance of class to the socialist project.[4] I see the NGO sphere as telescoping both emerging processes of class differentiation in post-Soviet Ukraine, and the ways in which persons variably resist these differentiation processes. In the face of new state policies that shifted the criteria for calculating needs, deservedness, and ultimately social and economic class, the activists in NGOs such as Our House and For Life were struggling to prevent the development of a permanent underclass. They sought to position and reposition themselves (and the categories with which they were identified) for recognition and redistribution through both practical strategies (mutual aid activities, lobbying) and strategies of public re-education. Through all these efforts, representatives of devalued categories of citizens struggled to prove their social worth. The efforts of NGO organizers to assert the social worth of certain marginalized groups are indicative of what Jennifer Patico has called those telling moments where "tangible conflicts are instantiated between actors differently situated vis-à-vis nation, state, and market to define the worth of different kinds of activities and people" (2005:490).

Among the social activists I knew in Kyiv, accounting for the social worth of devalued categories of citizens (large families, pensioners, the disabled) often hinged on the assertion of claims and centered around "needs talk" (Haney 2002). In Ukraine's contemporary conditions of privatization, welfare reform, and state retreat, making claims for various forms of support (social, state, international NGO assistance) is a slippery business. Neoliberal economic reforms are accompanied by processes of privatization and individualization that privilege models of "active citizenship" and "productive citizenship" over socialist-era models of citizenship based more on entitlement and the state's responsibility toward citizens. Concomitantly, citizens who received special recognition under socialism (mothers of many children, veterans, retirees) risk being moved into the category of "nonproductive," and therefore potentially "undeserving" of state assistance. To counter this positioning, women like Svetlana and Sofiia had to scramble to assert themselves as deserving of recognition and worthy of state support. As they felt themselves sliding into a stigmatized "low-class" identity, these women sought both to procure material benefits for themselves and their consociates, and to counter the new definitions of "deserving" citizenship. They mobilized accounts of their own social worth to deflect others' negative assessments of them, such as "they are giving birth to the poor" or "they are bread beggars" (Rus. *nakhlebniki*). In their claims making, Svetlana, Vira, Sofiia, and other women strove to resuscitate the Soviet-era formulation of class differentiation, one that was based not so much on citizens' productive potential or economic capital but on access to cultural and social capital, and claims to entitlement. These activists stressed the state's obligation to care for their "needs," as they defined them. These entitlement-based claims may ultimately have little resonance in the new Ukrainian political economy. To understand the shifting politics of claims in post-Soviet Ukraine, and why the advocacy efforts of Svetlana, Vira, and Sofiia have proved unsuccessful, it is necessary first to understand the shifts between Soviet and post-Soviet formulations of class difference.

In the Soviet Union, real differences in income between more- and less-educated workers were small, yet a distinction between the intelligentsia and the "working class" was central to perceptions of difference, often labeled as one's "level of culture" (*kul'turnist'*).[5] Therefore, social differentiation was based not primarily on monetary capital but rather on cultural and social capital, which were assessed by calculating education and qualifications, manners, taste, "knowledge," social ties, and access to information and resources (Bourdieu 1986). In today's conditions of neoliberal market reforms, and an increasingly stratified society in terms of socioeconomics, this system of social differentiation has changed. Income and material wealth are slowly becoming the common criteria for distinguishing between "classes," and the success of reforms in Ukraine is being gauged in part by donor governments according to the growth of the Ukrainian "middle class." However, a certain amount of cultural capital is still crucial to qualify as a member of the elite, or even as "middle class." Although the situation has changed as more Ukrainians move into the market sphere and engage in business activities, during the early years of postsocialism many were highly skeptical of the new cliques of very wealthy "businessmen" (*biznesmeny*) and the trappings of their wealth.[6] Those years saw the rise of Ukrainian nouveaux riches ("New Ukrainians") who had access to a range of goods and services not available to the average Ukrainian, such as lavish meals in expensive restaurants, the ubiquitous black Mercedes Benz or SUV, protection services, and medical care in Kyiv's numerous privatized clinics. More often than not, wealthy New Ukrainians were not afforded respect by their less privileged compatriots (except out of fear)—they were ridiculed for their poor taste and tacky lifestyles, and criticized for their conspicuous consumption. Because the New Ukrainians were perceived to be lacking "culture" and education, to have poor taste, and to exhibit bad manners, they were actually perceived as "low class," despite their material wealth.[7] By denigrating the New Ukrainians as wealthy yet "uncultured" and dim-witted, people asserted their own "culturedness," intelligence, and good taste, thus indicating that cultural capital is still an essential part of calculating class in post-Soviet Ukraine, despite the growing importance of economic criteria. In their efforts to stem the tide of class differentiation, activists such as Svetlana and Sofiia capitalized on this fact in their descriptions of themselves as impoverished, yet cultured and intelligent, women.

Another way some of the activists I knew sought to argue for enhanced class identities despite their growing material impoverishment involved genealogical research to trace one's (elite, they hoped) roots. People in the former Soviet Union commonly know little or nothing about their ancestors, given the waves of repression they and their families have lived through, and the secrecy with which many people subsequently guarded their family history. To be a person of noble descent was a dangerous, potentially fatal personal characteristic. In an atmosphere of political freedom and heightened interest in Ukrainian and Russian history, many of my friends in Ukraine were eagerly seeking out information on their "family origins." When, during our life history interviews, Zoia realized how little she knew about her ancestors, she began writing to relatives to ask for any information and stories they could tell her. She related the unfolding revelations to me in subsequent interviews, and pulled out old boxes of photographs to complement the histories. Having learned that her ancestors were members of the Russian, Polish, and Georgian nobility, Zoia even became involved in a local "nobility club" in Kyiv that sought to resurrect the prerevolutionary nobility. Svetlana and Vira also spoke of their families' past in life history interviews; Vira especially emphasized that her grandparents had been landowners of note deprived of their estate during collectivization. Post-Soviet interest in genealogy lends further clues about strategies people are undertaking to locate themselves within changing hierarchies of class.

Despite the emergence of economic capital as an increasingly important criterion for calculating one's class, social capital also remains a key aspect of class identity. In the shortage economy of the Soviet Union, networks (called *blat* [connections, or "pull"] in Russian) were important mechanisms for social stratification. One's *blat* networks consisted of relatives, acquaintances, and friends who were placed in positions affording them access to goods and services in shortage. One could obtain most anything *po blatu,* including consumer goods, trips to sanatoriums, good medical care, and access to entertainment (e.g., theater tickets). Catherine Wanner writes that, "to obtain something *po blatu,* or with the help of connections, means that one plugs into a vast network of contacts and utilizes the access or leverage they might have to obtain needed goods or services. . . . The right *blat* connection can produce power, access, and protection—things that money often cannot buy" (1998:52–53). Regarding the origins and functions of *blat,* Alena Ledeneva notes:

> *Blat*-like phenomena resulted from the particular combination of shortages and, even if repressed, consumerism; from a paradox between an ideology of equality and the practice of differentiation through privileges and closed distribution systems. In so far as those who had no privileges in the state distribution system could by-pass rationing and queuing it had an equalizing as well as stratifying effect. It therefore had a bearing on the society's egalitarian claims and its actual inequalities. (Ledeneva 1998:36)

After socialism, when there is an ample supply of goods yet a deficit of money, *blat* connections are no longer vital for obtaining deficit goods and services. Researchers such as Ledeneva have found that *blat* as a phenomenon has lost much of its significance, and the younger generation of Russians, for example, may not be familiar with the term or the practice.

However, people in other, various situations still utilize such connections. Those unable to cope with the new market, and those who have been most marginalized by its introduction, continue to mobilize the ideology and practice of "mutual help," in which networks and shared assistance are crucial for everyday life; this was the main idea undergirding the activities of the "mutual-aid associations" in my study. Catherine Wanner finds that, in post-Soviet Ukraine, *blat* networks continue to serve two other main functions besides obtaining goods and services: cutting through "bureaucratic inertia and stonewalling" and "locating meaningful employment that pays a living wage" (1998:52). A certain shift in the focus of *blat* networks, however, does reveal the emergence of money as a new source of power; namely, *blat* networks have shifted away from access to goods toward possibilities for accumulating income. In other words, *blat* is mobilized as a form of social capital that has the potential to produce economic capital.

For NGO organizers, social networks were a crucial form of social capital. Activists relied on developing successful social relations in order to become part of the "circle" of international NGO advocacy (what Ivana called a group of "girlfriends, brothers, sisters, and so on"), gain access to information on potential sponsors, grant competitions, and other opportunities, and lobby local bureaucrats for concessions and "partnership." Of course, all my informants had social and cultural capital in some form. Ivana had worked her way into the NIS-US Women's Consortium, and she had working relations with individuals at various international foundations in Kyiv as well as the U.S. Embassy. Maryna knew folks at Counterpart and the Consortium, and her work with the nationwide coalition for disability rights NGOs allowed her to expand her networks considerably. They knew the language of civil society, grants, and empowerment that had become fashionable and crucial for success in the new NGO sphere. Sofiia was a founding member of the Civil Parliament of Women of Ukraine, and she had published articles in the parliamentary newspaper *Uriadovyi kur'ier,* which gave her some recognition among political elites. Svetlana and Vira enjoyed good relations with a few politicians who had sponsored their organization (in exchange for members' votes), and some current and former members of their organization were well placed to help with advice and sponsorship opportunities. But in the changing milieu of post-Soviet market transformation, social welfare reform, and civil society building, some types of social and cultural capital were more highly valued and more useful than others. The capital that Sofiia, Svetlana, Vira, and other marginalized activists had at their disposal was not sufficient to propel them into the limelight of NGO organizing, or, in some cases, even to convince state bureaucrats that they deserved recognition and certain benefits and entitlements.

Indeed, some of my informants commonly criticized those groups whose main goal was to acquire humanitarian assistance and state benefits for members as "user" (*spozhyvchi*) organizations. Under assistance and "benefits" they grouped a range of tangibles and intangibles, such as humanitarian aid from local and foreign sources, welfare payments (for large families and sick persons, for example), and food subsidies. In criticizing "entitlement organizations," activists were really judging the sense of entitlement that many Ukrainians (and these NGO leaders, in particular) felt vis-à-vis the government. The Soviet guarantee of social protection from birth to the grave, they pointed out, was incompatible with the new market conditions in Ukraine. These activists thought that reliance on state-provided benefits made people lazy. They faulted certain groups for failing to "progress" or "develop." Maryna was especially vocal on this point:

> As for organizations for "children victims of Chernobyl," there are way too many of them. . . . Mostly they concentrate on getting "health trips" [Rus. *ozdorovlenie*] and humanitarian aid [Rus. *gumpomoshch'*], lots and lots of it. There are such organizations in every region of the city. But they don't try to grow; they don't try to participate in some activities [Rus. *aktsii*] in the third sector, no self-development; that is, they have one specific goal, either health trips, or humanitarian aid. Let's say if tomorrow humanitarian aid were halted, these organizations would cease to exist because they don't pursue any other goals.

Maryna went on to contrast her own organization, Lily, with the "slew" of mutual-aid associations in Ukraine, and criticized other groups for failing to take advantage of resources involving projects, grants, seminars, fund-raising, and "social business." Organizations for large families bore the brunt of many such criticisms. Informants who saw themselves as Westward-looking devalued organizations such as Our House, because they "just ask for handouts." One activist who knew Svetlana and Vira said that these two women "could solve all their problems if they would just get a job." This was an elitist narrative that failed to recognize the structural constraints faced by Svetlana and Vira, two middle aged women with mediocre educations and three children apiece (Svetlana was also a single mother). Other activists said that large families had been "spoiled" by humanitarian aid and implied that they were indolent. It is notable that many of the activists who criticized "entitlement" groups *themselves* received various pensions and subsidies monthly from the government. Their critiques thus were designed in part to inform me (and other interlocutors) of ways in which, even though they received welfare, they "actively" sought to support themselves through initiatives such as grant-supported projects and other "progressive" endeavors. Such evaluations fail to recognize that the ethos of entitlement is not necessarily a passive one; it is, however, a different way of conceptualizing citizen-state relations, one that calls for a strong social safety net and a strong state. By characterizing mutual-aid associations and other organizations that focused on articulating claims for recognition and redistribution to the Ukrainian state and other institutions as "user" organizations, other activists effectively de-politicized the work of these groups.

Thus, as NGO activists who were plugged into transnational NGO development networks espoused powerful modernizing narratives on civil society, democracy, self-sufficiency, and individualization, they positioned others negatively through anti-Soviet talk criticizing the Soviet past and those who they believed still clung to it. A Soviet social order was thus created, one that was devalued and effectively marginalized from the resources offered to activists who were fluent in "project speak" (Sampson 1996) and who moved in more elite NGO circles. To put this situation in context, and to understand the devaluing of Svetlana, Vira, and Sofiia's claims, I must outline further some of the emerging legislation that helped set in motion the differentiation these women were experiencing. In the discussion that follows I focus particularly on the largest social insurance program, pension reform, about which my informants—middle-aged and elderly women—were especially concerned. Pension reform is particularly indicative of the emerging narratives on personal responsibility and state withdrawal that buttress social insurance reform in postsocialist Ukraine.

Reform and Responsibility

Social insurance reforms are confusing, especially in a context where personnel and state policies are continuously changing and budget deficits prevent the enforcement of new or revised legislation. As of 2005, four state social insurance programs were in place: unemployment; temporary disability, and expenses related to maternity leave and funerals; compensation for industrial accidents and occupational diseases resulting in disability; and pension insurance, for example, retirement and permanent disability. As of early 2007, a fifth program on mandatory health care insurance was still in the planning stage. The primary component of the social protection system is the pension system, which was projected to constitute 85.81 percent of the mandatory state social insurance system in 2005 and involve 13.5 million recipients.[8]

Studies indicate that the overwhelming majority of persons in formerly Soviet countries (90 percent in one study) expect governments to be responsible for old-age pensions. Indeed, old-age pensions were (and still are by much of the populace) seen as an earned benefit, as delayed remuneration for services rendered (Buckley and Donahue 2000:256). This perception may be particularly strong in Ukraine today, given many people's recent experiences of working for years at state (and nonstate) enterprises without pay during the crisis years of the 1990s. Lest they end up ineligible for retirement pensions because of patchy work histories, many individuals chose to stay on the job even when they were not paid for months or years at a time.[9] In this way, millions of people constituted an essentially free labor force. Given this past experience of constituting "volunteer" labor, many see the provision of an old-age pension as the least they deserve from the state. A major problem with Ukraine's pension system is that there are too many pensioners (14 million) and not enough workers to support them (16.5 million). The ratio of pensioners to workers is 85 percent, one of the highest in the world, making pension reform an extremely pressing issue (V. Iatsenko 2005).

Given this situation, despite citizens' expectations of state-provided old-age pensions, postsocialist countries are, in reality, seeking ways to privatize their pension systems at least partly by means of multi-tiered schemes (Lipsmeyer 2003:559–560). Such a scheme has been introduced in Ukraine: legislation effective January 1, 2004, created a three-pillar pension system intended to make individuals much more personally responsible for the nature and size of their old-age pensions. Note, however, that the new three-tier pension system exists on paper but the reform process has been extremely slow. Budget deficits and frequent personnel changes are partly to blame, as well as perceptions that the new system is not viable. In January 2004 pensions were recalculated according to newly implemented formulas, but the real increases in pensions were so small that the new system was deemed unsatisfactory. The second and third pillars of the pension system have not been fully developed (N. Iatsenko 2006); the second pillar is scheduled to take effect only on January 1, 2009. The election of a new Parliament in September 2007 is sure to affect pension reforms, and the three-pillar system may or may not be further pursued. Nevertheless, it is useful to examine the characteristics of ongoing pension reforms, since they are indicative of discourses of differentiation and the rearrangement of state-citizen obligations.

The Soviet pension system was a pay-as-you-go (PAYG) system, with each generation of workers effectively paying the pensions of their contemporary retirees. It was a solidarity system with current workers paying for the retirement of those workers who had gone before them. One pillar of the new proposed three-tier system is the old PAYG, so an element of the solidarity system is retained. The second pillar is an accumulation system of mandatory state pension insurance; during their work years, insured individuals are to pay into personal accounts in the Accumulation Fund, funds they will draw out gradually upon their retirement. The third pillar is a nonstate pension system consisting of individuals and their employers making voluntary contributions into private pension funds (individual retirement accounts), to top off the first and second pillars. The sizes of old-age pensions in the new system are planned to be linked much more closely to individual workers' actual wages and years on the job than was the case under the Soviet system. As stated in one informational brochure on pension reform, "He who makes no contributions will not receive a pension. He who pays in larger contributions for a longer period of time will receive a higher pension proportional to the person who pays in smaller contributions or works for a shorter time."[10] The new pension system is thus a personalized, differentiated system that emphasizes each citizen's responsibility for working toward a maximal retirement pension. The retirement age is low in Ukraine— fifty-five for women and sixty for men—and citizens are encouraged to choose a late retirement so as to facilitate more pay-ins and higher pensions.[11] Other differentiation processes are also evident: the minimum monthly old-age pension is set at the minimum subsistence level (410 UAH in 2007, or about $81), but some can receive higher pensions for "distinguished merits" (for some disabled persons, for example). There are also higher "academic pensions" for individuals who worked in research institutions, and for those formerly employed as state administrators, lawyers, judges, journalists, parliamentarians, and others (V. Iatsenko 2005). Under the new system, state social assistance for those not eligible for pension benefits (those who made no pay-ins or did not work at all) will be means tested, which is new for Ukraine.

Pension reform has the potential to render certain categories of workers extremely vulnerable, including those with short official work histories, those who work an incomplete day, and persons who are not officially registered as workers at their place of employment (and thus do not pay into the Accumulation Fund), persons (almost exclusively women) who have taken long child care leaves, and the chronically unemployed and underemployed (most of whom are also women). Overall, pension reforms are likely to disadvantage women, since sex and wage discrimination in the labor market is so rampant, and many women have been ushered out of the workforce with the reassertion of a patriarchal ideology. Baskakova's analysis of Russian pension reform—a two-pillar system encompassing PAYG and retirement savings—holds for the Ukrainian case as well:

> Given these conditions [of discrimination against women in the sphere of employment], and the shrinking earning power of women compared to that of men, the new pension system means that a woman's average pension based on her retirement savings will be smaller than that of a man. Although it was conceived as gender-neutral, the new system may in fact increase secondary discrimination against women pensioners. (Baskakova 2000:63)

Ella Libanova, deputy director of the Institute of Demography and Social Research of the National Academy of Sciences of Ukraine, predicts that pension reforms in Ukraine will mean that the average woman will receive only 50 percent of the pension a man does (N. Iatsenko 2006). This is because of wage differentials (women's salaries only constitute between 45 percent and 70 percent of men's), and women's shorter work histories (women only need twenty work years to retire, and many take several years off for child care leave). Libanova notes that the current low retirement age for women works against them in additional ways, because many are forced to retire at fifty-five, especially skilled workers in relatively high-paying jobs. The marginalizing effects of pension reform for my informants—women NGO activists who worked long days with no official employment record or salary—will likely be very significant.

Official government publications on pension reform note widespread skepticism among the population about the third tier of the proposed new system—the personal savings accounts. Citizens' aversion to making voluntary contributions to pension funds are framed in terms of their "lack of awareness," apathy, conservatism, and "Soviet-era expectations." In fact, one study of pension reform is entitled *Pension Reform: From Apathy to Personal Responsibility*.[12] Publications such as these evince a certain frustration that citizens have not immediately taken to the idea of large personal investment in one's retirement (something the state previously took care of through the solidarity system). Rarely is it acknowledged in official discussions of pension reform that Soviet citizens who had created a savings account in state banks for retirement or for a "rainy day" (people like Sofiia, Svetlana, Vira, my friend Lidiia, and many others in the Soviet Union) lost their entire life savings owing to monetary reform, bank failures, and inflation. Many are still reluctant to squirrel money away in banks, preferring instead to invest in durable goods or simply hide their extra cash somewhere in the home. Furthermore, personal investments in mutual funds and stocks are a new phenomenon in post-Soviet countries such as Ukraine, and many citizens are skeptical of them after they were burned in the series of pyramid schemes and failed voucher programs that characterized the early 1990s.[13] These constraints are not noted in official discussions of social insurance reform.

Stephen Whitefield (2003) found that in Ukraine the populace generally supports a shift to targeted, needs-based assistance, but this support depends on which categories of citizens are under discussion. For example, in Whitefield's 1998 survey of two thousand persons, it was found that 37.7 percent of respondents believed that the state should support all families with three or more children, and 58.2 percent believed that only needy families in this category should receive support.[14] Only 1 percent believed that no large families should receive state assistance. According to 64.3 percent of respondents, the state should support all pensioners; 33.2 percent favored targeted assistance for needy pensioners only. All persons with disabilities should receive support, in the view of 77.2 percent of respondents, and only needy disabled persons should receive state assistance, according to 20.6 percent (Whitefield 2003:413). Therefore, among these three categories, respondents saw the state as particularly responsible for supporting all disabled citizens, whereas many preferred targeted assistance only for needy, large families.

Despite high levels of support for disability pensions among the general populace, targeted assistance may well guide disability policy in Ukraine's future. Friends of mine who receive disability pensions were worried in 2005 about legislation in the pipeline that would require a "reevaluation" of the status of each citizen who currently receives disability benefits. Faced with the prospect of a decrease in their disability pensions, or the revocation of pensions altogether, they felt the ground shifting under their feet. Provisions are also looming that would prohibit certain categories of citizens with disabilities from working and receiving a pension at the same time. My friends were afraid that no allowances would be made for their physical difficulties in getting to work and working a full day, or for wage disparities often encountered by disabled workers. They would have to choose employment or a pension; they could no longer have both. Indeed, in 2007 the Ministry of Labor and Social Policy announced plans to prioritize professional rehabilitation and job placement for persons with disabilities. Support of the disabled is thus shifting from blanket entitlements and pensions to technical assistance in the form of education and training, and the provision of equipment and services (e.g., prostheses, automobiles, and telephone and internet service). This assistance is designed to facilitate employment and economic self-sufficiency.

Two aspects of social insurance reform are especially important in this discussion of claims and class. The first is the emphasis on "personal responsibility" as state representatives seek to ease the burden of an expensive welfare system. This is indicative of the processes of privatization and individualization that accompany market reforms. The second is the changing language and mechanisms of the state's redistributive apparatus, as plans for "targeted assistance" take shape and new criteria are introduced for citizens to qualify for social welfare. As Lynne Haney so carefully outlines for the Hungarian case, "while the size of a state's redistributive apparatus clearly matters, so too does its interpretation of need; while it is critical to ask 'who gets what' in a given welfare state, it is equally important to interrogate the terms of inclusion and exclusion" (2002:241–242). Income and class are slowly becoming the most important criteria for sorting claims in Ukraine; welfare becomes stigmatized, as it is offered not on the basis of one's entitlement but according to the extent to which one is "needy." This "materialization of need" (Haney 2002) has a profound impact on how citizens' claims of social worth and entitlement will be received, and foists new class identities on those judged as "needy."

(Re)producing Claims

In the late 1990s, faced with the tide of social welfare reform that was slowly washing away universal benefits and leaving instead needs-based assistance, NGO activists like Svetlana and Vira made it a priority to protect the interests of their constituents and themselves as mothers of many children. Although their status as officially unemployed women seemed to indicate that they would easily qualify for assistance via needs-based assessments, they were nevertheless in precarious positions. Svetlana's two eldest children were aging out of the system, and soon she would receive a pension for only her youngest daughter (and this as a single mother, as she would no longer qualify as a "mother of many children"). Svetlana thought this was unfair—her son was a university student and she had borrowed large sums of money from relatives to put him through school. He did not contribute to the family budget; rather (in Svetlana's words), he helped drain it. The same was true for his eldest sister, who was taking secretarial courses and was not working. Vira's situation was slightly better: her husband was a small business owner. Still, he supported the family of five on his salary, since Vira was unemployed and their daughters were still in school. Moreover, in the late 1990s Vira's husband's monthly salary was only 47 UAH (around $12 at the time), not enough for him to pay into the pension fund (to draw an eventual old-age pension) and not enough for the family to receive a housing subsidy. It was unclear to Vira whether her family would qualify for needs-based assistance. Neither Svetlana nor Vira was eligible for unemployment benefits, since they had turned down jobs they had been offered through the unemployment office, jobs where the salary would have equaled their cost of transportation to and from work. Both women were extremely worried about how they would support themselves in their old age; with reforms tying old-age pensions to wage amounts and length of service, their pensions would be tiny or nonexistent. So they were desperately trying to assert their claims as persons deserving of recognition and redistribution from the state and from society at large. This was essential for them personally as mothers, and also as NGO activists as they sought to garner support from the state, businessmen, and foreign sponsors for their organization.

Amid the impending implementation of income tests and needs-based social assistance, Svetlana and Vira were caught in a bind. Differentiation processes entailed in welfare reform are characterized by shifts in focus between what people (now "clients") contribute to society (making them "deserving"), and what they lack (making them "needy"). In their claims making, then, the women were negotiating "needs talk" from two sides. On the one hand, they sought to position themselves as needing assistance as members of a vulnerable category of citizens (mothers of many children, and, in Svetlana's case, single mothers). To do this, they focused on their poverty and emphasized that they were "needy." On the other hand, in the context of new processes of welfare stigmatization, where being "needy" is seen as a personal shortcoming, Svetlana and Vira also had to calculate and demonstrate their social worth. Therefore, the women had to emphasize the contributions they made to society. They needed to be both deserving and needy, because it was unclear how the scales of reform would tilt.

Svetlana and Vira based most of their claims on their status as mothers.

These NGO activists had come to womanhood in a pronatalist, socialist state, where their role as mother was prioritized. As mothers who were each raising three children, Svetlana and Vira felt strongly that they were owed entitlements. During our interviews, Svetlana frequently calculated the various types of government pensions she had received during her maternity leaves, the same allowances on which any mother in the Soviet Union would have depended. The sense of entitlement she felt was universal to all working Soviet women, who were promised a range of benefits to help them reconcile their roles as both workers and mothers. Lynne Haney's description of the maternalist claims that women were accustomed to espousing in the Hungarian socialist welfare system also applies to the Soviet Union:

> These policies trained women on how to stake a claim in the welfare apparatus and on how to emphasize their identities as mothers when couching their appeals. They taught women that as mothers and caretakers, they had "special" needs. What is more, their needs were transformed into social rights through an entitlement system that guaranteed specific resources for mothers. (Haney 1999:154)

Svetlana and Vira saw no reason why, in postsocialism, their roles as mothers should have diminished in the eyes of the state. However, in the late 1990s, their emphasis on their status as mothers had less and less resonance, and their stories often echoed those of Haney's informants in Hungary who desperately asserted, "But we are still mothers!" (Haney 1999, 2002). It is important to note that during those years their motherhood-focused claims were devalued both by representatives of the social welfare system and by international foundations that supported women's NGO initiatives in Ukraine. The maternalist nature of their claims and self-identity was seen as out-of-date and out-of-step with the feminist mandate promoted by these organizations. Representatives of feminist-oriented international NGO development organizations operated on the assumption that a "rights" platform was incompatible with maternalist organizing. This assumption overlooked the fact that women like Svetlana and Vira were using a motherist argument to fight against discrimination of certain categories of women (mothers of many children, single mothers), but this was not interpreted as a "rights" platform by representatives of donor organizations, who dismissed their maternalist stance as backward.

It seems curious that the voices of women who had several children would be dismissed by the state in the context of Ukraine's ongoing demographic crisis. At the level of official rhetoric, pronatalist policies have been articulated ever since World War II in an effort to maintain and increase population levels. However, in our interviews, Svetlana and Vira told me a different story. They recognized that "mothers of many children" were privileged in Soviet discourse, and they were nostalgic for the entitlements and subsidies they had been extended, but they were also quick to point up the discrimination they had faced under the socialist regime. In spite of the Soviet state's pronatalist ideology, they told me, large families had always been treated ambivalently. The women attributed the contemporary poor treatment afforded them by state and business representatives to stereotypes of large families that had existed during Soviet times. Vira said:

> When the big crisis happened a few years ago, *mnogodetnye mamy* [Rus., mothers of many children] were despised. We could buy four kilograms of sugar instead of only one, because we had three children. People in line said, "They have babies, but who will feed them?" I tried to explain to them that I pay for what I get, so what difference does it make to them? I'm not taking food out of their children's mouths; they get their "norm," too. But they still hated us.

Svetlana added, "Whatever government office we go into, we always hear, '*Narozhdaiut nishchikh*' [Rus., 'They are giving birth to the destitute']. People can't stand *mnogodetnye*. They think we are parasites, that we can't do anything except have babies."

Given Svetlana's and Vira's descriptions of the stigmatization of large families, it is ironic that, among the elite classes in Ukraine, having many children has become quite fashionable. President Yushchenko has five children, for example, and the wealthy businessman and powerful parliamentarian Petro Poroshenko has four children. There is certainly a perception in Ukraine that large families are either very rich or very poor, a dichotomy that positions only certain social strata (the wealthy, self-supporting elite) as possessing a real right to have many children. Although Svetlana and Vira indicated that they had been poorly treated both during and after socialism, the root of this stigmatization had shifted. If during the Soviet period large families were shunned primarily in times of shortage, in postsocialist Ukraine poor families with many children were seen as inherently nonproductive and thus, as Svetlana put it, as a "ballast on society." So when their claims to special recognition as mothers were devalued, these women sought to emphasize their productive potential as well.

They did so primarily by emphasizing their role as workers, both during and after the Soviet period. In our interviews, both women spoke at length about their work histories—they had received a technical education (commensurate to a two-year degree in the U.S.) and worked at various blue-collar and semi-skilled jobs. During the late 1990s, they were fighting hard to establish an identity as "employees," even though they were officially unemployed and did not receive a formal salary as NGO organizers. This was a pressing issue, since, as persons recognized as "volunteers" by representatives of the state apparatus, no provisions were being made to ensure their retirement pensions. According to Svetlana and Vira, state bureaucrats regarded them not merely as "unemployed" but rather as *tuneiadki* (Rus.), literally "female spongers" or "female parasites."[15] The women thought this was ironic, since they had searched for work in earnest but had been unable to find jobs paying a living wage. According to Svetlana and Vira, when they went to the Kyiv City Administration to plead their case and convince the authorities that, as "social workers" working fourteen-hour days, they were in fact "employed" and should be given certain benefits (specifically, they wanted to be allowed to pay into the pension fund), the response of the woman in charge of their case was as follows: "Social [Rus. *obshchestvennaia*] work isn't considered to be 'work'; it is a hobby. We thought that you were prosperous ladies, that you didn't have anything to do, and in order to get out of the house and away from housework, you decided to dabble in social work." The two women, both of them nearly destitute, laughed at this (most certainly sarcastic) characterization of themselves as "prosperous ladies," probably a reference to the wives of factory directors and other elites during the early Soviet period (the *obshchestvennitsi*) who were volunteer social workers. They realized that the caseworker was making fun of them, and their appeals to receive state benefits as bona fide "employees" were brushed aside. It is important to note that, even when the women emphasized their productive potential as workers (rather than their reproductive potential as women), these narratives were nevertheless shot through with thoroughly gendered talk. Svetlana frequently described herself as a "workhorse" and detailed her grueling life as a blue-collar factory worker (which included lifting boxes that totaled two tons a day), but she took care to emphasize that she had undertaken this work "as a good mother."

Accounting for Social Worth

As they sought to secure support for themselves and other large families, women such as Svetlana and Vira were marginalized as "low-class" and their social worth was questioned, but not primarily because they were poor. Rather, they were stigmatized because they drew on Soviet-era discourses of state support, entitlement, and "needs" that are an anathema to the perceived "transition" to a free market society. The neoliberal ideology of the new free market economy labels these women (welfare mothers, retirees, and others) as nonproductive and non-deserving. They were thus veritably excluded from elite NGO circles, whose members shared narratives of self-empowerment, entrepreneurship, productive citizenship, and self-sufficiency. Recognizing their marginal position, these women used talk to shore up their sense of self-worth and to initiate public reeducation. In navigating the shifting meanings of "needs" and deservedness, they focused on their intense suffering as they spun out stories of hard work, shaming, and discrimination. Therefore, they emphasized their impoverishment and neediness even as they stressed their past and potential productive contributions to state and society. While relating their experiences of sudden and extreme poverty, the women were eager to convey that the mere fact of their poverty did not make them deserving of the cruel treatment they often faced from state officials and business representatives.

Many of my conversations with Svetlana revolved around her attempts both to account for her poverty and to resist the way she was categorized as "low-class" in post-Soviet Ukrainian society. Her narratives were strikingly different from those of activists like Ivana and Maryna, since Svetlana's hinged not on ideas of democracy and self-empowerment but on suffering and entitlement. Svetlana continually emphasized how she had suffered through the years, sometimes slipping into the speech genre of "saints' lives" described by Nancy Ries in the Russian context (1997:140–154). Articulating her stories of suffering, I think, was one way she sought to generate moral capital in a political economy that had left her by the wayside.

Svetlana had been the victim of two broken marriages; her first husband, whom she called "a weak man," beat her and even had his friends stab her when she threatened to leave and take their two small children with her. After their divorce, he stalked her and the children, and once attempted to kidnap their son from a playground. Her second marriage was short-lived; her husband decided to remarry his former wife, leaving Svetlana, then several months pregnant. When her daughter (and third child) was born, she simply wrote "single mother" on the birth certificate. She did not want to see the baby's father again, so she decided not to take him to court to prove paternity. This freed the father from any child support payments or responsibility for the child, something Svetlana later regretted (she had made the decision before perestroika, when she had 3,000 rubles in savings and, in any case, received 75 rubles a month from the state for the new baby).[16]

Svetlana also described in detail how hard she had worked to support her three children independently, and how she had accumulated personal savings before perestroika and the economic collapse. As she listed the various blue-collar jobs she had held, Svetlana countered popular stereotypes of "mothers of many children" and "welfare mothers" who supposedly do not work, only have babies, do not think about the future, and only live in the moment. Svetlana emphasized, however, that the economic crash of the late 1980s meant that all her hard work and planning was for naught. Almost everyone in Ukraine experienced the same near-overnight destitution and panic. Svetlana portrayed herself as no different from others and yet stressed that, as an overstretched single mother, she had few material possessions at the time, which made her situation especially precarious. In her words:

> Within two months I became destitute. Inflation totally ate up my savings. After that my savings would have bought nothing more than a box of matches. After I had worked so hard and economized—I could have bought a box of matches or ridden on the trolleybus one time. My savings turned into soap bubbles.

If, as others did, Svetlana had foreseen the economic crash and used her savings to buy durable goods (such as furniture, appliances, or building materials), her situation would have been better. But with the crash her savings quickly melted away, and Svetlana, still a single mother, remained destitute despite attempts to find work. She stayed on the rolls of the local unemployment office but gave up hope of finding a viable job. She saw no alternative but to depend on state allowances as a single mother, her first husband's alimony payments (which he rarely paid), and her daughter's small monthly allowance from the state as a "fatherless" child. Her role as the director of Our House was also a survival strategy, since any humanitarian aid the group acquired would go to her family as well.

Svetlana wanted to prevent her children from slipping into the underclass that she felt she was becoming part of, and she saw education as key. Her son, a teenager in the late 1990s, was a student at an institute in Kyiv. Svetlana had borrowed large sums of money from relatives, friends, and acquaintances to pay for his tuition, and was pinning all her hopes on his receiving a good job upon graduation. The debts she had incurred caused her great stress that often escalated into health problems. Svetlana and Vira were incensed when legislative changes threatened to bar families of three or more children that included university students from receiving state benefits as "large families." When they protested, the response of case workers was demeaning:

> SVETLANA: Do you know what they told us? The "ladies" [Rus. *damy*] who take care of that? They said, "It is a luxury to get an education. Let them go and work." Where? Not having a specialty and not having an education? Who will they work as? Racketeers, or at the [stock] exchange [Rus. *birzha*]? Who can they work as?
> VIRA: So it's like before, [people think] "They are creating superfluous [Rus. *lishnie*] people." Superfluous for society. That was the woman who was supposed to be defending the interests of our families. If she has such an opinion of us, what can we expect from everyone else?

Svetlana and Vira interpreted the case workers' position that teenagers from poor families should "go and work" instead of receiving an education as evidence of the differentiation of large families as "low-class." They responded in the interviews with attempts to counter negative stereotypes about large families that were prevalent in the popular imagination. They spoke of members in their organization who were accomplished musicians, and they showed me the artistic work of children from large families who had won art competitions. They described their members as "cultured people" who came from "old Kyivan families" that represented the "impoverished intelligentsia." The women often noted that the privatization of education and the offering of "extracurricular classes" in music, dance, and art on a for-fee basis (subjects that were a standard part of the curriculum in Soviet times) meant that children from large families and impoverished families in general missed out on opportunities to develop their creative and performance skills and learn about high culture.

Despite the women's continued attempts to "shake things up," as they put it, and insist on the rights of large families as a deserving category of citizens, they were fighting an uphill battle. The organization Our House had been unable to pay 4,000 UAH ($1,100) to the state in rent arrears, and the office was requisitioned in 2001. When I met them again in 2002, Svetlana and Vira assured me that their organizing activities had been interrupted only temporarily, but meanwhile they had sought official employment. Svetlana had gone to work for a crisis hotline, a job she found emotionally rewarding but physically demanding—she had to work twenty-four-hour shifts and was not allowed to lie down. Her salary was very low, just $100 a month (less than half the national average). Vira remained unemployed. With the advocacy efforts of Our House all but suspended, the seventy large families the organization represented were left to fend for themselves.

"Whose children are we?"

Like Svetlana and Vira, Sofiia and her fellow retirees at For Life articulated their claims in terms of their entitlement as members of a category the state had always recognized as deserving of state support. They had been taught that all dutiful citizens would be taken care of by the state after their retirement—old-age pensions were perceived as an earned benefit. As Sofiia once put it, "If the state paid me what it owes me, I wouldn't be called *maloobes-pechennaia* [Rus., insufficiently provided for] or *nishchaia* [Rus. destitute], which are really the same thing, but different labels are applied depending on one's perceived intelligence." Many of the women's claims were based on the conviction that the members of For Life and other retirees had sacrificed significantly for the state—many had served in World War II and all had impressive work records. The members of For Life found it unconscionable that the postsocialist transition was leaving an entire category of citizens—the old and retired—destitute. They were angry that, in Ukraine, being elderly was synonymous with being marginalized. These elderly women emphasized that their generation had borne the brunt of hardships during World War II and Stalin's Terror, and had sacrificed much to nurture the generation of men and women who now ran the country. They felt it a mockery of their sacrifices that the state and its representatives were abandoning them through the adoption of tough-love policies withdrawing state entitlements, subsidies, and adequate pensions from categories of citizens such as the elderly. They articulated these complaints in a letter to one deputy of Parliament:

> Whose children are we? Our parents died on the battlefields. We defended them [those in power today], we educated them for free, gave them medical treatment for free, and now they are making us pay, they are making our grandchildren pay for their education; they are making us pay for everything.[17]

This was a complex claim. In asking "Whose children are we?" these elderly women emphasized that they grew up without parents,[18] and they were reminding the current generation of able-bodied workers that they should feel some responsibility for taking care of the elderly (as figurative children). If the question is read, "Whose children are *we*?" it could be inferred that these retirees were protesting what they perceived as the state's focus on supporting children and childhood instead of caring for the elderly generation. The final phrase, "they are making us pay for everything," referred to the hard facts of the new market economy, where socialized medicine and free education are being phased out, but also hinted at the idea of atonement. It implied that younger generations in Ukraine were consciously penalizing the older, Soviet generation for the mistakes of the past, making them pay for everything that went wrong during Soviet state socialism.

Sofiia's narratives revealed much about how the elderly in general were positioned negatively by representatives of the state. The elderly, said Sofiia, were seen as "beggars," and bureaucrats treated them as if they were stupid and worthless. Many elderly people were impoverished and had to wear threadbare clothing, which contributed to this image. Sofiia connected the Ukrainian state's neglect of her organization to pervasive stereotypes attributing "outdated ideas," wrinkles, slow speech, and "Soviet mentality" to the elderly, all of which effectively marginalized this group as "beyond help." State officials had no patience, she said, for the supposed tendency of the elderly to approach them shabbily dressed and to shuffle around, heads down, while rambling on in their speech. Organizations serving elderly persons found it difficult or impossible to garner state support, because, as one former employee of a Western funding agency put it, they were "the wrong contingent, because of their age." The disempowering effects of these processes were devastating for Ukraine's elderly population. During the 1990s, the residents of Kyiv were the only members of the elderly population that received their dismal pension payments regularly; retirees in other cities and in rural areas languished for months without receiving their pensions. On the other hand, many elderly people in cities—who did not have access to the farm fresh products their rural compatriots did—subsisted almost entirely on bread and milk, the cheapest food items available. In 2002, Sofiia told me that living conditions had worsened considerably for her members since I first met the group in 1999. She used herself as an example: although she only received a monthly retirement pension of 120 UAH, the medicines she needed cost between 300 and 400 UAH a month. "Where am I supposed to get that money?" She complained that the elderly were being "squeezed out" and that bureaucrats were "walling themselves off from us," putting up barriers via office workers and guards who would not let her and her members into government buildings.

In this context, Sofiia and her constituents put great energy into making claims for their own social worth. They constantly educated me and other interlocutors as to the contributions they had made to society as workers, mothers, soldiers, and wives. Special events were dedicated to these endeavors, such as the "holiday" called "My Years, My Wealth" to which the women invited me in 1999. (Sofiia joked that each special event the group undertook was called a holiday, because "you never know if it might be your last.") At the celebration, I sat near a small group of international aid workers (the only other invited guests besides For Life's members who had shown up) and listened as the women stood up and proudly related their most significant life experiences. One woman, Olha, had been a surgeon during the Second World War and had reconstructed the damaged faces of wounded Soviet soldiers. She had pinned her medals of honor for her military service onto the formal navy and white dress that she had selected for the occasion. Others described how they had cleared the rubble from Kyiv's streets after the war and had assisted in rebuilding the city. Some focused their testimonies on the achievements they had made in their careers—the group consisted of teachers, professors, scientists, engineers,

Figure 14. "C'est la vie." Differentiation in Kyiv, 2005. Photo by Nikolai Zhdanov.

and doctors. The women talked about their children, grandchildren, and great-grandchildren with pride. The event gave the women the opportunity to provide accounts of their social worth as individuals and as members of certain categories (retirees, elderly women, war veterans, professionals). Indeed, Sofiia used the verb "account" (Ukr. *zvituvaty*) to describe the organization's motivation for holding the celebration. Of note is that local (Ukrainian) representatives of the state had not seen fit to attend the celebration or even to acknowledge the invitation. Bureaucrats who chose to ignore them and their accounts effectively silenced the women's voices and dismissed their claims.

In her own efforts to "shake things up," Sofiia tried to instruct her members on how to effectively engage state representatives and how to make successful claims. For some of the women, she explained, pensions had been incorrectly tabulated; these women were entitled to a larger pension than they received. Others might have been overcharged for their apartment rent. A major goal for Sofiia, then, was to instruct members on how to defend their rights by effectively approaching the relevant state officials and articulating their claims.

Sticking Lemons in Their Mouths

Sofiia once related what she saw as the major abuses against the elderly by indifferent bureaucrats:

> I . . . always look at every meeting, every conversation, every person, analytically. Once I watched how an elderly person conducted herself [in front of a government official]. All the elderly are used to walking into a room and immediately drawing their head down into their shoulders. For some reason they consider themselves to be more defenseless [Rus. *uiazvimye*] than others. And that director sat there [and barked in a gruff voice], "What?" And she just stood there, defeated. "What?" [repeated the director]. "I don't have it." He listened [and said]: "Go to that office. There they will handle it" [note: using the singular, informal form of address for "you," a sign of blatant disrespect when addressing the elderly]. She went to the second office, she told her story, she talked and talked. The second one listened to it all. "No! Go to another office . . ." But she could have [been told that at the outset and not wasted her breath] . . . All of them [listened first and then turned her away].

This was the first of many bureaucratic horror stories (Herzfeld 1992:4) Sofiia was to tell me, and in this tale she introduced key aspects of her struggles to empower elderly women. She emphasized the indifference of bureaucrats, who would sit and listen to the elderly person's timid requests and stories, and then pass the buck to another bureaucrat. In his study of bureaucratic indifference, Michael Herzfeld has noted that, "indifference is the rejection of common humanity. It is the denial of identity, of selfhood" (1992:1). I learned through listening to Sofiia's narratives that it was precisely this denial that she was resisting when she encountered bureaucrats on behalf of herself and her "girls" (as she called her members), and when she spoke about such encounters. She was concerned with helping her organization's members to make themselves visible and to voice their claims to state functionaries effectively, but her endeavors ran deeper. Sofiia took on state functionaries in order to personify for them a "real live elderly person" so as to disrupt stereotypes of the elderly, and assert their rights.

In Sofiia's many bureaucratic horror stories, she highlighted the dehumanizing tactics bureaucrats utilized, their complete inability to interact with citizens —especially with the elderly—and the rampant irresponsibility, negligent attitudes, and corruption that plagued government institutions. During these encounters, Sofiia initiated a reeducation of government bureaucrats as she sought to reform the rude, uncaring bureaucratic culture in postsocialist Ukraine. According to Sofiia, she often told bureaucrats, "My wish for you is that you will acquire some tact in interacting with people, because you surely do not possess it." She sought to teach by example: "With my quiet conversation, my politeness, and my age, I introduce them to the culture of social interaction." Needless to say, most government representatives perceived Sofiia's presumption to "teach" them "the culture of social interaction" as an unwelcome intrusion. Her ability to relate the vivid details of these fraught interactions resulted in many hours of hilarious, colorful interviews.

It is significant that Sofiia was most concerned with helping *women* confront state officials and voice their claims. Women comprise the majority of Ukraine's elderly,[19] as life expectancy for women is almost a full ten years higher than for men.[20] Sofiia acknowledged that it was harder for elderly women to be taken seriously by bureaucrats—most of whom were men—and that it was more difficult for women to attain positions of power in Ukrainian society. Sofiia's own lack of political backing and connections made her struggles for recognition and redistribution that much more difficult. In one narrative, for example, Sofiia recalled how she had made a heated speech at a roundtable meeting on Ukrainian social services sponsored by the United Nations. The meeting, she said, which was held on the premises of the Ministry of Ukraine on Family and Youth (in 1998, the ministry was "reduced" to a state committee), was "just like during Soviet times," with representatives of the different ministries reciting unwritten and unverifiable "reports" (Rus. *otchyoty,* literally "accounts") in front of one another. The main attraction for the participants, said Sofiia, appeared to be the lavish buffet that awaited them after the meeting. Sofiia said:

> When I saw [them heading for the buffet], I stood up. . . . Even though I am intelligent, I can be unpredictable. I said, "You'll excuse me . . . we were invited and we were promised the floor. So I am taking the floor. Everything that you just reported—did you prepare it in your office? [You must not have spoken to a single elderly person.] Who checked it for you? Show me. I am prepared to sit with you— you can watch me sleep, and eat, and you can verify your reports on me [a real live elderly person]. Do I have enough money from the pension that you assigned me? Furthermore, I don't at all understand why we are in this building [Ministry of Ukraine on Family and Youth]. In this organization, there is not a section, not even a person, who works with the elderly." And I also talked about what we do. I said, "We conducted lessons, the only ones [of their kind] in Ukraine, for an entire year,

every Wednesday. We didn't miss in winter or summer. We had a ceremony with the help of the UN. They supported us ..." I said, "We brought all of you invitations, and you didn't even respond. You aren't interested." I didn't abuse my time on the floor but I said that. When I finished it was as if a bomb had dropped.

Other interviews with Sofiia were filled with similar stories in which she related how she had confronted government officials with her criticisms, and how she had (mostly unsuccessfully) made persistent requests for government assistance for her organization. Many of her narratives seemed like hopeful attempts to counter the ways in which she and her fellow retirees were constantly silenced. Sofiia ended one of her stories proudly with the phrase: "[After I'm through with them] they often look as if I've stuck a lemon in their mouths." She told me this story after a general meeting, when several of her members were still in the office. Sofiia's fellow members who were listening to her lively narrative laughed and nodded their heads in approval. Sofiia was enjoying her performance and began to tell me other ways in which she had "shamed" bureaucrats. One of these stories involved her savvy use of the Ukrainian language. Sofiia liked to "trip them up," she told me, by speaking in Ukrainian, the official language of the new Ukrainian state. She said:

> Ha! You know, I go up to them and speak perfect Ukrainian, and you should see the looks on their faces! No one expects a Jew to know Ukrainian as well as I do. But I studied in a Ukrainian school, and I was a good student. I have a knack for languages. And you know, the policy is that all government workers should speak Ukrainian at work. But they can't do it! You should hear the garbled mess that comes out of their mouths. They are caught off guard, they feel silly, and they lose themselves. I'm telling you, they don't expect that from me![21]

The cultural logics that positioned a Jewish woman as a kind of precarious "Ukrainian" also meant that Sofiia and her organization were not able to get onboard the Ukrainian nationalizing project. This was because of two specific factors: the group's focus on the elderly population and the assumed "Jewish profile" of the organization. Although For Life was not actually a "Jewish" organization, many in government and the NGO sphere assumed that Sofiia and her organization served mostly Jews because of Sofiia's Jewish background and her previous involvement in Jewish organizations. And how was it possible, the thinking went, that a Jewish organization could have a mandate suited to raising Ukrainian national consciousness? The organization's narrow focus on the problems of old age was also a major barrier. Although the group did attempt to connect itself with the nationalizing project—one event, called "Grandmothers for Children," emphasized the important role of elderly women in nurturing the youngest generation of Ukrainians—most of Sofiia's efforts to articulate her group's agenda to the rubrics supported by development programs (Ukrainian and international) had been unsuccessful. She told me:

> The Year of the Elderly [1999] is over and no one wants to work with elderly people anymore. I have learned to talk about the "healthy nation" and a "healthy popula-

tion," but no matter how I put it, I can't make it work.[22] When they say "a healthy nation," they mean the reproductive nation, that is, those who are still in their reproductive years. And we are too old. When they say "a healthy nation," they have children in mind. But children could never be healthy if we hadn't nurtured them.

Therefore, Sofiia recognized that her group, which in the eyes of the state could contribute only marginally to "(re)producing" the new Ukrainian nation, and which was sometimes positioned as representing a different (Jewish) "nation" all together, was an unlikely candidate for any support from "nationalizing" sources.

Similarly, programs initiated by international organizations and foundations clearly had not been designed with the needs of elderly persons in mind. Sofiia and her members had attended seminars sponsored by Counterpart and the NIS-US Women's Consortium, and had found them useful, but none of the grant assistance offered by these organizations suited the purposes of For Life. The group had thought about trying to take advantage of the new trend in civic organizing, namely, "women in business," but ultimately decided that becoming "businesswomen" was beyond their mandate. "We could open a kiosk, or something like that, and sell something to support ourselves," said Sofiia. "But which of our members wants to sit in a kiosk all day, freezing in winter and boiling in summer? We are elderly, our health is poor—that is too much of a burden for us." She had heard about loans being offered to NGOs (probably the social enterprise program of Counterpart) but was unwilling to take this risk—she did not want to go into debt because it would be unfair to put this pressure on the members of the organization. Sofiia became a certified trainer through an international NGO development organization, but she had few opportunities to conduct trainings. In 2000, she informed me by letter that she might be offered a position with the State Committee on Small Business Development as a trainer for courses on "elderly persons in business" or on "how to make money," but I later learned that this opportunity never materialized. Sofiia was the oldest trainer I knew in Ukraine; I found a photograph of her in a newsletter that depicts her along with her "graduating class" of newly certified trainers. She is the only trainer with grey hair, and the only one who looks to be over forty-five years old.

The year 1999 was declared the "Year of the Elderly" by the United Nations, and For Life was awarded a grant of $20,000 from the UN for a project titled "Toward a Healthy Way of Life and an Active Old-Age." This grant represented the only major foreign funding the organization received. But either because of a misunderstanding or bureaucratic red tape, For Life received only about half the money it had been promised. Also significant, the support Sofiia's group received from the international community was based more on the personal goodwill of a few foreign aid workers than on grant programs. Several young aid workers from the United States took the organization under their wing during the late 1990s; they sponsored food and clothing drives, and helped members with medical bills and office equipment. These sympathetic young people recognized their own grandparents in Sofiia and her "girls," and they were troubled that pensioners had been abandoned by both the Ukrainian state and the international development industry. Though grateful for the support of these Americans, Sofiia did not let up in her efforts to seek out recognition and support from other sources. During the summer of 2002, when I returned to Kyiv for follow-up research with the organization, For Life was engaged in intense lobbying efforts protesting proposed legislation to withdraw from retirees the privilege of free public transportation. Such a policy, said Sofiia, would "hang" her. She depended on the fresh fruits and vegetables she grew at her small dacha outside Kyiv for survival, and she could never afford the bus fare there and back for her frequent trips. The women lamented that, if free transport were withdrawn, they would be stuck between their own four walls, unable to travel around or outside the city. They were lobbying legislators in writing and in person to prevent the bill from passing.

Because there were no grant programs for which the organization's mission was truly suited, the group devised creative ways to tap into funding opportunities. Members applied for grants to carry out projects only indirectly related to their original mandate, such as a pilot project on homelessness developed by For Life in 2002. Sofiia wrote to me at that time, explaining that this program (which would involve the rehabilitation of sixty homeless women in Kyiv) suited the organization because of its "ability to interact with degraded populations." The organization's members would integrate homeless women into discussion groups on mutual aid, cooperative work, and self-evaluation, and would invite them to their cultural events. At a general meeting of For Life that I attended in the spring of 2005, the group was discussing plans for developing a new project on preventing drug abuse among the city's youth. Their conversation centered more on protecting themselves and their elderly neighbors from violent addicts than anything else. As I listened to these plans, I could not help but reflect on the curious ways the organization had diversified its goals since the late 1990s, even though most of the faces around the long table remained the same.

"Benefits don't fall from the sky"

In describing how these NGO activists have articulated claims and espoused "value narratives" (Patico 2005:491) to argue for their social worth and resist being positioned in devalued class identities, I do not mean to imply that they were somehow stuck in a Soviet past or a "socialist mind-set," unaware of the transforming political economy and changing ideologies of worth swirling around them. On the contrary, these women were keenly cognizant of postsocialist processes of differentiation that positioned them on the losing end of "transition," and they were astute observers of others' opinions of them as needy pensioners and mothers of many children. They were not some "old Soviet guard" who longed for a return to the Soviet Union or to state socialism. Perfectly aware that others might perceive them this way, activists like Sofiia,

Svetlana, and Vira were careful to emphasize ways in which they were precisely "not Soviet." Sofiia, in particular, articulated many criticisms of the Soviet system. She detested lateness ("lack of punctuality"), a slovenly characteristic which she believed the Soviet system instilled in people. Even while iterating a discourse of entitlement, Sofiia also emphasized self-reliance and initiative. When explaining why she sought out members who were active, enthusiastic, hard workers, Sofiia said: "Benefits don't fall from the sky. That was during Soviet times." She told her elderly constituents that it was every individual's responsibility to prepare herself for old age, and she sought to convince them that they should be ready to rely only on themselves. At almost every meeting of For Life that I attended, I heard Sofiia tell her members: "Don't come here if you just want to sit around and socialize. This organization is for active people, and we only need those who do their part." In step with these ideas about self-sufficiency and individual initiative, Sofiia believed that people should receive rewards in proportion to how hard they had worked. Consequently, as the director of For Life, Sofiia did not treat all her members the same—they were rewarded according to their own contributions to the organization and the other members. These rewards came in the form of periodic allowances (cash payments) from private donors—Sofiia divided up these payments in increments as she saw fit and presented them to members.

Thus Sofiia, in her own way, engaged in the practice of differentiation, reproducing the processes of differentiation occurring in Ukrainian society at large and within the smaller worlds of NGO organizing and claims making. Ironically, in this way, she perpetuated some of the very processes of exclusion and marginalization that For Life was designed to stave off. Svetlana and Vira also launched a project of differentiation when they undertook a "needs assessment" of their organization's members that mirrored, eerily, case workers' "reviews" which they themselves would likely face as mothers of many children. In a 1999 interview, Svetlana described her motivation for differentiating her "needy" members from the non-needy:

> Once I visited one of our member families (they had five children) and I was shocked to see how well they were living. They had *Evroremont* (European-style repairs), a computer, and beautiful furniture. When I saw this family that I was working "to help," it made me ill [Rus. *mne plokho stalo*]. They could have helped [others] themselves, and here we were running around to find "help" for them. . . . I went about in a trance for about a month. I thought, "Svetlana, why in the world do you need this? What are you doing this for?" Here I was—and I fall into the poorest category of the families of our organization—here I was running my legs off to find help for such families, and then I find out that they are living the high life and could have helped others themselves! I took it really hard. . . . [After the experience we had with that well-off family] we immediately called a meeting of the organization's officers and decided to do an evaluation of all the families. We went around to each family and assessed their needs. About four or five of them we felt do not need help from the organization. But we didn't take any of them off our membership roster.

They are still members, and their children can participate in our holidays and trips, but we excluded [Rus. *iskliuchili*] them from our help.

In conducting her own "needs assessment" of member families, Svetlana was both a subject and an agent of state institutions mandated to undertake "differentiation" of social assistance as part of social insurance reform. Her participation in this project—one that she and other "mothers of many children" resisted on other levels—reveals the complex nature of the politics of recognition and redistribution in postsocialist Ukraine. It also shows how NGO activists have become both subjects and agents of the reform process, which has led to the formation of somewhat contradictory personal and social identities. As Svetlana and Vira worked in their office and interacted with other impoverished heads of families, there was a sense of the common struggles of the underclass of the newly poor. They delighted in each other's stories of scraping by and making do. These sessions escalated into veritable storytelling matches: Who was the ultimate mama-heroine-trickster? Whose creative means of surviving destitution would prevail? But when Svetlana and Vira scoured the capital city for sponsors, knocking on doors asking for "support," suddenly they were "low-class," "insolent" women "giving birth to the poor." In other contexts, they were administrators of a particular kind of social justice, bureaucrats in their own right who were empowered to assess the relative "need" of their clients in Our House.

To assert their claims, these NGO activists at times emphasized their needs and right to entitlements as special categories of citizens. However, they also leveraged the language of self-sufficiency, differentiation, and active citizenship that increasingly informs the social contract in conditions of market reform. Although they did tend to draw on ideas of entitlement in their "value narratives," it should be noted that entitlement is not necessarily a passive stance. In asserting their own social worth and that of others like them, and in engaging in lobbying efforts and claims making, women like Svetlana, Vira, and Sofiia saw themselves as taking a stance of active citizenship. Ultimately, however, their efforts met with little success.

The narrative accounts of these activists, understood in their "etymologically rich sense" as both narration and bookkeeping (Stark 1994), allow us to track the postsocialist creation of difference, and the material effects of exclusion, including the marginalization and disempowerment of certain categories of citizens (namely, those viewed as "unproductive"). Although these women worked hard to carve out their own place in the new political economy, they failed in establishing a higher status for themselves in the society and securing the material benefits that go with it. At the end of my initial fieldwork in December 1999, both organizations were hanging on by a thread. The activities of Our House were (temporarily, Svetlana and Vira assured me) suspended in 2001; their office was requisitioned by the state and sold to a private firm. Subsequently, the members of Our House were compelled to pursue survival strategies as individual families. It was around that same time that the members of For Life finally received a coveted new office (with twice the space of their original meeting space), but they continued to receive little in the way of funding or support from any state or non-state sources. It was unclear how long the organization could hang on with so little support for their claims. One activist I knew said that "user" organizations like the mutual-aid associations for large families, pensioners, and veterans would "fade from view" once the economic situation in Ukraine improved and people "outgrew" these NGOs. This vision of the happy postsocialist march to capitalism obscures the forms of differentiation that are occurring in the country at large, and in the NGO sphere as well. It is comforting to tell ourselves that privatization and democratization benefit all of society, but the stories of Svetlana, Vira, and Sofiia tell a different tale. Their stories complicate rosy assessments of "reform" and "civil society building," because they present the stark reality in which entire categories of people seem to have fallen through the cracks.

Excerpts from Interview Transcript, May 11, 1999

SVETLANA: Sometimes we have to go around and argue for our claims. We have to prove that the [bureaucrats] aren't right. That our demands are valid. That we are right and they aren't. This calls up a wave of animosity—not toward all [the families] but toward ourselves, personally. So we make a lot of enemies for ourselves, defending the interests of everyone. Because we found the courage. We get asked: "How could you conduct yourselves so poorly?"

VIRA: "How could you demand health trips for children? How could you demand it? Health trips are for people in the administration, for cadres . . ."

SVETLANA: And the funniest thing is that sometimes they confuse those children we represent through the organization with our own children. They say, "We gave your children a health vacation!" Which children, exactly? Those in the organization. "No, your own children," [they answer]. If you are talking about my own children, let me inform you that they sat on the asphalt in the city all summer. But for those vacations that you gave to the others, thank you. "This year, your children (meaning our own children) won't see a health trip like that." Is that normal? Our own children suffer because the cadres get angry at us. Sometimes it's better not to stick your neck out.

Then, each time they find out that we have managed to get something somewhere [Rus. *dobilis' chego-to*] and that we gave it out to people, they cross all our people off their list. "They already got something." Excuse me. You have a budget. You are given money from the budget for the work you carry out. We have practically no relation to your budget. You don't even relieve us from paying rent. We are a humanitarian organization. You could at least free us up from rent.

When we have a pre-election wave of humanitarianism, everyone declares, "Ah, impoverished people, the needy, oh, the elderly, children, Chernobyl victims, they all need help." And now at the end of May after the election they will forget all their promises. They'll say, "Girls, you understand, all the money was spent during the election campaign." To ask for help from another person you have to break something [inside you], and we were able to do it only thanks to one thing. We had to tell ourselves, "I am not doing this for myself. Behind my back, depending on me, there are many children, hundreds of children." Because neither Vira nor myself will go to ask for help for our own families. Even if we have it very bad. Until a person does this, he is reaching upwards. But when he breaks, it's like the person begins to fall downwards. When a person stretches out his hand and says, "Help me, for the grace of God," that means something has broken. And even for all the children, we didn't do it gracefully at first.

You come, and they let you in the office. The person who sits behind the table—the director of the bank, or the manager of the bank, or the director of some store or restaurant—it doesn't matter who it is. This is the person to whom you have come to ask for help. You haven't stepped over the threshold yet, but he already knows whether he will give you something or not. If he is a polite person, he will invite you to sit down, and he will say, "You know, we have our own difficult circumstances" or "Our firm doesn't engage in such things." [He says it] with respect. You say, "Excuse me, please," and you leave. He addresses you like a fellow human being.

But there are other scenarios. They will throw you out: "Swindlers [Rus. aferisty] are nosing around." "Avantiuristy [Rus. risky adventurers], who want money." That is an insult: we never ask for money. We do have a bank account, and if money is transferred to the account it is earmarked: for buying food. For health vacations. And we can't spend a kopeck anywhere else. We don't ask for money. "Can you give us help of some kind? Can you donate some of your manufactured goods? Or in some other way? It isn't important how. Anyway you can." But no, they had to insult you. In the beginning, when we began to go around, they called us swindlers, or avantiuristy. You won't shout back at them: "I'm not like that! I'm a good person!"

VIRA: And you haven't even come there for yourself, or even for your own children . . .

SVETLANA: You leave and sit down, your heart hurts, your face is red, you are nervous, and you can't even speak to one another.

VIRA: Yes, you can't look at one another, because you know as soon as you do you'll start crying. You have the feeling that they have hung their big Mercedes around your neck, and poured filth all over you, and that everyone around heard it, and they approved. And you feel like, "But we aren't at fault! We aren't like that!"

4 Movin' On Up: Social Activism and Upward Mobility

March 13, 2006

I can't help but smile as I read Lidiia's letter: "In 2003 Ivana went to work at the new publishing house Leleka—now she is director of the division for children's books."[1] Leleka! Last Christmas a friend sent my young son some books published by Leleka, and they quickly became his favorites. After that we bought up all the Leleka children's books we could find. Who would have guessed that Ivana played a major role in developing those wonderful books!

I had lost touch with Ivana and recently asked Lidiia to track her down. I spoke with Ivana on the phone in 2002, and we agreed to meet later in the summer in Kyiv, but again I was unable to reach her. I found out later that her daughter had died in an automobile accident shortly after our telephone conversation, and Ivana was immobilized with grief. I was never able to reach her by phone again and feared we had lost touch for good, until Lidiia finally found her in Kyiv. I'm actually not all that surprised that Ivana has become a businesswoman. During our last long interview in November 1999, she told me that she had been thinking for some time about going into business, and she envisioned a connection with children and education. Leleka seemed a logical outcome of those plans. In her conversation with Lidiia, Ivana attributed her ability to make the leap into business to the skills and self-confidence she accrued via her NGO leadership roles. As Lidiia wrote me:

> Her former NGO work did a lot for her personally—she learned to believe in herself, she learned to interact with people, and to listen to people—especially young people. . . . That work gave her the opportunity to see herself from the outside; she recognized in herself a leader, and she received her calling. She saw that she is a good manager, analyst, and marketing expert [Rus. *marketolog*], and endless opportunities opened up for her.

Elastic Elites

By now it is no secret that "civil society building" in Eastern Europe and other locales has led to the creation of a veritable NGO industry that seems all tangled up in itself—a self-perpetuating system of grants, seminars, round-tables, conferences, fund-raising (and on and on) that sustains the livelihood of thousands of local and foreign development workers in "transitioning" states like Ukraine. The professionalization of the NGO sphere means that much civil society development aid ends up benefiting only a small segment of the population rather than "trickling down" to the elusive "grassroots," to those citizens who are most vulnerable and marginalized. This point has not been lost on anthropologists, who have been well situated and eager to critique the NGOization of civil society in post-Soviet countries where small cliques of savvy post-Soviets have been able to get on and stay aboard the international NGO gravy train. There is apparent variation across the region as to who makes up these local NGO cliques and clans, and whether they are preexisting elite groups or groups actually formed by the very injection of foreign aid into a given country or region. Some critics have emphasized that these NGO elites tend to be "professionals already groomed in Soviet times" (Mandel 2002:285), already existing political elites nicely poised to hoard aid and information (Ishkanian 2000; Wedel 1998), whereas others argue that civil society development projects actually structure a somewhat unpredictable recipient community of elites (Abramson 1999a). A degree of opportunism is certainly invariably present: for Russia, Julie Hemment has noted that civil society's "participants are less often dissidents and politicos, the intellectual architects of the anti-Communist revolutions, but young people intent on developing their careers" (1998:34). In either case, anthropologists working in the region are attuned to the fact that rhetorically "grassroots-focused" endeavors to promote civil society development and democratization are top-heavy and elitist.

Ruth Mandel (2002) and Steven Sampson (2002) have penned some of the most pointed critiques of what Mandel calls the "new stratum" or "new cadre of local development professionals" (2002:286). Sampson calls them "Euro-elites." Working in Kazakhstan, where she served briefly on the board of one international NGO development organization (Counterpart), Mandel details the slow yet methodical migration of individuals in low-paid government jobs to the NGO sphere. These professionals, she argues, have internalized "new value systems" shaped by development agendas and have developed social capital including skills such as fund-raising, political know-how, and lobbying. Mandel asserts that members of this "new stratum" are rendered virtually unemployable by their own governments, because the skills they acquire, and the open and flexible work styles to which they become accustomed, are not easily applied to local contexts. Pay differentials is another big issue, and Mandel documents that many NGO professionals eventually seek out opportunities to emigrate abroad to take more lucrative jobs. Mandel calls these national elite NGO cadres a "sustainable" and "unexpected by-product of Western 'transition aid'" and the "human fallout of international development aid" (2002:279). Those who remain in-country, Mandel states, now form a parallel structure to that of the state, often perceived as rival rather than complementary, and sometimes encroaching on or taking over the state's responsibilities.

Like Mandel, Steven Sampson (2002) identifies "Euro-elites" as "project elites," the flexible, young, Anglophone staff of Western donor projects who are "wage earners working for foreign projects." Sampson argues that "their entire world is externally focused, and for many, the ultimate strategy is emigration or at least intense participation in global civil society networks." He believes this is a "decapitation" process whereby "a potential national elite goes missing." Also like Mandel, Sampson sees the "Euro-elites" as unlikely to take up government work in their home countries, because they are "trying to maintain their niche" (2002:310).

No doubt these critiques document real and important processes, and force us to consider whether international interventions to promote "democratization" are themselves at all democratic (Rivkin-Fish 2004). Such nuanced and critical portraits of the NGO industry certainly cloud romantic visions of civil society and "empowerment," but surely this is not the entire picture. In my research I, too, have documented the practices of competition, exclusion, elitism, even betrayal that permeate the world of NGOs in postsocialist states, and I know with certainty that "Euro-elites" exist. However, I agree with Julie Hemment that glossing all NGO activity as an "elite" activity "screens out a great deal of complexity" (2004:328). The power of the ethnographic approach is precisely that it allows us to examine this complexity and thus avoid generalizations about people's motivations and experiences. Critiques of development pitfalls and aid gone wrong are important, but we should not lose sight of the human face of the phenomena we describe; nor should the wide range of variation in experience be overlooked in order to make a point. Furthermore, as Hemment argues, just as development initiatives have unintended effects, so might our revisionist accounts of civil society building. She notes a recent trend in which "liberal triumphalism has been displaced by talk of how Russia is 'lost' and is a 'failed project,'" a turn that "could pave the way for scaling back support and the eventual withdrawal of aid agencies from Russia altogether" (2004:314). Like Hemment, I am troubled by this prospect. I have met scores of dedicated social activists making a huge difference in their communities, and I would hate to see them lose what little support they have from the international donor community. Despite the reservations I have about many NGO development interventions as they have played out in Ukraine, I still think that overemphasizing abuse of aid, failed assistance projects, careerism, and cynicism in the NGO world is dangerous when not balanced with a view of the local contexts and histories in which these interventions unfold.

The very diversity of activists' experiences makes this a crucial project. To be sure, a large number of activists are losing out because the international donor community sees their agendas as invalid or superfluous, and because they have not been quick to "repackage themselves" (Abramson 1999a:245) to take advantage of emerging and shifting opportunities. But neither are all social activists "Euro-elites" seeking to emigrate who thus have a "decapitating" effect on the national political elite. Indeed, try as I might, I have found it quite impossible to characterize my informants who did move in transnational NGO circles as elite cadres detached from local agendas; although they did pursue funding opportunities dictated by donors that at times steered them from their original mandates, these activists mostly maintained trajectories consistent with their professional expertise and the perceived needs of their target groups. Because

Ivana was a teacher, her NGO work was driven predominantly by education. Although Maryna did "grow out of" Lily of the Valley, she continued to work with disability issues at increasingly higher levels. Unlike the "new stratum" of indigenous development professionals profiled by Mandel and Sampson, who stood in opposition to local structures and seemed virtually unemployable in their home states, both Ivana and Maryna eventually moved into professional careers rarely available to women in Ukraine: business for Ivana, and high-level government administration for Maryna. In a context in which it has been extremely difficult for women to enter the business sphere, get elected to political office, and secure high-ranking appointments in the state administration, it is worth thinking about how rising through the ranks of NGO leadership might facilitate these types of career moves for women in Ukraine and other postsocialist countries. If we recall that the stated goals of many international development aid programs targeting East European women are to facilitate women's economic empowerment and foster women's successful integration into official power structures, perhaps Ivana and Maryna are, in fact, positive examples of successful development outcomes.

In this chapter I focus on Ivana's life story to add a human face to the story of upward career mobility or, "springboard" potential, that NGO development "transition aid" has offered some individuals. Ivana was able to move from her position in 1999 as a high school teacher who ran a small NGO (Hope) for troubled girls on the side, through paid positions as a trainer for international NGO development organizations, an administrator in Kyiv's technical schools, and a lecturer in a teachers' college, eventually to land a job as a marketing representative for a large publishing house, where she became director of the Kyiv branch in 2004. This is an impressive career progression in any context, and especially so in "transitioning" societies like Ukraine where economic crisis severely curtailed the labor market until very recently, especially job opportunities for women. It might be easy to dismiss Ivana as an opportunist who walked the walk and talked the talk of NGO development for a time in order to launch her own business career down the line. But if we take seriously Ivana's explanations of her own motivations for undertaking various projects, and her descriptions of how NGO work and training programs helped her change her worldview and develop valuable skills and expertise, a far more complex picture emerges.

Ivana's story is not a clear-cut case of manipulation and strategic "grant eating." Nor is it a story of a native NGO professional adopting whole scale a "new value system shaped by development agendas" (Mandel 2002:286). If Ivana did develop a new value system—and I believe she did—it was a complex value system informed by her experiences as a woman who came of age in the Soviet Union; the networks she developed as an NGO activist in postsocialism; the ideologies and practices circulating within these networks; and her own personal and family circumstances, among other influences. The way Ivana framed her stories about her life, and the motivations she articulated for undertaking NGO and development initiatives, revealed a melding of "Western" ideologies of active citizenship, individualism, and women's rights with more localized ideas on the Ukrainian national project and "traditional" gender roles. Ivana's hybrid identities and narratives made it difficult to pin her down with a static label, and she constantly surprised me. Ivana frequently used "Soviet" expressions in her speech, but she also manipulated transnational NGO phraseology and thus littered her narratives with Ukrainianized English words (*prohresyvno, preventatyvno, interaktyvno,* and *partnerstvo,* to name just a few). She described her "calling" to work with people by referring to several different roles: her position as a Komsomol leader in the Soviet Union, the fact that she was a woman "naturally" drawn to addressing social problems, and her new-found aptitude for leadership as a trainer for international foundations. Furthermore, Ivana's life story reveals that her dramatic career shifts began long before the fall of the USSR. It is crucial to note that—at least as she told it—Ivana's decision making and strategizing in terms of her work life were always informed by how she saw herself as a *woman* with particular gifts and responsibilities. This was as true of her post-Soviet NGO and business career moves as it was of her career decisions in socialist Ukraine. It is significant, however, that Ivana inserted a narrative of "rights" into her career talk and plans after her interactions with the NIS-US Women's Consortium. Well connected and well respected by the international donor community of transnational NGOs in Kyiv, Ivana was exposed to a range of modernizing narratives on feminism, entrepreneurship, civic education, and others. As she negotiated her own identity as a woman and a leader, she managed to localize many of the "imported" ideas. She was able to successfully capitalize upon the opportunities offered by NGO development initiatives while screening these ideas through a sort of cultural and personal sieve, picking out the choice nuggets and putting them to use, while allowing the less relevant and less useful ones to filter through.

Tracking Ivana's life story allows me to pick up the threads of discussions initiated in chapter 2 on Ukrainian NGO-graphy, international development interventions targeting women in Ukraine, and the concomitant differentiation of women in Ukraine's "third sector." I knew Ivana longer than I knew any other key informant, since I met her very soon after I arrived in Kyiv for extended fieldwork in February 1998. I was in close contact with her throughout two years of research during 1998 and 1999. And thanks to my friend Lidiia's detective work, I was able to track Ivana's career as a social activist and professional up to 2006. My firsthand observations of the changes in Ivana's life during the late 1990s were complemented by stories of previous experiences that she related to me during several life history interviews. Her story is a vivid example of how women with access to lucrative networks in the NGO sphere are able to develop the social and cultural capital necessary to expand their expertise and enter careers that are normally quite inaccessible for Ukraine's women. She described her experiences in ways that brought into vivid relief how leadership training seminars and interactions with a broad range of persons helped her "realize herself" as a woman and as a leader.

An Engineer of Human Souls

Ivana's life story was constructed to reveal how her priorities "as a woman" had changed throughout her lifetime, and how at various points in her life she had reevaluated her role as a worker and a mother. In the stories she told about the twists and turns her career path took over the years, Ivana emphasized the sacrifices she had made as a mother for her children. Other narratives revealed additional ways in which she believed she had denied herself in order to keep her family together, including a refusal to emigrate when she had the chance.[2] Ivana said that her original career goal was to become an atomic physicist, a profession dominated by men. When, for reasons she did not explain, "that dream washed out," she studied to become a mechanical engineer instead. She was one of only two women in a group of twenty-nine students. At the time, said Ivana, she chose a male-dominated field "to become an equal with men. Back then, people were supposed to be inspired by specialists, not by women." Ivana thus provided commentary on the Soviet gender contract, which promised women equality with men by offering equal work opportunities. Ivana emphasized that the Soviet ideology had elevated the value of workers, and she even portrayed her marriage as being founded on a working relationship. Ivana told me, laughing, "When I got married I tried to find a person who would understand me as an engineer, not as a woman."

For ten years, Ivana forged a very successful yet unfulfilling career as a mechanical engineer. She also entered graduate studies in engineering. When her children were old enough to go to preschool, she began to reevaluate her career choice and her role as a woman in the family and in society. She found great difficulty in reconciling her engineering career and her responsibilities as a mother. Her career, though prestigious, was not lucrative (her husband, who was a prominent construction engineer, made much more money than she did). She decided that her career was not benefiting her family; on the contrary, her children were "suffering" from inadequate preschools because she was working and could not look after them adequately. Because it was unheard of for a Soviet woman to leave work and become a stay-at-home mother, at first Ivana tried to reconcile her career and her child care responsibilities by doing her engineering work at home, a feasible strategy since most of her work involved drafting. She found this solution unsatisfactory, however, because her work still took her away from her children.

So, to the absolute shock of everyone around her, Ivana decided to quit her engineering job and her graduate studies. She started working as a nanny (Rus. *vospitatel'nitsa*, literally "upbringer") in the preschool that her children attended. Ivana implied that she would have preferred to quit working altogether, but since unemployed persons were considered "parasites" under the Soviet system, she was forced to work outside the home. The best solution she could think of was to work at her children's preschool, so at least she would be near them all day. This career trajectory represented a dramatic decline in prestige, which Ivana fully recognized.

In some ways, Ivana's story up to this point provided commentary on the Soviet regime's failed project to emancipate women. Although great strides were made to provide men and women with equal educational opportunities, and women theoretically were given access to careers on a par with men, women remained disadvantaged. The less prestigious professions were dominated by women, their opportunities to occupy elite posts in all professions were constricted, and women were paid less than men (Lapidus 1978:161–197). Additionally, although women were given (supposedly) equal work opportunities/ responsibilities, few strides were made to alleviate their domestic work burdens. Women like Ivana, who were on the fast track in their careers, faced great conflicts in how to divide their energy between work and home. Soviet promises to collectivize tasks of domestic drudgery such as child care, laundry, and cooking did not materialize, and women were left to shoulder the ubiquitous double burden.

Ivana explicitly criticized Soviet policies toward women, work, and the family. She described her dissatisfaction with work policies that prevented mothers from reconciling their professional and familial responsibilities. She stayed in her engineering job—which she saw as detrimental to her children, who "suffered" in their preschool—longer than she should have, she said, because "we were taught to think about the motherland [Rus. *rodina*] first, and only then about the family." According to Ivana, Soviet policies governing work in general and the quality of work produced by Soviet workers were also to blame for the lack of fulfillment she experienced in her career and for the "wasted" time she spent at work away from her children. All these factors led her to change her line of work. On the other hand, Ivana also narrated her career move from engineer to nanny as having more "personal" origins. Namely, she said it was a strategy to be true to herself and to fulfill her more "womanly" inclinations. She evaluated her choice of work and later career changes in the following terms:

> More than likely, when I was choosing a profession, my goal was to, somehow, stand equally with men. But later, throughout my life . . . I totally rethought my position on those matters. I want to be a woman, I want [people to] be inspired [by me]. . . . But back then, engineering was very prestigious, very fashionable. . . . But with time, I rethought all that. I wanted more contact with people, and to find a more womanly [Rus. *zhenskaia*] specialty, in order to create closer contacts with people. Not to be an engineer, not to be a person who understands lathes [Rus. *stanki*] and instruments, but to be an "engineer of human souls." That is what attracts me most, and suits me, as a woman.

Ivana inferred that trying to enter a "masculine" profession had been a mistake, and in a curious borrowing from Stalin, who called Soviet writers "engineers of human souls" (the phrase was used frequently in a series of speeches at the 1934 Soviet Writers' Congress), Ivana described a certain softening of her career aspirations (or she was just making a joke!). When her children started elementary school, Ivana decided not to go back to engineering, and she studied to become a teacher. She explained this career choice as reflecting the realization that her calling was to work with people—especially children—and to disseminate knowledge, activities that she said also suited her as a woman.

This same narrative line figured into Ivana's explanations for why she got into public life through social activism. She saw herself first and foremost as a woman, as someone who was taking up "womanly" roles and responsibilities in promoting social change. As Charlotte Linde (1993:72) has noted, in relating life history narratives, people often pause to take an evaluative stance, thus indicating how they would like their comments and the experiences they are describing to be interpreted. This was certainly true of Ivana, whose evaluative comments were often critical of a Soviet gender ideology that had placed more focus on production than on families, and that had championed women as workers above all. Most important, she indicated that in trying to establish herself as a professional and thus focusing narrowly on her career goals (something she believed the state had encouraged—indeed, forced—her to do), she had nearly failed to "realize herself" as a woman. She said, for example, "Back then I tried to prove myself as a worker; now I am proving myself as a woman." At the same time, however, she did portray her decision to leave engineering to become a nanny at her children's preschool as a personal sacrifice. Her now grown children (sixteen and twenty-one at the time), she said, recognized that she had given up her scientific career "to focus on their development," and that she had devoted "all her creative energies" for their well-being "at a time when other mothers were writing dissertations." Therefore, she said, her children had pledged their support for her NGO activities, and they helped her with this work in many ways. When describing her social work, Ivana often emphasized that for her it was a "family endeavor," and that her husband also contributed much of his time and expertise to her projects.

This arrangement was new for me, because many of the women NGO activists I knew were single, widowed, or divorced. Ivana was one of only three of my eleven key informants who were married, and she was the only one whose husband had become involved in her NGO work. Their story of cooperation, however, was not that straightforward. As Ivana described the evolution of her marriage, the theme of transformation was also dominant. During the early years of their marriage, Ivana characterized her husband's attitude toward her as one of disrespect. Even though she had established herself as a qualified engineer, she said, her husband treated her as if she "were nothing without him." The only reason she stayed in her marriage, she said, was for the sake of her children; her husband had refused to "give" her the children if she left him. After a series of events through which Ivana was introduced to what she called "traditional, aristocratic" ideas concerning the family and women's "natural roles" (ideas that conflicted with the official Soviet gender discourse), Ivana said that her views of herself as a woman, wife, and mother had changed. After this turnaround, she said, she commanded more respect from her husband, who began to treat her "totally differently." "Clearly changes took place within me," she reported, "that caused him to change his attitude towards me. For me these were the most key changes in my psychology, in my psyche, in my worldview. For me, this was a colossal change." It was after this series of events that she made the final decision to become a high school teacher, a profession, she said, that allowed her not only to pass on knowledge to students but to help them sort out personal and family problems. She described her career change from engineer to nanny to teacher/counselor as representing a journey from a "mechanical" mind-set to a "humanistic" one. Such humanistic endeavors, she asserted in her narrative, were best pursued by women because of their more "emotional natures." She thought the same was true of social activism, since women, she said, were naturally more suited to addressing social issues because of their caring, patient approach to resolving problems.

A Stormy Life

Ivana might have been caring, but she certainly did not seem very patient. She was always eager and excited, and practically bounced out of her chair when a new idea struck. During our life history interviews, she described her life as a series of "turnarounds" (Rus. *povoroty*), a characterization that seemed very fitting. During the two years that I followed her in Kyiv (1998–99), these transformations became inscribed on her body as her appearance gradually changed. Her light brown hair became more and more tinged with gray, a change she commented on frequently. She wore her mature mane with pride, however, and did not dye her hair, a very unusual choice in Ukraine, where few women give in to nature when it comes to their hair color. Ivana also started to dress differently. By 1999, she no longer wore the spike-heeled, knee-length, black leather boots she had been wearing when I first met her; nor did I see her in close-fitted tailored suits and two-inch, high-heeled pumps which she had worn earlier to teach high school students. Her dress was more casual now. She usually wore a simple skirt and sweater, and always wore boots or shoes with no heel. Such clothing, she told me, was more suited to the mobile and hectic lifestyle she was now leading.

Many of these surface transformations seemed indicative of the deeper changes that Ivana sought to make in her life. In all our interactions, including recorded interviews, casual meetings, and telephone conversations, Ivana was constantly working on her sense of self. When talking about her current work life, Ivana had several favorite themes: how busy she was, her positive (and improving) personal qualities, and her networks. Frequently referring to her life as "stormy" (Rus. *burnaia*), Ivana stressed the frenzied pace at which she lived each day. She often complained about a lack of sleep and said that each of her days was "planned to the minute."[3] She described her activities as important, exciting, and fulfilling, and she emphasized the positive impact the work she did was having on Ukrainian society. Many of my informants were shy about being interviewed, and thus played down our interviews by calling them "just conversations." Ivana, on the other hand, took our interviews seriously, and always called them "our work." She saw in them an opportunity to articulate her views on a range of topics, and she used interviews as brainstorming sessions to generate new ideas.

I suspect that Ivana's transformed appearance reflected the influence of the people with whom she had begun to surround herself as she became increasingly involved in development work. These included well-placed NGO activists in Kyiv, some of them American or Ukrainian representatives of donor organizations such as ACTR/ACCELS, the Soros Foundation, and others.[4] Her relaxed, more casual, and "natural" appearance approximated the dress and image of Westerners (especially Americans) living and working in Kyiv. It seemed to me that, for Ivana, these changes were indicative of the "progressive" (a word she often used to characterize her new colleagues) tone of her current lifestyle. She was an expert name dropper, and she constantly told me about important people she had met in connection with her work, including Ukrainian politicians and high-ranking representatives of the U.S. Embassy in Kyiv. Ivana proudly described the colleagues with whom she had written grants and carried out projects; she emphasized their academic credentials and prestigious posts in academic institutions. On several occasions, she strategically took me along to meetings with persons who were likely to be impressed that she had made an American acquaintance (something still rare in the late 1990s). Ivana often introduced me to her colleagues as an "American correspondent" (journalist), a description that, though inaccurate, emphasized my interest in Ivana's activities and indicated to others that I saw her as a source of expertise.

During the late 1990s, many of Ivana's activities were related to civic education, a program that came from the United States via the Civic Education Project, a nonprofit voluntary organization designed to enhance the development of higher and professional education in societies engaged in political and economic transition.[5] She took part in the Civic Education Project both as the director of Hope and in her capacity as a government employee in the Ukrainian system of vocational education. By writing and receiving grants through Hope, Ivana could channel these monies to implement programs in the state's notoriously underfunded and underdeveloped vocational schools. To me this was one of the most striking aspects of Ivana's organizational activities, and the arrangement debunked the commonly held perception that NGOs exist in exclusively antagonistic relationships with state institutions. Ivana's middle-person position meant she was well placed to serve marginalized girls coming through the vocational schools (called professional-technical, or "proftech" in Ukraine) as both an NGO activist and a state employee.

In Ukraine, the vocational education system is very much a "second-tier" or "second-best" structure, and it has a poor reputation. People commonly perceive that vocational schools, which offer courses starting in the ninth grade, mainly service poor children of neglectful parents. Vocational schools are seen by many educated persons as an alternative high school for children who are too "delinquent" or "low" to receive an education in regular schools, and who have no ambition to study at a university. It was true, Ivana said, that most students in the vocational education system came from poor families, and many were from abusive households. "Students in proftech are usually from orphanages or from poor families; they don't have the chance to get a higher education because they have no money . . . they have few opportunities," she said. Given their disadvantaged position in Ukrainian society, Ivana saw these students—especially girls—as a critical target for humanitarian and "enlightening" activities. In an interesting arrangement, Ivana was able to combine her duties as the director of Hope and as a state employee of the proftech education system, even as she became more and more involved in the Civic Education Project. I emphasize this point to stress Ivana's aptitude for networking and placing herself in strategic positions, but also to show how she sought to remain mission-focused as she did so.

In the late 1990s, Ivana was working with other Ukrainian colleagues to develop educational materials on civic education (civics, basically) for proftech students, and she was developing and carrying out training seminars for lecturers in proftech institutions. The goal of these initiatives—for which the working group had received financial and technical support from the Civic Education Project—was to introduce concepts of civics and active citizenship to vocational education students, and to train faculty how to teach these new subjects, "so students will know how to defend their rights." As part of her own preparation for this work, Ivana had gone through a series of "trainings" as a participant, most notably seminars on "women in leadership" and "women's small business" sponsored by the NIS-US Women's Consortium. Eventually she established her reputation as an experienced and reliable trainer, and became a paid trainer for the Consortium.

Ivana frequently mentioned the ideas and methodologies that she had learned as a participant and leader of trainings, and the positive effects they had on her personal life and at work. She told me that attending the seminars had boosted her self-image and strengthened her self-confidence. In this sense, the seminars had effectively "trained" Ivana to become a better leader:

> I began to look differently at some problems—life positions and so on—after those seminars. For me it was one of those turning points in my life. . . . I had many complexes [Rus. *byla zakompleksovannoi*] for a long time . . . and after those seminars I felt more confident, more literate professionally, in order to socialize with people on a certain level. . . . Earlier I was unable to pick up the receiver and speak with a stranger. Now it is the easiest thing for me. In front of any rank of person, no matter who it is . . . I can speak on the same level as they and feel absolutely competent talking about those issues that I want to share or discuss. This is proof that I have become adequately confident in myself.

Learning about "women's rights" and completing exercises designed to heighten self-esteem were the aspects of the seminars that Ivana had found most personally relevant and empowering. Ivana indicated that she had invited other women to get involved in the seminars and that these women had also experienced "positive personal changes" as a result of their participation. Ivana connected the transformations she had experienced as a result of the trainings with the broader personal transformations she believed her social activism had engendered:

> I am glad, after all, that my life isn't gray; my days are not gray, rather they are full. Sometimes I have days that are planned down to the minute. . . . I see that people around me get charged with my enthusiasm. . . . I'm very happy, truly, that I gained some confidence. . . . Earlier I walked around like this, [with my head hunkered down], and now I walk with a raised head. That is, I can look people in the eyes. Earlier I couldn't look people in the eyes, because I thought that I was a freak [Rus. *urodka*]. I had a mass of complexes that I developed in childhood, and which my husband supported for a while. And now I know that I can do . . . things that not everyone can. So these are the things that have happened to me recently—good events, good changes, you could say.

Ideas about individuality, self-realization, women's human rights, and women's leadership that Ivana had encountered through the Consortium-sponsored trainings had led her to seek avenues for expanding her social work and engaging in strategies for "self-improvement." In connection with her activist endeavors, she began studying psychology and English. She was thinking about pursuing an advanced degree in the psychology of pedagogy, an endeavor that would allow her to participate in a range of academic exchange programs in the United States for NIS scholars. Ivana also revealed that she had an "unrealized dream" to open her own small business through which she would address problems of education and health. She envisioned several projects (for example, opening sanatoriums for treating ill children) that could serve as the "first step" in establishing her own business. As was the trend for women interested in business, Ivana's preferences indicated her desire to focus on services traditionally provided by women, in this case the care of sick children. In embarking on a career (business) not traditionally associated with women's "attributes," Ivana, like other women, intended to take up tasks that *were* traditionally "female." Such strategies indicate how various feminist and "traditionalist" ideas were woven together by activists as they carved out a space for themselves in Ukrainian society and as they acted on the basis of these ideas. For her part, Ivana resisted what she called the "aggressive" methods of the Consortium's seminars, which, I learned, was her way of criticizing the approach to gender roles promoted in the trainings:

> SP: When you went to those trainings, they were on gender, right?
> IVANA: Yes, gender and women's leadership.
> SP: Did they change how you think about relations between—
> IVANA: The sexes?
> SP: Yes. Or, did they reinforce what you already thought?
> IVANA: In principle . . . about me, right? It changed me a lot. At last I was able to talk about myself, about what I am proud of. What qualities in myself I can be proud of. I could talk about my accomplishments, or about what I am proud of in life in general. I took away many positive things for

myself. I found my way in life; I was able to become a leader in some ways. I became convinced that I have the right to have my own opinion. I have the right to insist on my rights. I have the right to insist on my own positions. That was very important for me.

But I also changed some things in those trainings [when I began to conduct them myself]. There were a lot of aggressive presentations that don't suit our mentality. So now when I conduct the trainings, I conduct them a bit differently; I plan them a little bit differently.

Other conversations with Ivana revealed that, when she later conducted the "women in leadership" seminars herself, she softened the presentation of material on the cultural construction of gender roles. She did not agree that gender roles were "culturally produced" but believed, instead, that women and men were inherently "different," and that these natural differences had equipped women and men for success in different spheres:

> If you look at politics here, women have not held high political offices. That's not right. Who, if not a mother, if not a woman, knows the problems of the family in a state? Who can change things, if not a "mistress of the house" [Rus. *khoziaika*]? We say that the leader of the country can be, and should be, a woman. A lot in the state, and in the family, depends on her. [She provides] a cultural and spiritual base. After all, a woman is the keeper of the hearth. But to be honest, I am strongly against all aggressive methods. One must not behave so aggressively. It must be done diplomatically, and with a lot of wisdom and patience. And, to tell the truth, all the same a woman must remain a woman, even though she must strive for equality. But for rational [Rus. *razumnoe*] equality, for rational and fair, tolerant equality. No matter what, a woman is a mother; she is the origin of spirituality and emotion, right? And peace and calm depends, in the end, on a mother, a woman. If a woman is a leader, I think she will bring harmony to society, which is not happening now. So I believe that in society—and in our Ukrainian society—a woman is harmony, she is harmony in everything—in society, life, the family, the Verkhovna Rada, and the government administration.

Embedded in this narrative was a critique of what Ivana saw as "radical" feminist approaches that challenged traditional gender roles. For Ivana, the ideal woman-leader embodied all the qualities traditionally associated with womanhood—harmony, culture, spirituality, patience (versus aggressiveness), and emotion. Though not directly stated in these terms, Ivana's description of women's special leadership qualities articulated ideas about "gender peace," a new term coined by Ukrainian researchers (Zhurzhenko 2004:31). This emphasis on women's roles as mothers and nurturers of the nation differed significantly from the messages of leadership seminars, which emphasized women's rights. In this way, "imported" ideas about women, leadership, women's rights, and gender were localized by NGO trainers and activists like Ivana, who adapted these narratives to local understandings of men's and women's roles in social and political life.

Ivana had also begun to link her success in NGO development, education, and social work to qualities that were stressed in the Consortium trainings as necessary for success in leadership and business: creativity and "cooperative" approaches to planning and decision making. As she reflected over her career history, she pinpointed ways in which her own creative qualities and cooperative inclinations had benefited her work and made her especially suited for certain tasks. She also discussed innovations she had made in the classroom as a high school teacher and later as a trainer for the Consortium. The ability to innovate, she believed, made her unique:

> I was not only a teacher who passed on knowledge of the subjects [I taught].... All the lessons that I taught—from the first day to my last day as a teacher—were nontraditional. They were interesting lessons because they didn't take place between a teacher and a student, but [between] "partners" in the lesson. Students and I communicated [Rus. *vzaimoobogashchalis'*]. We pulled out new information from different sources. The lessons were more like a discussion. We had "interactive" [Rus. *interaktivnye*] lessons, not lessons where I give you knowledge and tomorrow you return it, having memorized it, or something ... rather, there was communication.... When I reached a certain moment, I understood that I must organize my life and my work to include a bigger circle of people to whom I can pass along that knowledge, those abilities and skills [Rus. *navyki*] that I received.

Ivana went on to relate how her innovative and "communicative" or "interactive" approach in the classroom had allowed her to enter the larger world of NGO development and work in the city education administration.

The processes of introspection, individualization, and skill building promoted by international NGO development initiatives are all present in Ivana's reflections on the "turnarounds" in her life and in her career. After a lengthy hiatus in her work as she dealt with her cancer and her daughter's tragic death, Ivana did pursue the business career she had been considering for some time. Not insignificantly, she took her NGO expertise with her, and she also maintained close working ties with state educational institutions. She thus stretched herself three ways to enact the very sort of state–market–NGO partnership promoted by many civil society development programs in the region.

Maryna's NGO career also took twists and turns from the late 1990s but landed her in quite a different place. In 2006, Maryna reflected back on her social activism. She said she had accrued valuable skills, especially experience interacting with people from "all levels of life"—from "regular people" to members of the government administration. She left Lily of the Valley in 2002 as expected, and in 2003 she also quit her work with the Ukrainian-wide NGO coalition of disability rights organizations, where she had headed up the division for women's NGOs. Maryna applied for and obtained an administrative job in the Verkhovna Rada, where she worked for almost two years on the auditing commission. She then switched jobs to a high-level post in the auditing commission for the city of Kyiv. Maryna told me in the spring of 2006 that she hopes to move to a job in the Ministry of Labor and Social Policy where she will work on drafting legislation on disability and Chernobyl affairs. Curiously, this would bring her full circle, since one of her first achievements as an NGO leader with Lily of the Valley was working with a team that drafted and pushed through legislation guaranteeing several hundred of Kyiv's children status as Chernobyl victims. But now Maryna would be working on legislation and social justice issues from a much more privileged position, as a government insider. She continues to work with the resource center Mist that she founded years ago, focusing mostly on conducting leadership trainings for directors of women's and disability rights NGOs.

Success and Struggle

I continue reading Lidiia's letter:

Ivana heads the division for publishing children's books and textbooks. They are developing their own innovative methodological approaches—"Learning through play," with collections of methodological materials for elementary school teachers, preschool teachers, and parents. Right now Ivana is planning a roundtable on this subject. She has not abandoned her NGO work. In 2003, she worked on a gender project, and she is still the director of the civic organization Hope. Through the publishing house she organized an NGO/resource and consultation center that involves children, teachers, and parents in developing and testing new books. She works closely with the state Pedagogical Institute, where students and faculty also participate in developing and disseminating the new methodologies and books. She says she loves the work, but it is a heavy load—sometimes she works twenty hours a day.

Are Ivana's and Maryna's success stories? I think so. By rising through the ranks of civil society development initiatives, Ivana was able to capitalize on opportunities to acquire skill sets and ways of evaluating her own personal qualities and expertise in order to launch a successful career in educational publishing. Because Ivana's path to business zigzagged through grants and projects, and through networks of NGO elites, it might be easy to be skeptical of her motives. But in roundabout fashion perhaps Ivana's successful leap into the role of businesswoman actually achieves one of the goals of transition aid: to help secure the emergence of a new middle class of entrepreneurs and property owners who, as stakeholders, "demand and create a stable and secure democracy" (Mandel 2002:281) as a precondition for civil society. That she has been able to succeed where few women do in Ukraine is certainly significant. The same is true of Maryna, who gradually worked her way into a career in high-level government administration and lawmaking. In this capacity, she will be taking up many of the same advocacy issues she has all along (disability, Chernobyl) but from the other (more powerful) side of the table.

Of course, it would be ill-advised to extrapolate from the experiences of just a few social activists, but these women's stories do point to some successes of development interventions to facilitate women's empowerment in postsocialist states. Their achievements should not be over-romanticized, since both Ivana's and Maryna's career trajectories were also filled with much frustration, self-doubt, and a lot of grueling work. Most striking to me about both women (and especially Ivana) is their ability to filter and localize concepts introduced in development interventions (women's rights, innovation, flexibility, self-improvement) and insert them into their own life strategies in effective and productive ways. This ability, perhaps, made Ivana more prepared to compete both in the world of NGO politics and in the new market economy. Maybe she has become the ideal "innovator" à la the classic definition of the entrepreneur. She certainly impressed my friend Lidiia, who wrote after meeting Ivana: "Interviewing women like her is not work, but pleasure. I bow to people like this who are really working for the good of Ukraine and its future (and children *are* our future). Thank you for the chance to meet people like this, it is such a balm for me. I am proud we have such women in Ukraine."

There is, of course, another darker side to this story. NGO development aid appears to have helped women who already had some valuable social and cultural capital (networks, education) to leverage themselves into better careers, whether inside the transnational NGO community or in other spheres. But aid does not appear to have helped the most vulnerable women improve their situation. Like so many transnational development programs, the initiatives Ivana had springboarded herself through were extended to certain categories of citizens unequally. This has engendered a process of differentiation whereby NGO leaders and other women who espouse a neoliberal, individualist model of empowerment and possess the requisite capital are privileged over those who operate according to more collectivist (read: "Soviet") modes of social action (such as mutual aid) and who value ideas of entitlement. As Ivana increasingly became involved in the world of civic education and women in leadership, she became part of a different social order, one that included powerful institutions such as international foundations, government agencies, and various groups of foreigners. Not all women activists—and certainly not all women—had access to the sorts of trainings and seminars sponsored by the NIS-US Women's Consortium and other groups. Marginalized women such as Svetlana and Vira, the directors of an organization for large families—a quite stigmatized category—were not plugged into the Western-oriented networks of the Consortium and similar organizations. They did not know much at all about the lucrative world of "projects" and grants, and were not on the fast track to becoming NGO elites or moving into lucrative and satisfying careers, unlike some of my informants. The contrasting stories of women like Ivana, Maryna, Svetlana, and Vira are indicative of the emerging politics of class difference in Ukraine, and illustrate how the international NGO development industry has contributed to post-Soviet processes of differentiation of citizens and their claims. While Ivana and Maryna pursue rewarding careers in business and politics, Svetlana and Vira are still waiting for their middle-class fantasies to come true.

Conclusion: *Dyferentsiatsiia,* Democracy, and Development

"It's too early for us to die"

I spent four months in Ukraine during 2005, and in late April I called Sofiia on the telephone. We had not spoken in some time, and there was a lot to catch up on. I asked Sofiia how she was feeling. She laughed, "Well, as I told my doctor last week, even though I'm nearly seventy, it's hard for me to get used to the idea that I'm getting old." I asked how she felt about the Orange Revolution—did it produce some changes? Sofiia was not optimistic:

> I have been working in this sphere for eighteen years, and I don't see it getting any easier. On the contrary, things are getting harder and harder. From the tribune everyone is talking about "democracy," but there is a lot of dishonorable conduct [Rus. *neporiadochnost'*] nevertheless. Now it's even harder for us to get our voices heard than it was before. It doesn't smell of democracy around here.

A few days later, I attended For Life's weekly meeting. I entered the hubbub of the organization's office and immediately spotted Sofiia, seated at her customary spot at the head of the long conference table. She was wearing a lovely periwinkle turtleneck sweater that accentuated her blue eyes. She motioned for me to go sit next to her, and another chair was pulled round to the head of the table to accommodate me on her right. I noticed that she had lost weight, and she brought this up herself when she briefly told me that she had been ill during the winter and had to have heart surgery. During the two-hour-long meeting Sofiia was a woman on a mission. Little was said about the group's current projects, letter writing campaigns, and upcoming events. Rather, Sofiia stood up for about half an hour imparting a pointed and impassioned plea that the members of For Life think hard about what contributions each of them was making to the organization's work. "Don't come here unless you are ready to work. I don't want to see a single one of you coming in here out of habit, just because you felt like it. This is a collective, but most of the work has always been left to me." After going on in this vein for some time, Sofiia realized that she had dampened the mood of the gathering, which was to include a birthday celebration for three members with May birthdays. So she ended on a note of encouragement: "Let's all use our knowledge, of which we possess a great deal, for the benefit of our group!"

That said, the birthday congratulations began. Fancy canapés and small pastries were produced, and everyone was offered a tiny glass of fortified wine. Sofiia drank only mineral water and quietly placed most of her treats on my plate. The three birthday girls were all very dressed up: they wore jewelry, makeup and pretty hairdos, and had donned their finest blouses and sweaters. They were congratulated with flowers, cards, and chocolates, and several women read original poetry they had written for the occasion. These emotional gestures lent an atmosphere of mutual respect and support, and the three honorees reciprocated by giving short speeches. They stressed the importance of the organization's members in their lives, and mentioned by name special women whom they especially revered for their various excellent personal qualities and the good examples they set for others. The lone man in the organization, a musician, began to play tunes on his bayan (button accordion), and the women all sang along. Everyone's favorite was a song from the Second World War about marching to the front: "It's the road to the front, yet we fear no bombs. It's too early for us to die—we still have work to do at home!"[1] During the last chorus the women sitting closest to me at the table changed the words to, "It's too early for us to die—we still have work to do *in the fund!*"

During the birthday celebration, Sofiia and I continued to talk in low voices. She confided to me that she had grown weary and could no longer devote so much of her energy to For Life. She felt overburdened by her activist duties and said she wanted more time to spend with her relatives, whom she never got to see. Sofiia admitted that she did not have the strength to continue her work at the pace she was used to, a pace her members had grown to expect. "I am trying to transfer the director's chair to someone else, but no one will take it." At one point during the birthday celebration, Sofiia remembered something she had brought to show the other women; she had found it at home when cleaning out some boxes. She rummaged in her purse for a small folding card (Rus. *udostoverenie*) identifying her as a "brigade member cooperating with the police." The women responded with delight: "I have one of those, too!" "I haven't seen that in ages!" The card was issued after the war to people who helped clear the rubble from the bombed-out city of Kyiv. I snapped Sofiia's picture as she proudly held the small card up for all to see, a childlike smile spread out across her face.

Ten days later, Sofiia died. She had gone to spend the weekend at her dacha outside Kyiv, to get her vegetables and flower gardens going for the growing season. She died there, inside the small house, alone, of a heart attack. A day went by before a neighbor found her. Before the members of For Life even knew she had died, Sofiia was buried in a town where some of her relatives lived, hundreds of kilometers from Kyiv. Several weeks later, a group of For Life's members hired a bus and made the long journey to visit Sofiia's grave. Later, the women invited me to the customary forty-day remembrance gathering (Rus. *pominki*), which they held in For Life's office. Several years earlier a journalist from one of Ukraine's most popular newspapers had written a full-page piece on Sofiia and For Life, and we invited her to the *pominki*. Another journalist was contacted—his article in a major city newspaper about For Life had been published just a month earlier. Both journalists promised to attend the *pominki* and write an article in commemoration of Sofiia and her work. Neither one showed up. My friend Lidiia, who also knew Sofiia and went to the *pominki* with me, lamented: "The administration hasn't reacted to her death like they should have. They haven't taken note." Sofiia's death also seemed to go mostly unobserved in the NGO community; the group received few condolence calls or inquiries of any kind. For Life's members were at a loss. The assistant director cautiously took over the reins of the organization, but it was not at all clear how long the group would hold together without Sofiia's strong leadership. With Sofiia's quiet death, retirees—and many of Ukraine's women—lost their staunchest advocate, but this loss was ignored. Besides For Life's members and a few friends in Ukraine and the United States, hardly anyone even seemed to notice.

Transforming the Housework of Politics

Michele Rivkin-Fish, in her book *Women's Health in Post-Soviet Russia: The Politics of Intervention* (2005), tracks the processes of privatization and individualization that accompany market reforms in Russia to examine the structural violence that has been wrought on the Russian health care system and its workers since the collapse of state socialism. She explores women's health initiatives to document the ideologies and practices of *razgosudarstvlenie* (Russian for "the withdrawal, or disinvestment, of government") that characterize the current thinking of many Russians about health care and society in general, and which also drive international health development interventions. Rivkin-Fish convincingly argues that many Russians see circumventing the state or evading collective action as the best way to heal themselves: "Rather than engaging oneself with official state spheres and struggling for influence over policymaking, efforts to improve health involved disassociating oneself from arenas marked as 'official,' working informally to cope with constraints generated by the state, and locating 'transition' in one's own attitudes, behaviors, and commitments" (2005:6–7). Rivkin-Fish stresses the depoliticizing nature of this discourse of personal responsibility, moral reform, and "working on oneself," and shows how this powerful rhetoric on the moral rectitude of the individual—a rhetoric bolstered by international development interventions—makes collective mobilization around health issues difficult or impossible in post-Soviet Russia. She warns of the inadequacy of approaches to women's health that rely on notions of personal responsibility that are overly privatized and individualized, since "personal and privatizing strategies repeatedly produced less than actors hoped" (2005:212).

Rivkin-Fish's findings resonate with my study of women's social activism in Ukraine, although I have approached questions of privatization, individualization, and collective action from a slightly different angle. Whereas Rivkin-Fish trained her lens on Russian health care professionals, administrators, and patients (and international development cadres) to explore the ideologies of "de-governmentalization" and privatization that motivated Russian citizens to *detach* themselves from state structures, I have examined processes of individualization and privatization as played out in the lives of women social activists, many of whom specifically articulated themselves *to* state institutions to advocate for social justice and secure recognition and entitlements. Unlike the Russian reproductive health activists and others interviewed by Rivkin-Fish, most of the women I interviewed did not actively strive to insulate themselves from the state and politics. Indeed, they faced representatives of the state head-on in their calls for redistribution after socialist collapse. For some groups, however, especially those that based their demands on notions of entitlement as they reached out for "the familiar allocative state of before" (Verdery 1996:214), these efforts were not successful. Their claims were not legitimated, and these women and the groups they represented were marginalized even further from positions of power. Sofiia's unheralded death was a sad and poignant illustration of processes of privatization and differentiation through which citizens are being encouraged to forge their own personal solutions to postsocialist economic and social crises, leaving them to fend for themselves and develop personal safety nets, or fall through the cracks. Similarly, when Our House folded (after the group's premises were requisitioned by the state), the organization's members were compelled to pursue survival strategies as individuals and families, without the backing of the civic organization. The argument could be made that Our House served its purpose in helping impoverished large families until they could regroup, and that the support Our House offered its constituents is no longer needed by most. Svetlana herself acknowledged in early 2006 that life had improved for many of Our House's member families. Ironically, however, life has not improved significantly for Svetlana, who continues to struggle financially to support her family, and suffers serious health problems. It is difficult not to be troubled by the silencing of women such as Svetlana and Sofiia, who spent the last decade or more advocating for vulnerable and marginalized populations, struggling to prevent the development of a permanent underclass of the disadvantaged.

At the same time, it is hard not to admire the successes of women like Ivana and Maryna, who have forged rewarding careers in business and government after climbing through the ranks of local and international NGOs. NGO activism has allowed some women to establish themselves in lucrative and prestigious professions, and thus suggests some possibilities for women's socioeconomic success after socialism (Ghodsee 2005; Johnson and Robertson 2007). For those who are plugged in to the right networks, able to access and utilize opportunities and ways of thinking and speaking that circulate through the world of international NGO development, NGO activism can prove life-changing. In the spring of 2006, Maryna, who had left most of her activism activities behind for a paid job in the government administration, characterized her NGO days as "the peak of her life." Her assessment echoed the self-transformation narratives of Ivana and other activists I interviewed in Kyiv. But it is impossible for me to contemplate these women's successes without thinking about Svetlana and her "cross" of NGO activism, or Sofiia and her unfinished and unheralded work. One might view NGOs as a kind of reservoir, a temporary holding tank for both the potential winners and losers of "transition." On the one hand, as the concerns of particular categories of citizens are rendered invalid and social support for them is scaled back or withdrawn, NGOs are compelled to move in to take up the slack on the part of the state. This is particularly true of the NGOs that focus on mutual aid and "social problems," and tend to be led by women. If the stories of For Life and Our House are any indication, however, those organizations that fail to attract local, state, or international support for their advocacy efforts will be gently ushered out of advocacy work. On the other hand, with the interventions of international development organizations targeting NGOs as a forum through which to empower postsocialist citizens, some activists (many of them also women) who have the right credentials are funneled through professionalizing channels to emerge as successful NGO cadres, businesswomen, or government administrators.

As a site of postsocialist transformation, NGO activism has thus produced important, often hidden effects. Paramount among these is the formation of new, often elite socialities as others are disbanded. This process is reflected in the contrasting picture that materializes when NGO "Euro-elites" are juxtaposed with the leaders of now defunct or marginalized organizations like Our House. By combining ethnographic analysis of women activists' lives and narratives with an examination of broader processes of sociopolitical change (here, primarily, economic crisis and social welfare reform), I have been able to explore a few of the ways in which "democratization" and accompanying processes of privatization and individualization have led to a sharpening of social inequalities in postsocialist Ukraine. Individualization entails a process by which, "in the form of their own lives, people must take individual responsibility and blame for—and often cope alone with—what used to be handled collectively as a class destiny" (Beck and Beck-Gernsheim 2002:48). Many of the women described in my book were engaged in social justice struggles to stave off the atomization of particular social groupings and the unraveling of state support for them, but with mixed success. Most have scaled back operations dramatically or have gone under; some appear to exist in name only. Today the most vital organization explored in this book is Lotus, the NGO founded by Zoia and her son, Sasha, to provide services and information to Kyiv's population of wheelchair users. The group survives thanks to transnational advocacy networks with disability rights groups in Sweden and Canada that developed over the past decade, as well as support received from local businesspersons with disabilities. Internet contacts and access to Web resources (developed by Sasha, a computer expert) play a major role in the NGO's successful work today. The group has received little support from local or national government, or from international development agencies working in Ukraine.

What do the little histories of these women and their NGOs tell us more broadly about postsocialist Ukrainian society and democratization? The struggles and life stories of the women in this book show how postsocialist transition is not only about reforming economies and state institutions. It also entails changing persons and detaching them from certain relationships. Although processes of privatization, personalization, and individualization certainly are integral to the story I have told here, I also have explored trajectories of *differentiation* to shed further light on the rearrangement of state-citizen relationships in postsocialist Ukraine. Differentiation can be detected in official proclamations and laws governing social politics, in the "development" interventions of international organizations, and in citizens' changing ideas about entitlement and "needs." These three sites of differentiation all coalesce in the social justice struggles of NGOs, making these community organizations a fruitful jumping off point for analyses of differentiation processes and the social disparities they produce as Ukraine enters the global market economy. The little histories of the groups examined here include chapters on the privatization of social problems, the entrenchment of new social hierarchies, and processes of individualization and privatization as activists are cut loose from state support, and encouraged to tap into ideologies and strategies of self-reliance. As criteria for deserving citizenship shift, and as opportunities for advancement are offered to groups of citizens and groups of women unequally, processes of differentiation are enacted that result in new forms of social inequality. Perhaps, in this way, "differentiation" is actually a more honest way of talking about "democratization."

As state institutions are scaled back and rearranged, vital questions about state-citizen relations are being asked, and NGOs are one forum where the new social politics are hashed out. Which identities will be perceived as valid in the new Ukraine, and upon what criteria will citizens be deemed deserving or not of state support? What possibilities will citizens be offered to act upon the ideologies of self-reliance, entrepreneurship, and personal initiative that are emphasized increasingly by state representatives and that are tied to development aid? Will increased social spending really represent greater state support for vulnerable populations, or are differentiation and targeted assistance ways to tighten government purse strings and shrink the social safety net further while giving the appearance of a more compassionate social politics? Proclamations and procedures for increased social spending that emerged during 2005–2007 (especially during the 2006 and 2007 parliamentary elections) may point to an impending re-governmentalization of the social sphere in independent Ukraine. I suspect, however, that the ideology of targeted assistance, differentiation, and "reevaluation" will prevail in the context of the market economy, and that the processes of *dyferentsiatsiia* documented here will continue to escalate.

These processes uncover dynamics of class differentiation in postsocialist states upon which anthropologists and other scholars of culture and society need to train their lenses more rigorously. It is particularly important to track the making of classes within the domain of "civil society," since this amorphous realm of social life has been so romanticized and so championed as the potential cradle of democratization and empowerment in postsocialist states. Groups such as Our House and For Life have been doing precisely what celebratory visions of "civil society" ask them to do—organizing for their rights, putting pressure on states, participating in the political process—but they have failed. Their claims are dismissed, and the large families and retirees these groups represent may find themselves sliding into a permanent underclass. As Susan Gal has noted, "While claiming the equality of individuals in the political realm, the idea of civil society obscures the economic and other social differences that, in practice, fundamentally constrain political participation" (1997:34). I have documented this ethnographically by exploring the very different outcomes of several women social activists, whose stories illustrate the complex processes of upward mobility and social dislocation that accompany market and social reforms in Ukraine. Focusing on differentiation thus sheds light on new breakdowns in national solidarity that go beyond the common one that envisions Ukraine exploding along language and ethnic lines.

Crucially, the ethnographic method has also allowed me to reflect on the various ways in which social activists have incorporated ideologies of personalization, privatization, and individualization into their own lives and organizing strategies. In response to social welfare reform, the constraints placed on their claims, and the neoliberal ideologies promoted by international development organizations and representatives of the Ukrainian state, these women began to change how they saw themselves and how they envisioned appropriate citizen-state relations. Zoia, for example, began to abandon the language of entitlement for strategies based on self-sufficiency and individual empowerment. During one of our first interviews, Zoia lamented that she and other NGO activists were taking up the state's slack and providing services to persons with disabilities that the state had wrongfully shirked. In a later interview, she articulated quite a different view:

> I was privy to a conversation when some Americans and Ukrainians were discussing the benefits that disabled people in Ukraine get. The [disabled] Americans discussed how they had been taught to work at an early age. We don't have that here. You know, in no other country are there benefits for the disabled. The disabled have to work just like everyone else. Our disabled people will do everything possible in order to receive benefits so they won't have to work.

Zoia's assessment that "in no other country are there benefits for the disabled" was, of course, erroneous. This statement did, however, reveal her stance that persons with disabilities needed to be as self-sufficient as possible. In line with this strategy, Zoia's organization, Lotus, promoted a system of "active rehabilitation" for people in wheelchairs, a program that was introduced to wheelchair users in Ukraine in the early 1990s by a group of Swedish activists. To a large extent it was Zoia's growing network ties with European NGOs for disabled persons, and also her ties to international foundations in Ukraine, that had informed her thoughts on benefits, entitlement, work, and charity. Inherent in her critique was disdain for the Soviet system of entitlements that she felt had made citizens "lazy" and dependent on the state.

Similarly, the activists who appear in this book began to incorporate ideologies of differentiation into their own worldviews and NGO practices, and thus became both agents and objects of the state's governmentality (Cruikshank 1999). When Svetlana and Vira carried out their own needs-based assessment of their NGO's members, and when Sofiia rewarded her organization's members differently according to her assessment of their contributions to the group's work, these NGO directors participated in processes of differentiation. This could be discerned at the level of personal identity formation as well. For instance, a follow-up interview with Svetlana during March 2006 revealed that she now sees herself in terms that diverge from those she articulated during the late 1990s. Svetlana, who makes a meager living as a counselor for a crisis hotline in Kyiv, now says that "social activism has become a hobby for me." When I heard this, I immediately thought back to previous conversations with Svetlana and Vira during 1999, when they complained that bureaucrats in the city administration had discounted their claims and taunted them, "We thought that you were prosperous ladies," and said they assumed the women's NGO work was "just a hobby." Now Svetlana does appear to "dabble in social work," as the bureaucrats suggested; she runs the nearly defunct organization Our House out of her small apartment and prioritizes her paid work as a telephone counselor. This move represents a broader process similar to that documented by Rivkin-Fish in Russia, in which postsocialist citizens are more likely to take up private, individual solutions for empowerment and survival than engage in collective action and articulate themselves to the "official" realm of the state.

My findings suggest that the NGO boom of the 1990s in Ukraine has not resulted in the widespread empowerment of vulnerable categories of citizens such as large families, the elderly, the sick, and the disabled, and collective action strategies have not succeeded in buffering the privatization of social problems. In some cases, the interventions of development organizations into local social justice struggles have either escalated processes of privatization and differentiation or actually fragmented local social movements. This process might be turned around if more sensitive and sustained efforts are made to foster coalition building among Ukrainian NGOs, which would give groups pursuing common goals a more effective political voice. Indeed, representatives of the Ukrainian state prefer to work with NGO coalitions rather than with separate groups, and strong coalitions of civic organizations are more likely to have their claims heard and considered in the halls of government. One example of successful coalition building includes the National Assembly of the Disabled of Ukraine, a coalition of more than fifty all-Ukrainian, regional and city-based disability rights NGOs. The Assembly has successfully lobbied for the passage of antidiscrimination legislation, has developed strong ties with advocacy groups in other countries, and has members in high political office who are able to advance the group's agenda. Rather than focusing aid efforts on small grants, trainings, and individual NGO projects, international development organizations might make a more positive impact by participating in and fostering NGO coalition building and lobbying efforts. Many of my informants said that one of the most useful aspects of the Counterpart and Consortium trainings they attended was the opportunity to meet NGO activists with similar goals and to develop their organizational networks. These opportunities could be better developed for coalition building purposes to help activists and the categories of citizens their NGOs represent wield a more powerful collective voice.

There is also more that can be done to help empower Ukraine's women, especially single mothers, mothers of many children, retirees, and others who face particular difficulties during the post-Soviet "transition." Contrary to popular expectations, NGO activism has not proven empowering for many of these women. If we continue with the example of Svetlana, it is difficult to see her as a woman who was "empowered" via NGO activism—she is in a low-paying job that threatens her already poor health, and she struggles mightily to support her family of five (new grandson included).[2] Those women who did emerge successful from NGO work found opportunities to retool, retrain, and apply themselves to more prestigious and lucrative spheres. Such opportunities are crucial in a context of social welfare reform in which "targeted assistance" and "reevaluation" procedures mean that citizens—many of them women, who are major recipients of welfare—are likely to be cut loose from state support. As this process escalates, it is critical that these persons have equal access to more and better tools and opportunities to support themselves and their families in the changing political economy. This needs to be implemented not through "projects" and small-scale, community-based approaches but rather in national programs. Efforts to extend opportunities to the socially and economically vulnerable (men and women) must be combined with broad-reaching economic reforms for job creation and job placement, and the enforcement of antidiscrimination labor laws already in place.

This is where international development organizations seeking to empower post-Soviet women could make a difference. But broader political realities and economic arrangements that disempower women socioeconomically are exceedingly difficult to remedy through "trainings" and small grants to women's NGOs. If one proposed solution to women's subordination is to foster an army of Ukrainian businesswomen, such a strategy is unlikely to prove successful in the absence of necessary economic and political infrastructures in the country. It is difficult to see how aid organizations could really improve women's (or men's) situation in the labor market without engaging in overt politics, something they are reticent to do. Also, as the example of Counterpart's social enterprise program illustrates, development initiatives that apply free market models indiscriminately, and fail to take fully into account local dynamics of class and gender ideologies, are bound to have problematic outcomes. As Kristen Ghodsee (2005:166) has argued for the Bulgarian case, social entrepreneurship does not resonate with many citizens in postsocialist states, because it displaces responsibility for basic rights (e.g., health care, child care, and education) away from the state and onto the "free market," women, and the unemployed. Creating a "market" for social services is the last thing many citizens—who expect the state to provide the basics—want.

Given these difficulties, international donors might pursue other ways of facilitating women's participation in the market economy besides (or in addition to) encouraging them to become "social entrepreneurs" or small business owners. Even though women are in a disadvantaged position in the labor market, few retraining efforts for unemployed women have been organized in Ukraine. Women would benefit from job training to allow them to search for work as professionals in the conditions of the new market. However, rather than indiscriminately applying Western business models and ideologies about women and work, careful attention must be paid to local economic and social realities. As Michele Rivkin-Fish (2004, 2005) has documented for the case of women's health in Russia, all too often "developers" enter a society with a ready-made vision of what locals need, and fail to take into account local contexts or engage in meaningful dialogue. This renders the very "democratizing" processes that development organizations seek to foster decidedly undemocratic themselves. Obviously, opportunities for job training, economic empowerment, and social protest need to be developed in dialogue with carriers of local knowledge, ideally with the intended recipients of the development interventions.

In Ukraine, part of this challenge lies in the fact that, when it comes to women's and gender issues, international NGOs have found it exceedingly difficult to work within local frames of gender. The maternalist character of many Ukrainian women's NGOs, and local visions of women's and men's respective qualities, roles, and potential contributions to society and the family, are unsettling to many Western feminist-oriented development NGOs. These groups tend to be suspicious of motherhood as a political platform, and perceive it as one that could backfire by relegating women's interests to the private sphere and the family, without offering women a real political voice. These are valid concerns. Too often, however, a knee-jerk negative reaction to the "traditional" gender ideologies espoused by many women in countries such as Ukraine leads representatives of development organizations and scholars to discount these women's voices and to devalue their own interpretations of their lives and the problems they face. As Aihwa Ong (1996:134) has noted, "After all, feminism and women's rights only make sense in terms of the imagined communities within which people live and, through their embeddedness in cultural relations and norms, decide what is good and worthwhile in their lives." Additionally, assuming that motherhood is an insufficiently political platform for women's rights ignores the fact that motherhood always and everywhere is a site for state intervention and surveillance. Such a stance also discounts the important histories of strong maternalist groups in Ukraine and other post-Soviet countries, particularly groups of Soldiers' Mothers, who have successfully turned maternalist politics against the state since 1989. Ignoring these facts, and automatically devaluing "maternal" politics, may choke off opportunities for helping women in Ukraine to voice their own claims and advance their own interests in ways that resonate with local populations. Moreover, as Alexandra Hrycak (2002:75) has documented, international development organizations that seek to empower Ukrainian women and yet implement programs that "presuppose a type of women's rights activism that is absent in the region, particularly at the grassroots" actually end up fragmenting and diluting the Ukrainian women's movement. What "developers" might find is that class-based identities and inequalities have more resonance than gender-based ones, and that fostering programs and protests centered on class may prove a more successful strategy.

Clearly, more opportunities for women's empowerment need to be sought beyond the realm of NGOs, which have not produced the far-reaching democratizing and empowering effects for postsocialist citizens that many anticipated. True, some women such as Ivana and Maryna have been able to emerge from NGO activism as successful career women and leaders, but too many women are left doing "the housework of politics" (Sperling, Ferree, and Risman 2001:1156) in mutual-aid associations and other caring-focused NGOs. In the absence of meaningful strategies for increasing women's participation in the realm of official politics, "civil society feminism" (Miriou 2004) has not substantially improved women's lot. Civil society feminism cannot succeed without a concomitant empowerment of women in the political sphere. With the obvious exception of Yuliia Tymoshenko, women politicians in Ukraine tend to fill token roles (as heads of "virtual parties," for example) and to populate the less important committees and ranks of government. A full sixteen years after Ukrainian independence, women still occupy only 7 percent of seats in the Ukrainian Parliament. In contrast, as of March 2005 women represented 20.7 percent of parliamentarians in Poland, 26.3 percent in Bulgaria, 21.7 percent in Croatia, and 15.7 percent in the Czech Republic (UNDP 2005:303–304). As I came to know many women social activists, I wondered how things in Ukraine might be different if these dynamic and dedicated women—with their leadership skills, knowledge of local problems, and savvy interpersonal and negotiating skills—populated the ranks of the Ukrainian government. Women in Ukraine need to be encouraged to see "official politics" as a viable career option, and they must be offered serious opportunities to seize meaningful political roles. But development organizations have been reluctant to support this agenda directly, preferring to work behind the scenes (offering women training seminars in "women in leadership," for example) via NGOs rather than interfere directly in local and national politics.

One obvious way to facilitate women's entrance into "big politics" would be the reintroduction of Soviet-era quotas, a strategy that was debated but shelved in Parliament during 2005. Some women I knew in Kyiv understood the logic of the quotas, but argued against quotas because they "would not guarantee that women elected to office will be qualified or even intelligent." Quotas might prove a useful temporary solution for addressing women's political inequality, but the strategy should be approached with caution. The quota route could develop similarly to what Mihaela Miroiu (2004) calls "room service feminism," a situation where states (such as Romania) have adopted ready-made policies to protect women's rights offered to them by bodies such as the European Union without a concomitant change in consciousness or real commitment to these ideals on the part of the state or the general population. Care must be taken to ensure that quotas do not perpetuate or even escalate the tokenism that often characterizes women's political roles in contemporary Ukraine.

Helping women capitalize on their perceived and real roles as "solvers of social problems," an identification that has heretofore led women to swell the ranks of certain types of caring and service-oriented NGOs, might also help women move into meaningful political office. Such a strategy may be criticized for shoring up stereotypes of women as "natural" caregivers while potentially muffling issues of women's rights, but women's roles as NGO leaders, advocates for vulnerable populations, and initiators of social justice struggles could serve as a convincing platform from which to propel them into the ranks of government in ways that resonate with local gender and class perceptions. NGO activists who see women as "naturally suited" for solving social problems, and who may also emphasize women's important roles as mothers and caregivers, are not passive recipients of a traditionalizing, nationalizing ideology. They possess valuable leadership and communication skills that they utilize to stake claims, lobby representatives of the state, and argue for the social worth of women and other categories of citizens. Women such as those profiled in this book, having worked with various marginalized populations at the intersection of state policy, international development, and NGO efforts, are well placed to engage with social welfare reform and critique processes of differentiation as concerned citizens, as social activists, as politicians, and as women. The development of far-reaching programs—through education, advocacy, media campaigns, and public education—to pave the way for women to enter the ranks of government might be the best road to empowerment for post-Soviet women in Ukraine. Having weathered processes of differentiation themselves, the women activists in this book, and many others like them, "still have work to do at home" as their own best advocates.

Notes

Preface

1. The literature on ethnographic fieldwork, roles, and ethics is vast. See, for example, Appell 1978; Cassell and Wax 1980; DeSoto and Dudwick 2000; Fluehr-Lobban 2003; Gupta and Ferguson 1997; Jackson 1987; Kulick and Willson 1995; Markowitz 2001; Rabinow 1977; and Wolcott 1995.

2. For consideration of the friend/consultant/informant conundrum, see Behar 1993; Berdahl 2000; Bruner 1990; and Silverman 2000.

3. See, for example, Silverman 2000; Farmer 1992; Singer 1994a, 1994b; and Farmer and Kim 2000.

4. Such engagements are explored in the volume *Chronicling Cultures: Long-term Field Research in Anthropology* (Kemper and Royce 2002). Examples also include the Sacha Runa Foundation initiated by Norman and Dorothea Whitten, which supports a medical-care delivery program in Amazonian Ecuador (D. Whitten 1996), the Kalahari Peoples Fund (Biesele 2003), and Paul Farmer's Zanmi Lasante in Haiti, which grew into the remarkable organization Partners in Health (Farmer 1992; Kidder 2003).

Introduction

1. Except where indicated, the names of all informants, and the organizations with which they were affiliated, have been changed to protect their privacy.

2. In most cases, my references to "Ukrainians" carry the meaning "people of Ukraine" or "people living in Ukraine" rather than connoting Ukrainian ethnics to the exclusion of other ethnic groups living in Ukraine.

3. Large or "many-child" families are those with three or more children, a shift from Soviet policy where a family with five children constituted a "large" family. The total fertility per woman in Ukraine declined from 2.2 children during 1970–75 to a projected 1.1 children during 2000–2005 (UNDP 2005: 232). This is the context in which a family with three children is considered "large." In Ukraine, there are about 497,000 "large" families, or 3.7 percent of the total number of families in Ukraine (Iaremenko and Balakirieva 1999:141).

4. Haney (2000, 2002) has written of similar situations in Hungary. She gives a poignant account of how welfare clients in postsocialist Hungary were stigmatized and treated deplorably by caseworkers. Haney writes, for instance, that, "'caseworkers' defensive attacks on their clients frequently descended beyond their presumed personality traits to their physical characteristics. The sight, the smell, and the feel of clients' bodies were common topics of conversation

among caseworkers. Many caseworkers used animal metaphors to describe their clients, referring to them as cattle and pigs. . . . Moreover, caseworkers spoke incessantly about the 'smell' of their clients. They often berated clients for not washing regularly. 'I used to wash before work,' a caseworker once remarked to me. 'Then I realized that there is no use, so now I clean myself as soon as I return from work.' . . . Given their disgust with the sight and smell of their clients, welfare workers avoided all contact with clients' bodies. . . . This may have been another reason for the security guards: These men handled the contaminated. . . . On one occasion an elderly client lost her balance and fell to the floor of one Gyamhotosag office. Unable to get up, she was forced to lie on the floor until a caseworker called a guard to help her up" (Haney 2000: 66–67).

5.   In February 2006, the average national monthly salary in Ukraine was $220.

6.   See also "Novi vidpovidi na stari pytannia" (New answers to old questions). *Sotsial'ne partnerstvo* 3(4): 5.

7.   I use the term "transition" with full knowledge of the limitations that concept carries. Like a host of other scholars (see Creed 1995; Hann 1996; Kideckel 1995; Stark and Bruszt 1998; and Verdery 1996) I take issue with the teleological constructs behind the notion of "transition." Like Stark and Bruszt, in place of "transition" (with the emphasis on destination) I prefer to analyze "transformations" (with the emphasis on actual processes) "in which the introduction of new elements takes place most typically in combination with adaptations, rearrangements, permutations, and reconfigurations of already existing institutional forms" (1998:83).

8.   See also Handrahan (2002) and Liborakina (1998) for similar arguments on women and NGOs in Kyrgyzstan and Russia, respectively.

9.   The "feminization" of the "third sector" of NGOs is common across post-socialist states. Nayereh Tohidi (2004) outlines the reasons why women in Azerbaijan are especially likely to undertake NGO organizing: women are excluded from opportunities to advance in politics and business; women have traditionally been responsible for mediating social problems; the civic arena is seen as less corrupt than official politics (and thus more appropriate for women); and women tend to possess vital networking and linguistic skills. These factors hold for the Ukrainian case as well. Lori Handrahan (2002:80) notes that 76 percent of the twenty-eight NGOs she surveyed in Kyrgyzstan were led by women, and 96 percent of her respondents believed that women were leading NGOs nationwide.

10.   In May 2000, for example, an event called "Kyiv Civic Organization Day" was held by Kyiv's Innovation and Development Centre to showcase the work of the various social organizations in the city. Of the 150 civic and charitable organizations represented at the exhibition, 40 percent were formed to protect the interests of children, families, and women; 68 percent of the organizations with such an orientation were directed by women (Innovation and Development Centre 2000a).

11.   Seminal studies on the negative effects of socialist collapse for women's lives include Bridger, Kay and Pinnick 1996; Bridger and Pine 1998; Buckley 1992, 1997; Einhorn 1993; and Marsh 1996. Although it is generally accepted that

women in Ukraine experience greater poverty than men do, a recent World Bank study (Dudwick, Srinivasan, and Braithwaite 2002) found little difference in women and men's susceptibility to poverty. However, the authors of the report acknowledge the difficulty of collecting and interpreting data on poverty in Ukraine, which is hard to disaggregate by gender. One significant finding of the study is that female-headed households with children are at greater risk for poverty than are other household forms. Thirteen percent of the population in Ukraine lives in female-headed households. Many of the women in my study, single mothers with children, were pursuing NGO activism as a survival strategy.

12. Interview with Volodymyr Semynozhenko and Mykhail Papiiev on Radio-Era FM, March 27, 2006, transcript retrieved from http://www.svidomo2006.org. ua/materials/964.html (accessed June 16, 2006).

13. Cabinet of Ministers of Ukraine, Decree 525-r (December 15, 2005), "On the Approval of the Pension System Development Strategy," p. 2; http://www. svidomo2006.org.ua/materials/964.html (accessed June 16, 2006). During the first quarter of 2007, the pension fund was apparently in the black. Some interpreted this as a temporary situation, a strategy to placate voters before the 2007 early parliamentary elections. The U.S. dollar to UAH exchange rate in July 2006 was $1 to 5 UAH.

14. People with disabilities are usually called "invalids" in Ukraine and Russia. Disability rights activists advocate using instead the terms "persons with special needs" (*liudy s osoblyvymy potrebamy*) or "persons with limited physical capabilities" (*nepovnospravni*). This language is gradually making its way into legislation.

15. See http://www.ukraine.ru/text/replic/273107.html (accessed June 16, 2006).

16. See http://www.svidomo2006.org.ua/materials/964.html (accessed June 16, 2006).

17. On April 1, 2006, natural gas prices increased 1.5 times in Ukraine, and rose further in September 2006. Electricity prices increased 25 percent in May 2006. Throughout 2006, tariffs on gas and electricity rose every three months. These increases resulted in rising costs of transportation and communications, including train tickets and local telephone calls.

18. See the article "Adresna dopomoha malozabezpechenym verstvam naselennia" (Targeted assistance to needy sections of the population), April 6, 2005, by the Ministry of Labor and Social Policy of Ukraine. Available at http://www. mlsp.gov.ua/control/uk/publish/article?art_id=39368&cat_id=34941 (accessed March 9, 2006).

19. My translation from the Ukrainian.

20. From the website of the Verkhovna Rada of Ukraine, http://portal.rada.gov. ua/control/uk/publish/article/news_left?art_id=67813&cat_id=33449 (accessed June 7, 2006).

21. See http://portal.rada.gov.ua/control/uk/publish/article/news_left?art_ id=69543&cat_id=37486 (accessed June 7, 2006).

22. See http://portal.rada.gov.ua/control/uk/publish/article/news_top?art_ id=64176&cat_id=37486 (accessed June 7, 2006).

23.   See http://portal.rada.gov.ua/control/uk/publish/article/news_left?art_
        id=56091&cat_id=33449 (accessed June 7, 2006).

24.   See http://www.mlsp.gov.ua/control/uk/publish/article?art_id=39368&cat_
        id=34941 (accessed March 9, 2006).

25.   During early parliamentary elections in 2007, representatives of the major par-
        ties all promised increases in childbirth allowances. Yushchenko's Our Ukraine
        proposed a childbirth allowance of 15,000 UAH for second and all subsequent
        children; Yanukovych's Party of Regions and Tymoshenko's BYuT both prom-
        ised 50,000 UAH for third and all subsequent children. A similar childbirth in-
        centive program has been implemented in Russia. Described in one newspaper
        article as a "revolutionary program of demographic development" (Kanaev
        and Gerashchenko 2006), the program entitles families to a payment of $9,600
        upon the birth of a second child, and for all subsequent children.

26.   "Pry narodzhenni dytyny uriad vyplachuvatyme visim z polovynoiu tyciach
        hryven' zhyvymy hroshyma" (Upon the birth of a child the administration
        will pay 8,500 UAH in real money). 5tv.com.ua (accessed April 10, 2005).

27.   Here I do not limit civil society institutions to NGOs but rather present com-
        munity organizations such as the ones I have studied as a particularly apt ex-
        ample of the links between social change and personal transformations.

28.   See, for example, Abramson 1999a, 1999b; Hemment 2007; Murdock 2003; and
        Rivkin-Fish 2004.

29.   Jews were present in Rus' during the Kyivan period in the 800s, and they moved
        into Ukraine during the sixteenth and seventeenth centuries in greater num-
        bers. To prevent Jews from competing with Russian merchants in the Russian
        Empire, the tsarist government forbade Jews to live in Russia proper. This
        meant that they were confined to the Pale of Settlement, which included the
        western borderlands of Lithuania, Belarus, and much of right-bank Ukraine.
        The Pale remained largely in effect until the Bolshevik Revolution in 1917.
        Jews suffered a number of pogroms at the hands of ultra-right Russian na-
        tionalist groups, and the relationship between Ukrainians and Jews was never
        a friendly one (Subtelny 1994:276–277). During World War II, the Soviet re-
        gime made no efforts to evacuate Ukraine's Jewish population and remained
        silent about the Jews' persecution. Most Jews in Ukraine fell into the hands of
        the Nazis, who established 50 ghettos and more than 180 large concentration
        camps in Ukraine. About 850,000 Jews in Ukraine were killed by the Nazis
        and their execution squads. In Kyiv, at Babi Yar, 33,000 Jews were executed
        in two days alone (Subtelny 1994:468). Between 1970 and 1997, more than
        422,000 Jews emigrated from Ukraine to Israel and the United States (Gitel-
        man 2000:143).

30.   The Great Terror refers to Stalin's attacks on all types of opposition (both real
        and imagined) to industrialize and collectivize the Soviet Union, and to de-
        stroy any form of self-government in the republics. Waves of repression began
        to roll across Ukraine during the early 1930s targeting Ukraine's political elite
        and cultural activists. It is difficult to determine how many people were exe-
        cuted and exiled, but in 1938 alone an estimated 170,000 Communist Party
        members in Ukraine were purged. During World War II, in Vinnytsia, a mass
        grave containing 10,000 bodies was discovered—they had been shot between

1937 and 1938. It is estimated that in the Soviet Union around 500,000 people were executed during 1937–39, and between 3 million and 12 million were sent to labor camps (Subtelny 1994:420–421).

31. In the Soviet Union, Jews were labeled as such in their passports under the category *natsional'nost'* (Rus.). It made no difference if a person was a Jew of Russian, Ukrainian, or Georgian background—for the state, "Jew" was the identity superseding all others. In the Soviet Union, the Russian term *grazhdanstvo* was used to denote citizenship, "which did not necessarily carry connotations of shared cultural or linguistic identity. In contrast, the term *natsional'nost'* . . . was primarily reflective of an individual's ancestry and determined independently of an individual's citizenship and residence in a particular sub-state political entity (republic, autonomous republic, etc.)" (Wanner 1998:11). The fixation of "nationality" in one's passport facilitated discrimination of Jews and other stigmatized "nationalities" (i.e., Roma, Chechens, etc.).

32. The ruble was the Soviet currency. The currency in independent Ukraine, as noted, is the Ukrainian hryvnia (UAH).

33. The retirement age for men is sixty. In a provision inherited from Soviet legislation, coal miners and other professional groups have a lower retirement age. To be eligible for a pension, most men must have a twenty-five-year work record, and women a work record of twenty years. In conditions of economic crisis, about 1.7 million pensioners, or 10 percent of those employed, continue to work (Góralska 2000:236).

   I attended approximately ten meetings of For Life between 1999 and 2005 and saw only two men—one was the spouse of a female member, and the other a musician who provided musical interludes at the weekly meetings.

34. Readers are reminded that For Life is a pseudonym for the group's name. The real name of the organization was more confrontational, and—like this banner—served as a direct criticism of the state's abandonment of the elderly population.

1. All Aboard the "Titanic Ukraina"

1. The monument and the Soviet ideology of "people's friendship" and "internationalism" are described in more detail by Catherine Wanner (1998:194–197).

2. In 1998 a two-room apartment in the Borshchahivs'ka district, on the outskirts of the city, cost $10,000; by 2006, the price was $50,000–$60,000. In the center of the city, the price of a two-room apartment rose from $18,000 to $80,000.

3. Although the ruble-dollar exchange rate was 1:1 during the late Soviet period, the real value of the ruble was relatively greater, and, because of price fixing, 3,000 rubles in the Soviet Union had much more purchasing power than did $3,000 in the United States.

4. Subtelny divides the political history of Kyivan Rus' into three phases (1994:41). The initial period, from Oleh's accession to power in Kyiv in 882 to

the death of Sviatoslav in 972, was characterized by rapid expansion. The second phase stretched from the reigns of Volodymyr the Great (980–1015) and Iaroslav the Wise (1036–54) until just after the reigns of Volodymyr Monomakh (1113–25) and his son, Mstyslav (1125–32). During this time, termed the "height" phase, the socioeconomic structure of society became more marked, law and order were more thoroughly defined, and Christianity was introduced. The decline of Kyivan Rus' began when Andrei Bogoliubsky of Suzdal captured and sacked the city of Kyiv in 1169. In 1240, the city was almost totally destroyed by Mongols.

5.   For detailed studies of Kyiv's immigrant communities, see publications of the Kennan Kyiv Project (Braichevska et al. 2004; Popson and Ruble 2000; and Ruble 2003, 2005).

6.   Nationalizing projects in Ukraine have been studied by a number of scholars; see Bilaniuk 2005; Wanner 1998; Wilson 2000; Wolchik and Zviglianich 2000; and Wolczuk 2000.

7.   See Wanner (1998:171–199) and Wilson (2000:223–228) for discussions of the re-branding of Ukrainian cityscapes since independence.

8.   See Ukraine's European Union website, which includes a section devoted to "Ukraine's Eurointegration Course": http://ukraine-eu.mfa.gov.ua/eu/en/publication/content/1985.htm (accessed May 18, 2006).

9.   The Russian is "*v odnoi ruke Svetka, v drugoi ruke—setka, szadi p'ianyi Ivan, a vperedi—Gosplan.*"

10. "Zarplata s nachala goda vyrosla na 30%" (The salary rose 30% since the beginning of the year) (2001:2).

11. Data from the UNDP, 2002 and 2005 Human Development Reports, available at http://hdr.undp.org/reports/ (accessed March 9, 2006).

12. Limited space permits only a cursory overview of the history of the "woman question" in the Soviet Union. Excellent, thorough treatments of the issues are found in Edmonson 1984, Stites 1978, Wood 1997, and others.

13. See Natalya Baranskaya's poignant essay, *A Week Like Any Other* (1969), for one of the first portrayals of women's quadruple burden in Soviet literature. Soviet and post-Soviet women's multiple family and work roles have been examined by a number of scholars, most of whom refer to the "double burden" (see, for example, Berdahl 1999; Buckley 1989; du Plessix Gray 1989; Lapidus 1978, 1982; Scott 1974; and Wolchik and Meyer 1985).

14. This assertion diverges from that made by Fodor (2004) for socialist Hungary, where, she argues, Hungarian women had ample access to positions of authority in the workplace, more than women in capitalist Austria, for example. Since women's participation in positions of workplace authority in socialist Hungary was "encouraged primarily in less prestigious and lower level positions," however, Fodor characterizes the gender regime in the labor force in Hungary as one of "limited inclusion" (2004:784–785).

15. See Zhurzhenko 2004, for further consideration of legislation pertinent to women and families in Ukraine in the 1990s, including the 1997 National Plan of Action for 1997–2000 on Improving the Status of Women and the Rise of Their Role in Society, the 1999 Declaration on General Fundamentals of the

State Policy in Ukraine Concerning Family and Women, and the 1999 Draft of State Family Policy.

16. Examples of such advertisements are cited by Bridger, Kay, and Pinnick (1996: 80): "Secretaries required: attractive girls with office experience, aged 18–22, at least 168 cm tall," and "Secretary/personal assistant required with knowledge of English, pretty girl under 25."

17. Moroz was again elected speaker in 2006.

18. The speech may be found at http://www.nbuv.gov.ua/fpu/2005/zp20050305.htm (accessed March 8, 2005).

19. See Hrycak 2005:81n36. These include Yuliia Tymoshenko, Rayisa Bohatyr'ova, Halyna Artiukh and Liudmyla Matiiko (Hromada), Nataliia Vitrenko (Progressive Socialist Party of Ukraine), Olena Bondarenko (Rukh), Halyna Harmash (Socialist Party of Ukraine), Inna Bogoslovska (Viche, and, later, Party of Regions), and Liudmyla Suprun (Electoral Bloc of Liudmyla Suprun).

20. For example, the singer Mary J. Blige began to sport a Tymoshenko-style braid during 2005, and wears the hairstyle on the cover of her 2005 album "The Breakthrough." Tymoshenko's appearance (especially her braid) is also a point of ridicule by those who oppose her. During 2005, on the central square of Donets'k, a handwritten sign read: "A waif with a braid approaches: 'You will be hungry and barefoot!'" (The couplet rhymes in Russian—"*Prishla kostliavaia s kosoi . . . Golodnyi budesh' i bosoi!*")

21. For comparison, in the United States in 1999, women occupied 13 percent of seats in the senate and 14 percent of seats in the house. At the ministerial level, women held 31.8 percent of the positions (UNDP 2001).

22. Matters of gender equality are the purview of the Department of Family and Gender Politics and Demographic Development. Again, women's issues are linked to "family concerns," reproduction, and the demographic crisis.

2. Ukrainian NGO-graphy

1. During the late 1990s, charitable and civic organizations in Ukraine were classified as such based on their goals and target groups, a distinction that is still operative. Charitable organizations are nonprofits that engage in charitable endeavors directed at specific target groups other than the organization's members. Civic organizations are also nonprofit organizations, but their activities are focused inward and directed more toward the organization's members (although outreach to nonmembers and other groups is common). Activities include ecological, cultural, health, amateur sport, educational, and scientific events. Legislation governing these organizational forms was solidified in 2003 in the laws "On Civic Organizations" and "On Charitable Actions."

2. Information comes from the website of the Innovation and Development Centre, http://www.idc.org.ua/index_en.php (accessed May 24, 2006).

3. See the U.S. Department of State fact sheet on U.S. Assistance to Ukraine for Fiscal Year 2005 (dated July 25, 2005), at http://www.state.gov/p/eur/rls/fs/50839.htm (accessed June 4, 2006).

4. See Truman's inaugural address of January 20, 1949, at http://www.yale.edu/lawweb/avalon/presiden/inaug/truman.htm (accessed July 11, 2006).

5. See, for example, Anderson 1996; Borneman 1992; Buchowski 1996; and Hann 1996.

6. Over dinner once in Kyiv I was discussing volunteerism with acquaintances. One young man, Bohdan, mentioned his plan to create a "fund" for Ukrainians who had suffered during World War II in forced labor camps. These (now very elderly) people, he told me, were entitled to reparations and needed "advocates." Touched by his concern, I mentioned Bohdan's plans later to his roommate, Roman. Roman laughed, and revealed that Bohdan was planning a "scam." He had conceived of the organization as a "front" and hoped that purporting to aid victims of war would attract money from the international community, especially from the Ukrainian diaspora in Canada and the U.S.

7. Armine Ishkanian (2000:19) heard similar narratives in Armenia, where some NGO activists also were referred to as "grant-eaters" (*grantagerner* in Armenian).

8. One volume on *Gender Aspects of Civil Service,* published by the Ukrainian Academy of Civil Service, the Center for Research on Administrative Reforms, and the Center for Study of Gender Education (Kravchenko 2002), necessitated a five-page glossary entry on "gender" and related concepts like "gender democracy," "gender equality," and "gender stratification."

9. See, for example, Abramson 1999a, 1999b, 2004; Fisher 1997; Hann and Dunn 1996; Helms 2003; Hemment 1998, 2000; Hrycak 2002; Hulme and Edwards 1997; and Lewis 1999. Fisher's (1997) seminal work has shaped the critical approaches taken by many anthropologists studying postsocialist civil societies. For critical accounts of civil society in Eastern Europe, also see Creed (1991) and Creed and Wedel (1997). Julie Hemment's (1998, 2000, 2004, 2007) work on NGOs, civil society, and transnational interventions in Russia is excellent; also see Armine Ishkanian (2003, 2004) on the multiple discourses deployed by women NGO activists in Armenia, and David Abramson's (1999a; 1999b) articles on civil society, NGOs, and corruption in Uzbekistan. Lori Handrahan (2002) has studied women's NGOs in Kyrgyzstan. In her work, Michele Rivkin Fish (2000, 2004, 2005) critiques international health development interventions in Russia. Janine Wedel's (1998) study of development aid to Eastern Europe gone wrong also includes mention of the complexities of civil society building in the region.

10. For a historical consideration of Ukrainian women in the public sphere, see Bohachevsky-Chomiak 1988. For studies of the contemporary women's movement in Ukraine, see Bohachevsky-Chomiak 2000; Hrycak 2000, 2001, 2002, 2006; Pavlychko 1992, 1996; and Smoliar 2000a, 2000b, 2000c. The Russian women's movement has been more thoroughly studied; see, for example, Browning 1987; Edmondson 1984; Kay 2000; Konstantinova 1992, 1996; Sperling 1999; and Waters 1993.

11. Gleason (2000:2) also examines democratic initiatives in Ukraine from a historical perspective. As evidence of the historical roots of civil society in Ukraine he cites the *zemstvo,* or "the local rural self-governing councils, which brought together hundreds of teachers, doctors and health care officials from

the late 19th century through World War I to bring education and a better life to the peasantry." He also points out that the Kyiv telephone book of 1912 listed 250 philanthropic and charitable organizations.

12. See, for example, Funk and Mueller 1993; Huseby-Darvas 1996; Ries 1994; Rubchak 1996; Sperling 1999; and Watson 1997.

13. In 1996, only three hundred women in the entire country were affiliated with NGOs identified as "feminist," whereas Zhinocha Hromada alone claimed fifteen thousand members (Hrycak 2000:22).

14. For a more detailed treatment of international NGO interventions targeting women in Ukraine, see Hrycak 2006.

15. See, for example, Ghodsee 2005; Hemment 2004, 2007; and Rivkin-Fish 2005.

16. Counterpart International, Inc. (also called Counterpart Foundation, Inc.) was founded in 1965 as the Foundation for the Peoples of the South Pacific, and it has been active in NIS countries since 1992. During its initial efforts in the region, the foundation, which received USAID funds to implement a range of programs in Ukraine and other postsocialist states, sought to strengthen indigenous NGO capacity and service delivery and to foster partnerships between U.S. PVOs (private voluntary organizations) and indigenous NGOs. During the time of my research, the focus had moved to the development of the small business sector and, in particular, assisting women entrepreneurs. Counterpart's current major project in Ukraine is the Accessible Ukraine Award Competition. The competition, which will present one annual award for the "friendliest place for the disabled," is intended to increase disability awareness and promote accessible architectural design. Overall, Counterpart's activities in the region have shifted to Central Asia, Afghanistan, and Iraq. David Abramson (1999b) details a training session sponsored by Counterpart that he attended in Kokland, Uzbekistan. Ruth Mandel (2002) discusses Counterpart in the context of Kazakhstan.

17. Since Svetlana Mishchenko is profiled in Alter (2002), I have not assigned her a pseudonym here.

18. See, for example, Abramson 1999a; Mandel 2002; Richter 2002; and Sampson 1996.

19. See Gidron, Kramer, and Salamon 1992; Pestoff 1998; and Uvin 2000.

20. Winrock International is a private nonprofit organization based in the United States that works to facilitate responsible resource management through programs to promote environmental protection, renewable energy, and leadership development. The NIS-US Women's Consortium was conceptualized as a way to link women's groups in the former Soviet Union with their counterparts in the West to share information and experiences through leadership training, economic empowerment and job skills training, and capacity building for NGOs. Winrock's sponsorship of the Consortium ended in 1999, but Winrock continued to support the Consortium in Ukraine as a "partner." Active programs implemented by Winrock in Ukraine include Women's Economic Empowerment; the Trafficking Prevention Project (TPP) in Ukraine; and Community Responses to Domestic Violence and Trafficking.

21. By the end of 1998, the Consortium had 216 member organizations, including

93 women's groups in twenty-six cities in Ukraine, 2 in Belarus, 4 in Moldova, 2 in Armenia, 1 group each in Azerbaijan and Uzbekistan, 91 groups in Russia, and 22 women's groups in the United States (Hrycak 2000:11). The Consortium has offices in Washington, D.C., and Moscow; the Kyiv office, which was opened in 1996, served as the regional hub for the West NIS (i.e., NIS countries besides Russia).

Hrycak (2002) also describes the work of the NIS-US Women's Consortium. She focuses on how the Consortium has lent little support to nationalist women's associations and welfare rights mothers' groups in Russia and Ukraine, preferring to work instead with experienced elite women activists (many of them academics) who have experience working with foreign institutions, are familiar with feminism, and "could frame their concerns in terms familiar to American activists" (2002:74). She concludes that, despite the Consortium's support of some important local initiatives, its programs "failed to support more classically grassroots community organizations" and instead has been "oriented toward highly educated professional women who might become future leaders" (2002:74).

22. In her introduction to the Consortium's training manual on Women in Leadership, Olena Suslova (1997:3), the Consortium's former director of training programs in Ukraine, states that the material was obtained from various sources, including trainings of other organizations and a number of meetings and roundtables. The expertise of the Global Women's Fund, the U.S. League of Women Voters, and Amnesty International were also utilized.

23. "U.S. Assistance Strategy for Ukraine 1999–2002" (Washington, D.C.: USAID, March 29, 1999), 10; quoted in Hrycak 2006:81.

24. Between September 1996 and May 1998, more than 1,503 women attended the Consortium's trainings. For the same period, trainings were attended by only 76 men (NIS-US Women's Consortium 1998).

25. It is noteworthy that, in the 1960s, researchers found that "the elected leaders of the peer collective [such as the Komsomol] are . . . likely to be girls (in the thirty or more schools, camps, and Pioneer palaces visited [by researchers in the late 1960s], there was only one instance in which the highest officer was a boy)" (Bronfenbrenner 1970:73). Reasons for this disparity are not explored, but the author implies that girls were socialized into leadership roles in the Pioneer and Komsomol because of traditional gender expectations that position girls and women as caretakers and "upbringers."

26. Catherine Wanner (1998:49) refers to this song (written by composer David Tuchmanov) as "one of the many forms of propaganda that bombarded individuals to remind them that they were Soviet."

In 2002, the Russian band Leningrad remade the song on their album "Pirates of the 21st Century." Called "WWW," Leningrad's song (which cleverly disseminates their real internet address) is an irreverent reflection on life in post-Soviet, postmodern times ("My address is not a house or a street, my address is www.leningrad.spb.ru"). I thank Joe Crescente and Brooke Swafford for bringing the song to my attention. The complete lyrics of "WWW" are as follows (translation by Joe Crescente):

I don't remember when I moved.
I was probably drunk.
My address is not a house or a street.
My address today goes like this:
W-W-W LENINGRAD S-P-B DOT RU
When a policeman stops me (and says)
"You're not registered anywhere!"
I calmly reply,
"My address today goes like this":
W-W-W LENINGRAD S-P-B DOT RU
When I get really drunk
I flag down a car (and say) "C'mon driver take me home
Just a sec, I'll show you the way":
W-W-W LENINGRAD S-P-B DOT RU

27. *Komsorgi* were responsible for organizing the activities of the Komsomol
     at the schoolwide level, and much of their free time was occupied by these
     Party-related activities. School-based Komsomol organizations held meetings,
     engaged in public service activities, arranged competitions, and organized rec-
     reational activities such as hiking and camping. The school's Komsorg oversaw
     all these events.

28. Counterpart Creative Center (CCC) Fund was one of the six partner organi-
     zations that comprised the Counterpart Alliance for Partnership (CAP). The
     center offered the following trainings for local NGO activists: project writing
     and management, NGO management, setting up social businesses, training
     for trainers, strategic planning, financial management, work with volunteers,
     public relations (NGOs' relations with government institutions, businesses,
     and the media), principles of NGO viability, conflict management, working
     with staff, human rights representation and advocacy, lobbying and coalition
     building, and strategies of working with the mass media.

3. Claims and Class

1. An *ekstrasens* is a type of healer believed to possess extrasensorial powers. The
    late 1980s and early 1990s saw an explosion of interest in such nontraditional
    healing practitioners throughout the former Soviet Union (Lindquist 2006).

2. See Caldwell 2004; and Rivkin-Fish 2005.

3. See Caldwell 2002; Dunn 2004; Ghodsee 2005; Humphrey 1995; and Patico
    2002, 2005.

4. Ukrainian sociology has also been slow to consider questions of class, even
    though class is a central question in sociology. The first sociological investiga-
    tion of class to appear in independent Ukraine was Kutsenko's 2000 Russian-
    language book *Obshchestvo neravnykh: Klassovyi analiz neravenstv* (Society of
    unequals: Class analysis of inequalities).

5. See Patico 2005, for a detailed analysis of shifting meanings of *kul'turnost'*
    (the Russian term) in the Soviet Union up to the late 1990s. Patico notes that
    "*kul'turnost'* (culturedness) came to refer in the early 20th century to a code

6. For descriptions of the newly wealthy in Russia, see Grant 1999; Humphrey 2002; and Ries 2002.

7. Stereotypes of "New Ukrainians" (like those of New Russians) almost never refer to women. Patico has proposed that "this may be related to the fact that being a New Russian implies not only wealth, but also particular activities (including crime) and displays (raspberry jackets, shaved heads, heavy gold jewelry) that are associated more with men than with women and very strikingly differentiate New Russian men from other Russian men" (2000:77). In St. Petersburg, Patico found that New Russian women were usually understood to be successful businesswomen or the wives and girlfriends of New Russian men.

8. Ministry of Labor and Social Policy of Ukraine, and Pension Fund of Ukraine 2005:4.

9. During research in rural villages in Western Ukraine during 1998 and 1999, I met collective farm workers who had not been paid for their labor in one to four years. Some workers grew accustomed to being paid with goods instead of money; for several years, my father-in-law in Rivne oblast' was paid in huge sacks of sugar for his work as a night watchman for a factory.

10. Ministry of Labor and Social Policy of Ukraine, and Pension Fund of Ukraine, in cooperation with the Committee for Pensioners, Veterans, and Disability Affairs, "Why Is Disability Insurance Reform Needed in Ukraine?" (n.d.).

11. Ministry of Labor and Social Policy of Ukraine, and Pension Fund of Ukraine, in cooperation with the Committee for Pensioners, Veterans, and Disability Affairs, "Why Should People in Ukraine Have the Option of Later Retirement? Why Should Retirement Age Be Identical for Women and Men?" (n.d.).

12. Report on the results of the public survey of attitudes as to pension reform conducted by the GfK-USM company in July–August 2005 and commissioned by the USAID/PADCO project "Ukraine: Pension Reform Implementation" (GfK-USM 2005).

13. See, for example, Katherine Verdery's (1996:168–203) analysis of the Caritas pyramid scheme in Romania during 1990–94; see, too, Eliot Borenstein (1999) on Sergei Mavrodi and his notorious MMM pyramid scheme that scammed millions of people in Russia in the early 1990s.

14. The survey was administered by Socis/Gallup and involved a national random sample that was representative of Ukraine as a whole.

15. *Tuneiadets*, or "parasite," is a Soviet era understanding. In Soviet discourse, practically every citizen was required to work and thus "make a contribution to society." Those who did not were labeled "parasites," and could be arrested and jailed. The idea of the *tuneiadets* arose from the false assertion that unemployment as such did not exist in the Soviet Union, in contrast to the United States and other Western countries. Homelessness was also officially nonexistent, although there were homeless persons in the Soviet Union.

16. During the early 1990s, 3,000 rubles was a large nest egg in the Soviet Union,

and 75 rubles a month was enough to take care of all the needs of Svetlana and her children.

17. The group was urging the passage of the Law on Social Protection of Children of War (No. 2195 IV), which was eventually adopted on November 18, 2004. The law, which promises some retirees an increase in pensions of up to 30 percent, was upheld in February 2006 by the Verkhovna Rada, overturning a presidential veto. Because of budget deficits, it is unclear whether the law will be enforced.

18. Between 20 million and 40 million Soviet citizens died during World War II. An estimated 5 million persons in Ukraine were killed, 2 million were deported to camps in Europe, 3.5 million were evacuated to other parts of the Soviet Union, and more than 10 million were left homeless (Wanner 1998: 191).

19. In 1995, there were nearly 2.5 times more women than men over the age of fifty-five. Among persons over seventy years of age, women outnumbered men 5 to 1 (Sayenko et al. 1995:13–14). In the general population, women also outnumber men 117 to 100 (Paliy et al. 1996:21). The general trend in Ukraine is toward an aging population; the proportion of persons over sixty years of age (the aging coefficient) was 18.5 percent (13.7 percent for men and 22.6 percent for women) (Paliy et al. 1996:14), an indication that "Ukraine is becoming one of the most aged populations in the world" (Steshenko 1997:22). In 2003, 13 percent of the Ukrainian population was over age sixty-five; this figure is expected to increase to 16.4 percent by the year 2015 (UNDP 2005:233).

20. In 2003, the life expectancy at birth for women was 72.5 years, and for men 60.1 years (UNDP 2005:300). This represented a dramatic decrease in life expectancy from 2001 (77.4 years for women and 64.1 years for men) (UNDP 2003:311).

21. See Bilaniuk (2005) for a detailed analysis of language politics in contemporary Ukraine.

22. Sofiia was referring to a new presidential initiative, Zdorov'ia Natsiyi (Health of the Nation), which focused on health care reform.

4. Movin' On Up

1. Leleka (Stork) is a pseudonym for the publishing house.

2. Ivana turned down a United States green card that she won in a green card lottery in 1996. She was the recipient of one of only fifty green cards issued to persons in Belarus and Ukraine that year, and thus she had the opportunity to immigrate to the U.S. with her entire family. Ivana turned down the chance, she said, because her husband's business was just taking off and she did not want to disrupt her daughter's successful university studies and promising position as an employee at a foreign firm in Kyiv. She portrayed the decision as a personal sacrifice she had made for the good of her family.

3. She told me, for example, "All my friends and colleagues know that they can call me anytime day or night. All I ask is that they give me one hour—from 6:00 to 7:00 AM—to get myself together!"

4. ACTR/ACCELS is a private, nonprofit educational association and exchange organization devoted to improving education, professional training, and research in Russia and other NIS countries. American Councils Kyiv has administered programs of the Bureau of Educational and Cultural Affairs of the U.S. Department of State since 1992. The Council cooperates with the Ministry of Education and Science of Ukraine with a focus on providing experience and skills to current and future leaders to help build democratic infrastructures and a market economy.

5. The Civic Education Project was founded in 1991 by a group of American scholars and professionals. Today the organization is active in twenty-two countries, plus the region of Kosovo and the Republic of Montenegro. The CEP facilitates exchanges between scholars and professionals in the social sciences; funding is provided for local scholars to develop curricula in the social sciences, and American educators are funded to teach courses in host country universities. The CEP receives most of its funding from the Higher Education Support Program of the Open Society Institute, a private operating and grant-making foundation and part of the Soros Foundations Network. Other funding comes from international organizations, foundations, corporations, governments, and individuals.

Conclusion

1. In Russian, "*Ekh put'-dorozhka, frontovaia, ne strashna nam bombyozhka liubaia, a pomirat' nam ranovato, est' u nas eshchyo doma dela!*"

2. In 2006, Svetlana's son completed two university degrees and found a job paying 500–600 UAH per month ($100–$115), far below what was then the national average of $220. He is still paying off university loans to relatives and acquaintances, but he also contributes his earnings to the family budget.

Bibliography

Abramson, David. 1999a. A Critical Look at NGOs and Civil Society as a Means to an End in Uzbekistan. *Human Organization* 58 (3): 240–250.

———. 1999b. Civil Society and the Politics of Foreign Aid in Uzbekistan. *Central Asia Monitor* 6:1–12.

———. 2004. Engendering Citizenship in Postcommunist Uzbekistan. In *Post-Soviet Women Encountering Transition: Nation Building, Economic Survival, and Civic Activism*, ed. K. Kuehnast and C. Nechemias, 65–84. Washington, D.C.: Woodrow Wilson Center Press.

Abu-Lughod, Lila. 1991. Writing Against Culture. In *Recapturing Anthropology*, ed. R. Fox, 137–162. Santa Fe, N.M.: American School of Research Press.

Akhaladze, M. G. et al. 1999. *Women Workers' Rights in Ukraine*. Kyiv: Ukrainian Institute for Social Research.

Alter, Sutia Kim. 2001. *Managing the Double Bottom Line: A Business Planning Guide for Social Enterprises*. Washington, D.C.: PACT.

———. 2002. *Case Studies in Social Enterprise: Counterpart International's Experience*. Washington, D.C.: Counterpart International, Inc. Retrieved from http://www.virtueventures.com/files/cicases.pdf (accessed December 24, 2004).

Anderson, David G. 1996. Bringing Civil Society to an Uncivilised Place: Citizenship Regimes in Russia's Arctic Frontier. In *Civil Society: Challenging Western Models*, ed. C. Hann and E. Dunn, 99–120. London: Routledge.

Appell, George N. 1978. *Ethical Dilemmas in Anthropological Inquiry: A Case Book*. Waltham, Mass.: Crossroads.

Averianova, Irina E. 1998. Pyrrhic Victory: The Feminization of Higher Education in Ukraine. *The Harriman Review* 11 (1–2): 31–35.

Bach, Jonathan, and David Stark. 2002. Innovative Ambiguities: NGOs' Use of Interactive Technology in Eastern Europe. *Studies in Comparative International Development* 37 (2): 3–23.

Baranskaya, Natalia. 1969. *A Week Like Any Other*. Translated by P. Monks. Seattle: Seal.

Baskakova, Marina. 2000. Gender Aspects of Pension Reform in Russia. In *Making the Transition Work for Women in Europe and Central Asia (World Bank Discussion Paper no. 411)*, ed. M. Lazreg, 61–68. Washington, D.C.: World Bank.

Beck, Ulrich, and Elisabeth Beck-Gernsheim. 2002. *Individualization: Institutionalized Individualism and Its Social and Political Consequences*. London: Sage.

Behar, Ruth. 1993. *Translated Woman: Crossing the Border with Esperanza's Story*. Boston: Beacon.

Berdahl, Daphne. 1999. *Where the World Ended: Re-unification and Identity in the German Borderland*. Berkeley: University of California Press.

———. 2000. Mixed Devotions: Religion, Friendship, and Fieldwork in Postsocialist Eastern Germany. In *Fieldwork Dilemmas: Anthropologists in Postsocialist States*, ed. H. DeSoto and N. Dudwick, 173–194. Madison: University of Wisconsin Press.

Biesele, Megan. 2003. The Kalahari Peoples Fund: Activist Legacy of the Harvard Kalahari Research Group. *Anthropologica* 45:75–88.

Bilaniuk, Laada. 2005. *Contested Tongues: Language Politics and Cultural Correction in Ukraine.* Ithaca, N.Y.: Cornell University Press.

Bohachevsky-Chomiak, Martha. 1988. *Feminists Despite Themselves: Women in Ukrainian Community Life, 1884–1939.* Edmonton: Canadian Institute of Ukrainian Studies.

———. 1994. *Political Communities and Gendered Ideologies in Contemporary Ukraine.* Cambridge, Mass.: Harvard University Press.

———. 2000. Women in Ukraine: The Political Potential of Community Organizations. In *Cultures and Nations of Central and Eastern Europe: Essays in Honor of Roman Szporluk,* ed. Z. Gitelman, L. Hajda, J.-P. Himka, and R. Solchanyk, 29–47. Cambridge, Mass.: Harvard University Press.

Borenstein, Eliot. 1999. Public Offerings: MMM and the Marketing of Melodrama. In *Consuming Russia: Popular Culture, Sex, and Society since Gorbachev,* ed. A. M. Barker, 49–75. Durham, N.C.: Duke University Press.

Borneman, John. 1992. *Belonging in the Two Berlins: Kin, State, Nation.* Cambridge and New York: Cambridge University Press.

Bourdieu, Pierre. 1986. Forms of Capital. In *Handbook of Theory and Research for the Sociology of Education,* ed. J. G. Richardson, 241–258. Westport, Conn.: Greenwood.

Braichevska, Olena, Halyna Volosiuk, Olena Malynovska, Yaroslav Pylynskyi, Nancy E. Popson, and Blair A. Ruble. 2004. *Nontraditional Immigrants in Kyiv.* Washington, D.C.: Woodrow Wilson International Center for Scholars.

Bridger, Sue, Rebecca Kay, and Kathryn Pinnick. 1996. *No More Heroines? Russia, Women and the Market.* London: Routledge.

Bridger, Sue, and Frances Pine, eds. 1998. *Surviving Post-Socialism: Local Strategies and Regional Responses in Eastern Europe and the Former Soviet Union.* London: Routledge.

Bronfenbrenner, Urie. 1970. *Two Worlds of Childhood: U.S. and U.S.S.R.* New York: Russell Sage Foundation.

Browning, Genia. 1987. *Women and Politics in the USSR: Consciousness Raising and Soviet Women's Groups.* Brighton and Sussex: St. Martin's.

Bruner, Edward. 1990. Introduction: The Ethnographic Self and Personal Self. In *Anthropology and Literature,* ed. P. Benson, 1–26. Urbana: University of Illinois Press.

Buchowski, Micka . 1996. The Shifting Meanings of Civil and Civic Society in Poland. In *Civil Society: Challenging Western Models,* ed. C. Hann and E. Dunn, 79–98. London: Routledge.

Buck-Morss, Susan. 2000. *Dreamworld and Catastrophe: The Passing of Mass Utopia in East and West.* Cambridge, Mass.: MIT Press.

Buckley, Cynthia, and Dennis Donahue. 2000. Promises to Keep: Pension Provision in the Russian Federation. In *Russia's Torn Safety Nets: Health and Social Welfare during the Transition,* ed. M. G. Field and J. L. Twigg, 251–270. New York: St. Martin's.

Buckley, Mary. 1989. *Women and Ideology in the Soviet Union.* Ann Arbor: University of Michigan Press.

———, ed. 1992. *Perestroika and Soviet Women.* Cambridge: Cambridge University Press.

————, ed. 1997. *Post-Soviet Women: From the Baltic to Central Asia.* Cambridge: Cambridge University Press.

Cabinet of Ministers of Ukraine. 2005. Decree 525-r, "On the Approval of the Pension System Development Strategy" (December 15, 2005). Retrieved from http://www.pension.kiev.ua/FILES/ENG/CM_decree_525_eng.pdf (accessed May 5, 2006; link no longer available).

Caiazza, Amy. 2002. *Mothers and Soldiers: Gender, Citizenship and Civil Society in Contemporary Russia.* New York: Routledge.

Caldwell, Melissa. 2002. The Taste of Nationalism: Food Politics in Postsocialist Moscow. *Ethnos* 67 (3): 295–319.

————. 2004. *Not by Bread Alone: Social Support in the New Russia.* Berkeley: University of California Press.

Cassell, Joan, and Murray L. Wax, eds. 1980. *Ethical Problems of Fieldwork.* Special issue of *Social Problems* 27:259–378.

Chukhym, Nataliia, and Marfa Skoryk. 2000. Genderni doslidzhennia v Ukrayini: Iaki zh perspektyvy? *Perekhrestia* 4 (9): 21–23.

Cohen, Jean L., and Andrew Arato. 1992. *Civil Society and Political Theory.* Cambridge, Mass.: MIT Press.

Cook, Beth, Chris Dodds, and William Mitchell. 2002. Social Entrepreneurship: False Premises and Dangerous Forebodings. *Australian Journal of Social Issues* 38 (1): 57–72.

Counterpart Creative Center. 2002. *Dovidnyk donors'kykh orhanizatsii ta blahodiinykh prohram, shcho pidtrymuiut' diial'nist' NUO v Ukrayini.* Kyiv: Counterpart Creative Center.

Creed, Gerald. 1991. Civil Society and the Spirit of Capitalism: A Bulgarian Critique. Presented at the Ninetieth Annual Meeting of the American Anthropological Association, Chicago, Ill., November 20–24, 1991.

————. 1995. The Politics of Agriculture in Bulgaria. *Slavic Review* 4:843–868.

Creed, Gerald, and Janine Wedel. 1997. Second Thoughts from the Second World: Interpreting Aid in Post-Communist Eastern Europe. *Human Organization* 56 (3): 253–264.

Cruikshank, Barbara. 1999. *The Will to Empower: Democratic Citizens and Other Subjects.* Ithaca, N.Y.: Cornell University Press.

D'Anieri, Paul, Robert Kravchuk, and Taras Kuzio. 1999. *Politics and Society in Ukraine.* Boulder, Colo.: Westview.

Danylenko, Tetiana, and Iuliia Nazarov. 2005. *Ukrayins'ka "zalizna ledi" Iuliia Tymoshenko ocholiuie uriad.* 5tv.com.ua, February 4, 2005.

Denisova, Tatyana A. 2004. Trafficking in Women and Children for Purposes of Sexual Exploitation: The Criminological Aspect. In *The Prediction and Control of Organized Crime: The Experience of Post-Soviet Ukraine,* ed. J. O. Finckenauer and J. L. Schrock, 43–51. New Brunswick, N.J.: Transaction.

DeSoto, Hermine, and Nora Dudwick, eds. 2000. *Fieldwork Dilemmas: Anthropologists in Postsocialist States.* Madison: University of Wisconsin Press.

Dovzhenko, Valentyna I. 1998. The Situation of Women at the Labour Market under Social and Economic Transformation: Possible Solutions. In *The Now Days Problems of Women at the Labour Market and Possible Decisions,* ed. V. I. Dovzhenko, I. L. Demchenko, U. M. Yakubova, and O. O. Yaremenko, 196–205. Kyiv: Stolytsya.

Dudwick, Nora, Radhika Srinivasan, and Jeanine Braithwaite. 2002. *Ukraine Gen-*

der Review. The World Bank, Social Development Unit, Europe and Central Asia Region. Retrieved from http://siteresources.worldbank.org/INTECAREGTOPGENDER/Resources/UkraineCGA.pdf (accessed June 25, 2006).

Dunn, Elizabeth. 2004. *Privatizing Poland: Baby Food, Big Business, and the Remaking of Labor.* Ithaca, N.Y.: Cornell University Press.

DuPlessis, Rachel Blau, and Ann Snitow, eds. 1998. *The Feminist Memoir Project: Voices from Women's Liberation.* New York: Three Rivers.

Du Plessix Gray, Francine. 1989. *Soviet Women: Walking the Tightrope.* New York: Doubleday.

Edmonson, Linda. 1984. *Feminism in Russia, 1900–1917.* Stanford: Stanford University Press.

Edwards, Michael, and Gita Sen. 2003. NGOs, Social Change and the Transformation of Human Relationships: A 21st-Century Civic Agenda. In *The Earthscan Reader on NGO Management,* ed. M. Edwards and A. Fowler, 38–49. London: Earthscan.

Einhorn, Barbara. 1993. *Cinderella Goes to Market: Gender, Citizenship and the Women's Movement in Eastern Europe.* London: Verso.

Farmer, Paul. 1992. *AIDS and Accusation: Haiti and the Geography of Blame.* Berkeley: University of California Press.

Farmer, Paul, and Jim Yong Kim. 2000. Limited Good and Limited Minds: Public Health Logic and the Survival of the Poor. Presented at the Ninety-ninth Annual Meeting of the American Anthropological Association. San Francisco, Calif., November 17, 2000.

Fisher, William. 1997. Doing Good? The Politics and Antipolitics of NGO Practices. *Annual Review of Anthropology* 26:439–464.

Fluehr-Lobban, Carolyn. 2003. *Ethics and the Profession of Anthropology: Dialogue for Ethically Conscious Practice.* 2nd ed. Walnut Creek, Calif.: AltaMira.

Fodor, Éva. 2004. The State Socialist Emancipation Project: Gender Inequality and Workplace Authority in Hungary and Austria. *Signs* 29 (3): 783–813.

Fowler, Alan. 2000. NGDOs as a Moment in History: Beyond Aid to Social Entrepreneurship or Civic Innovation? *Third World Quarterly* 27:637–654.

Fraser, Nancy. 1997. *Justice Interruptus: Critical Reflections on the "Postsocialist" Condition.* New York: Routledge.

Frejka, Tomaš, Marek Okólski, and Keith Sword, eds. 1999. *In-Depth Studies on Migration in Central and Eastern Europe: The Case of Ukraine.* New York: United Nations.

Funk, Nanette, and Magda Mueller, eds. 1993. *Gender Politics and Post-Communism: Reflections from Eastern Europe and the Former Soviet Union.* New York: Routledge.

Gal, Susan. 1997. Feminism and Civil Society. In *Transitions, Environments, Translations: Feminisms in International Politics,* ed. J. W. Scott, C. Kaplan, and D. Keates, 30–45. New York: Routledge.

Gapova, Elena. 2000. When Western Assistance Overlooks Cultural Values in FSU Gender Programs. *Give and Take* 3 (2): 10–11.

Gardner, Katy, and David Lewis. 1996. *Anthropology, Development and the Postmodern Challenge.* London: Pluto.

GfK-USM. 2005. Pension Reform: From Apathy to Personal Responsibility. Report on the results of the public survey of attitudes as to pension reform conducted by the GfK-USM company in July–August 2005 and commissioned by the USAID/ PADCO project "Ukraine: Pension Reform Implementation."

Ghodsee, Kristen. 2004. Feminism-by-Design: Emerging Capitalisms, Cultural Feminism, and Women's Non-governmental Organizations in Postcommunist Eastern Europe. *Signs* 29:727–753.

———. 2005. *The Red Riviera: Gender, Tourism, and Postsocialism on the Black Sea.* Durham, N.C.: Duke University Press.

Gidron, Benjamin, Ralph M. Kramer, and Lester M. Salamon, eds. 1992. *Government and the Third Sector: Emerging Relationships in Welfare States.* San Francisco, Calif.: Jossey-Bass.

Gitelman, Zvi. 2000. Native Land, Promised Land, Golden Land: Jewish Emigration from Russia and Ukraine. In *Cultures and Nations of Central and Eastern Europe: Essays in Honor of Roman Szporluk,* ed. Z. Gitelman, L. Hajda, J.-P. Himka, and R. Solchanyk, 137–163. Cambridge, Mass.: Harvard Ukrainian Research Institute.

Gleason, William. 2000. Civil Society and Democracy: Historical Reflections. *Ukrainian NGO Monitor* 1:1–2, 15.

Gnauck, Gerhard. 2005. Julia Tymoschenko: "Ich bereue nichts." Retrieved from http:// www.welt.de/data/2005/12/05/813087.html (accessed December 15, 2005).

Góralska, Helena. 2000. Funding of Social Benefits and the Social Service System in Ukraine. In *Economic Reform in Ukraine: The Unfinished Agenda,* ed. A. Åslund and G. de Ménil, 232–251. Armonk, N.Y.: M. E. Sharpe.

Gorbachev, Mikhail S. 1987. *Perestroika: New Thinking for Our Country and the World.* New York: Harper and Row.

Government of Ukraine. 2006. The Government of Ukraine's European Union website. Retrieved from http://ukraine-eu.mfa.gov.ua/eu/en/publication/content/1985. htm (accessed May 18, 2006).

Grant, Bruce. 1999. The Return of the Repressed: Conversations with Three Russian Entrepreneurs. In *Paranoia Within Reason: A Casebook on Conspiracy as Explanation,* ed. G. Marcus, 241–267. Chicago: University of Chicago Press.

———. 2001. New Moscow Monuments; or, States of Innocence. *American Ethnologist* 28 (2): 332–362.

Gray, Mel, Karen Healy, and Penny Crofts. 2003. Social Enterprise: Is It the Business of Social Work? *Australian Social Work* 56:141–154.

Gupta, Akhil, and James Ferguson, eds. 1997. *Anthropological Locations: Boundaries and Grounds of a Field.* Berkeley: University of California Press.

Handrahan, Lori M. 2002. *Gendering Ethnicity: Implications for Democracy Assistance.* New York: Routledge.

Haney, Lynne. 1999. "But We Are Still Mothers": Gender, the State, and the Construction of Need in Postsocialist Hungary. In *Uncertain Transition: Ethnographies of Change in the Postsocialist World,* ed. M. Burawoy and K. Verdery, 151–187. Oxford: Rowman and Littlefield.

———. 2000. Global Discourses of Need: Mythologizing and Pathologizing Welfare in Hungary. In *Global Ethnography: Forces, Connections and Imaginations in a Postmodern World,* ed. M. Burawoy, 48–73. Berkeley: University of California Press.

———. 2002. *Inventing the Needy: Gender and the Politics of Welfare in Hungary.* Berkeley: University of California Press.

Hann, Christopher M. 1996. Introduction: Political Society and Civil Anthropology.

In *Civil Society: Challenging Western Models,* ed. C. Hann and E. Dunn, 1–26. London: Routledge.

Hann, Christopher, and Elizabeth Dunn, eds. 1996. *Civil Society: Challenging Western Models.* London: Routledge.

Helms, Elissa. 2003. Women as Agents of Ethnic Reconciliation? Women's NGOs and International Intervention in Postwar Bosnia-Herzegovina. *Women's Studies International Forum* 26 (1): 15–33.

Hemment, Julie. 1998. Colonization or Liberation: The Paradox of NGOs in Postsocialist States. *The Anthropology of East Europe Review* 16 (1): 31–39.

———. 2000. The Price of Partnership: The NGO, the State, the Foundation, and Its Lovers in Post-Communist Russia. *The Anthropology of East Europe Review* 18 (1): 33–36.

———. 2004. Strategizing Gender and Development: Action Research and Ethnographic Responsibility in the Russian Provinces. In *Post-Soviet Women Encountering Transition: Nation Building, Economic Survival, and Civic Activism,* ed. K. Kuehnast and C. Nechemias, 313–333. Washington, D.C.: Woodrow Wilson Center Press.

———. 2007. *Empowering Women in Russia: Activism, Aid, and NGOs.* Bloomington: Indiana University Press.

Herzfeld, Michael. 1992. *The Social Production of Indifference: Exploring the Symbolic Roots of Western Bureaucracy.* New York: Berg.

Hofmann, Erin Trouth. 2006. Virtual Politics and the Corruption of Post-Soviet Democracy. *Kennan Institute Meeting Report* 23 (13): 1.

Hrycak, Alexandra. 2000. Women's Groups in a New Civil Society: Opportunities and Threats. Presented at the Fifth Annual World Convention of the Association for the Study of Nationalities, New York City, April 13–15, 2000.

———. 2001. The Dilemmas of Civic Revival: Ukrainian Women since Independence. *Journal of Ukrainian Studies* 26 (1–2): 135–158.

———. 2002. From Mothers' Rights to Equal Rights: Post-Soviet Grassroots Women's Associations. In *Women's Activism and Globalization: Linking Local Struggles and Transnational Politics,* ed. N. Naples and M. K. Desai, 64–82. New York: Routledge.

———. 2005. Coping with Chaos: Gender and Politics in a Fragmented State. *Problems of Post-Communism* 52 (5): 69–81.

———. 2006. Foundation Feminism and the Articulation of Hybrid Feminisms in Post-Socialist Ukraine. *East European Politics and Societies* 20 (1): 69–100.

Hubbs, Joanna. 1988. *Mother Russia: The Feminine Myth in Russian Culture.* Bloomington: Indiana University Press.

Hughes, Donna M., and Tatyana A. Denisova. 2004. The Transnational Political Criminal Nexus of Trafficking in Women from Ukraine. In *The Prediction and Control of Organized Crime: The Experience of Post-Soviet Ukraine,* ed. J. O. Finckenauer and J. L. Schrock, 61–90. New Brunswick, N.J.: Transaction.

Hulme, David, and Michael Edwards, eds. 1997. *NGOs, States and Donors: Too Close for Comfort?* London: Macmillan.

Human Rights Watch. 2003. Ukraine: Women's Work: Discrimination against Women in the Ukrainian Labor Force. *Human Rights Watch* 15, no. 4(D).

Humphrey, Caroline. 1995. Creating a Culture of Disillusionment: Consumption in Moscow, a Chronicle of Changing Times. In *Worlds Apart: Modernity through the Prism of the Local,* ed. D. Miller, 43–68. New York: Routledge.

———. 2002. The Villas of the "New Russians": A Sketch of Consumption and Cultural Identity in Post-Soviet Landscapes. In *The Unmaking of Soviet Life: Everyday Economies after Socialism*, 175–201. Ithaca, N.Y.: Cornell University Press.

Huseby-Darvas, Éva. 1996. "Feminism the Murderer of Mothers": The Rise and Fall of Neo-Nationalist Reconstruction of Gender in Hungary. In *Women Out of Place: The Gender of Agency and the Rise of Nationality*, ed. B. Williams, 161–185. New York: Routledge.

Iaremenko, O. O., and O. M. Balakirieva, eds. 1999. *The Family in Ukraine*. Kyiv: Studtsentr.

Iatridis, Demetrius S. 2000. The Social Justice and Equality Contexts of Privatization. In *Social Justice and the Welfare State in Central and Eastern Europe: The Impact of Privatization*, ed. D. S. Iatridis, 3–20. Boulder, Colo.: Westview.

Iatsenko, Nataliia. 2006. Ella Libanova: "U zhinky menshe trudovykh prav cherez nyz'kyi pensiinyi vik i nyzhchu, nizh u cholovikiv, zarplatu." *Dzerkalo Tyzhnia* 22 (601). Retrieved from http://www.dt.ua/2000/2650/53616/ (accessed September 27, 2007).

———. 2007. Prezydents'kyi prianyk. *Dzerkalo Tyzhnia* 25 (654). Retrieved from http://www.dt.ua/2000/2650/59763/ (accessed October 5, 2007).

Iatsenko, Volodymyr. 2005. Pensiina reforma: U poshuku zdorovoho hluzdu ta spravedlyvosti. *Dzerkalo Tyzhnia* 11 (539). Retrieved from http://www.dt.ua/2000/49592/ (accessed September 27, 2007).

Innovation and Development Centre. 2000a. *Den' Hromads'kykh Orhanizatsii Kyieva: Kataloh Uchasnykiv*. Kyiv: Innovation and Development Centre.

———. 2000b. *Guide to Foreign Funding Sources Available for Ukrainian Non-Profits*. Kyiv: Innovation and Development Centre.

———. 2001. *Hromads'ki orhanizatsii ta blahodiini fondy Kyieva*. Kyiv: Graffiti Group.

———. 2006. Website of the Innovation and Development Centre, Kyiv. Retrieved from http://www.idc.org.ua/index_en.php (accessed May 24, 2006).

International Organization for Migration. 2001. New IOM Figures on the Global Scale of Trafficking. *Trafficking in Migrants Quarterly Bulletin* 23.

Ishkanian, Armine. 2000. Gender and NGOs in Post-Soviet Armenia. *The Anthropology of East Europe Review* 18 (2): 17–22.

———. 2003. Importing Civil Society? The Emergence of Armenia's NGO Sector and the Impact of Western Aid on Its Development. *Armenian Forum: A Journal of Contemporary Affairs* 3 (1): 7–36.

———. 2004. Working at the Local-Global Intersection: The Challenges Facing Women in Armenia's Nongovernmental Organization Sector. In *Post-Soviet Women Encountering Transition: Nation-Building, Economic Survival, and Civic Activism*, ed. K. Kuehnast and C. Nechemias, 262–287. Washington, D.C.: Woodrow Wilson Center Press.

Jackson, Bruce. 1987. *Fieldwork*. Urbana: University of Illinois Press.

Johnson, Janet Elise, and Jean C. Robinson, eds. 2007. *Living Gender after Communism*. Bloomington: Indiana University Press.

Kanaev, Petr, and Ekaterina Gerashchenko. 2006. Dengi na rebyonka. *Vzgliad*, May 10, 2006. Retrieved from http://www.vz.ru/economy/2006/5/10/33073.html (accessed May 11, 2006).

Kay, Rebecca. 2000. *Russian Women and Their Organizations: Gender, Discrimination and Grassroots Women's Organizations, 1991–96*. Houndmills: Macmillan.

Kemper, Robert, and Anya Royce, eds. 2002. *Chronicling Cultures: Long-term Field Research in Anthropology.* Walnut Creek, Calif.: AltaMira.

Kenny, Sue. 2002. Tensions and Dilemmas in Community Development: New Discourses, New Trojans? *Community Development Journal* 37:284-299.

Kharkhordin, Oleg. 1999. *The Collective and the Individual in Russia: A Study of Practices.* Berkeley: University of California Press.

Kidder, Tracy. 2003. *Mountains Beyond Mountains.* New York: Random House.

Kideckel, David, ed. 1995. *East European Communities: The Struggle for Balance in Turbulent Times.* Boulder, Colo.: Westview.

Komykh, Nataliia. 2001. Genderni osoblyvosti motyvatsii pidpryiemnyts'koi diial'nosti. In *Gender i kul'tura,* ed. V. Aheieva and S. Oksamytna, 209-215. Kyiv: Fakt.

Konstantynova, Valentyna. 1992. The Women's Movement in the USSR: A Myth or a Real Challenge? In *Women in the Face of Change,* ed. S. Rai, H. Pilkington, and A. Phizacklea, 200-217. London: Routledge.

———. 1996. Women's Political Coalitions in Russia (1990-1994). In *Women's Voices in Russia Today,* ed. A. Rotkirch and E. Haavio-Mannila, 235-247. Brookfield, Vt.: Dartmouth Publishing.

Koval', Iarina, Natal'ia Mel'nik, and Elena Godovanets. 1999. Biznes dlia zhenshchiny kak retsept ot pessimizma i razocharovaniia v sebe. *Den'* 173, September 21, 1999.

Koval's'kyi, V. S., ed. 2002. *Zakonodavstvo Ukrayiny pro sim'iu.* Kyiv: Iurinkom Inter.

Kravchenko, Bohdan, ed. 2002. *Genderni aspekty derzhavnoyi sluzhby.* Kyiv: Osnovy.

Kravchuk, Robert S. 2002. *Ukrainian Political Economy: The First Ten Years.* New York: Palgrave Macmillan.

Kulick, Don, and Margaret Willson, eds. 1995. *Taboo: Sex, Identity, and Erotic Subjectivity in Anthropological Fieldwork.* London: Routledge.

Kulick, Orysia Maria. 2005. Women of the Orange Revolution. *Women East-West* 83: 12-13.

Kutova, Natalia. 2003. Gender Identity and the Ukrainian Nation-State Formation: Clinging to the Past. Presented at Gender and Power in the New Europe, the Fifth European Feminist Research Conference, Lund University, Sweden, August 20-24, 2003. Retrieved from http://www.iiav.nl/epublications/2003/Gender_and_Power/5thfeminist/paper_343.pdf (accessed September 27, 2007).

Kutsenko, O. D. 2000. *Obshchestvo neravnykh: Klassovyi analiz neravenstv.* Kharkov: Kharkov National University of Karazin Press.

Kuzio, Taras. 2002. Gender Issues Hijacked by "Party of Power." *Ukrainian Weekly* 11 (70).

———. 2005. Yushchenko's First Year in Office: A Western Perspective. Address at the University Kyiv Mohyla Academy, November 2005. Reproduced on the Ukraine List, Vol. 371, December 19, 2005.

Lampland, Martha. 2000. Afterword. In *Altering States: Ethnographies of Transition in Eastern Europe and the Former Soviet Union,* ed. D. Berdahl, M. Bunzl, and M. Lampland, 209-218. Ann Arbor: University of Michigan Press.

Lapidus, Gail Warshofsky. 1978. *Women in Soviet Society: Equality, Development, and Social Change.* Berkeley: University of California Press.

———, ed. 1982. *Women, Work, and Family in the Soviet Union.* Armonk, N.Y.: M. E. Sharpe.

Ledeneva, Alena. 1998. *Russia's Economy of Favours: Blat, Networking and Informal Exchange.* Cambridge: Cambridge University Press.

Lewis, David. 1999. Revealing, Widening, Deepening? A Review of the Existing and Potential Contribution of Anthropological Approaches to "Third-Sector" Research. *Human Organization* 58 (1): 73–81.

Lewytzkyj, Borys. 1984. *Politics and Society in Soviet Ukraine, 1953–1980.* Edmonton: Canadian Institute of Ukrainian Studies.

Libanova, Ella. 2001. Bidnist' v Ukrayini: Diahnoz postavleno—budemo likuvaty? *Dzerkalo Tyzhnia,* March 31–April 6, 2001. Retrieved from http://www.dt.ua/2000/2650/30585/ (accessed September 27, 2007).

Liborakina, Marina. 1998. The Unappreciated Mothers of Civil Society. *Transitions* 5 (1): 52–57.

Linde, Charlotte. 1993. *Life Stories: The Creation of Coherence.* New York: Oxford University Press.

Lindquist, Galina. 2006. *Conjuring Hope: Healing and Magic in Contemporary Russia.* New York: Berghahn Books.

Lipsmeyer, Christine S. 2003. Welfare and the Discriminating Public: Evaluating Entitlement Attitudes in Post-Communist Europe. *Policy Studies Journal* 31 (4): 545–564.

Mandel, Ruth. 2002. Seeding Civil Society. In *Postsocialism,* ed. C. Hann, 279–296. London: Routledge.

Markowitz, Lisa. 2001. Finding the Field: Notes on the Ethnography of NGOs. *Human Organization* 60 (1): 40–46.

Marsh, Rosalind, ed. 1996. *Women in Russia and Ukraine.* Cambridge: Cambridge University Press.

Marunych, V., A. Ipatov, O. Serhiieni, and T. Voitchak. 2004. Pliusy ta minusy indyvidual'nykh prohram reabilitatsiyi invalidiv. *Sotsial'ne Partnerstvo* 1 (1): 22–23.

Mauss, Marcel. 1938. Une Categorie de L'Esprit Humain: La Notion de Personne, Celle de "Moi." *Journal of the Royal Anthropological Institute of Great Britain and Ireland* 68 (2): 263–281.

Milanovic, Branko. 1998. *Income, Inequality and Poverty during the Transition from Planned to Market Economy.* Washington, D.C.: World Bank.

Ministry of Labor and Social Policy of Ukraine. 2005. Adresna dopomoha malozabezpechenym verstvam naselennia. Retrieved from http://www.mlsp.gov.ua/control/uk/publish/article?art_id=39368&cat_id=34941 (accessed March 9, 2006).

———. 2006. Summary of Work of the Ministry of Labor and Social Policy during the Fourth Parliamentary Convocation, March 30, 2006. Retrieved from http://portal.rada.gov.ua/control/uk/publish/article/news_left?art_id=69543&cat_id=37486 (accessed June 7, 2006).

Ministry of Labor and Social Policy of Ukraine, and Pension Fund of Ukraine. 2005. *Mandatory State Social Insurance and Pensions in 2004: Figures and Facts.* Kyiv: Ministry of Labor and Social Policy, Pension Fund, USAID, and PADCO.

Ministry of Labor and Social Policy of Ukraine, and Pension Fund of Ukraine, in cooperation with the Committee for Pensioners, Veterans, and Disability Affairs. n.d. Why Is Disability Insurance Reform Needed in Ukraine?

———. n.d. Why Should People in Ukraine Have the Option of Later Retirement? Why Should Retirement Age Be Identical for Women and Men?

Miroiu, Mihaela. 2004. State Men, Market Women: The Effects of Left Conservatism on Gender Politics in Romanian Transition. Address at Indiana University, Bloomington, January 23, 2004.

Mort, Gillian Sullivan, Jay Weerawardena, and Kashonia Carnegie. 2003. Social Entrepreneurship: Towards Conceptualisation. *International Journal of Nonprofit and Voluntary Sector Marketing* 8 (1): 76–88.

Murdock, Donna. 2003. That Stubborn "Doing Good" Question: Ethical/Epistemological Concerns in the Study of NGOs. *Ethnos* 68 (4): 507–532.

Mychajlyszyn, Natalie. 2004. *Ukraine: Crossroads Country Report.* Retrieved from http://unpan1.un.org/intradoc/groups/public/documents/nispacee/unpan016209.pdf (accessed June 14, 2004).

Myerhoff, Barbara. 1978. *Number Our Days.* New York: Simon and Schuster.

Myronivs'kyi, Viktor. 2005. Iak atestuvaty roboche mistse invalida? *Sotsial'ne Partnerstvo* 3 (4): 14–16.

Nader, Laura. 1969. Up the Anthropologist: Perspectives Gained from Studying Up. In *Reinventing Anthropology,* ed. D. Hymes, 284–311. New York: Pantheon.

Najafizadeh, Mehrangiz, and Lewis A. Mennerick. 2003. Gender and Social Entrepreneurship in Societies in Transition: The Case of Azerbaijan. *Journal of Third World Studies* 20 (2): 31–48.

National Information Service Strana.Ru. 2006. Yushchenko legko obshchat'sia s Putinym. Retrieved from http://www.ukraine.ru/text/replic/273107.html (accessed June 16, 2006).

NIS-US Women's Consortium. 1997. *Zhinoche liderstvo: Teoriia. Pidruchnyk dlia treneriv.* Kyiv: NIS-US Women's Consortium.

———. 1998. *Fourth Quarterly Progress Report, Year 2.* Arlington, Va.: NIS-US Women's Consortium.

Novi vidpovidi na stari pytannia. 2005. *Sotsial'ne partnerstvo* 3 (4): 4–5.

Ong, Aihwa. 1996. Strategic Sisterhood or Sisters in Solidarity? Questions of Communitarianism and Citizenship in Asia. *Indiana Journal of Global Legal Studies* 4 (1): 107–135.

Paliy, O., L. Artamonova, V. Zayika, G. Yeremenko, N. Narina, M. Oleksiyko, O. Rozdobudko, O. Sytnyk, V. Steshenko, and G. Shyriayeva. 1996. *Childhood and Motherhood in Ukraine: Challenges of Transition.* Kyiv: Central and Eastern Europe, Commonwealth of Independent States and the Baltics Regional Office UNICEF; UN Office in Ukraine.

Palyvoda, Lyubov, Oksana Kikot, and Olga Vlasova. 2006. *Civil Society Organizations in Ukraine: The State and Dynamics (2002–2005).* Kyiv: Macros.

Panina, Natalia, and Evhen Golovakha. 1999. *Tendencies in the Development of Ukrainian Society (1994–1998): Sociological Indicators.* Kyiv: Institute of Sociology.

Patico, Jennifer. 2000. "New Russian" Sightings and the Question of Social Difference in St. Petersburg. *The Anthropology of East Europe Review* 18 (2): 73–77.

———. 2002. Chocolate and Cognac: Gifts and the Recognition of Social Worlds in Post-Soviet Russia. *Ethnos* 67 (3): 345–368.

———. 2005. To Be Happy in a Mercedes: Tropes of Value and Ambivalent Visions of Marketization. *American Ethnologist* 32 (3): 479–496.

Pavlychko, Solomea. 1992. Between Feminism and Nationalism: New Women's Groups in the Ukraine. In *Perestroika and Soviet Women,* ed. M. Buckley, 82–95. Cambridge: Cambridge University Press.

———. 1996. Feminism in Post-Communist Ukrainian Society. In *Women in Russia and Ukraine,* ed. R. Marsh, 305–314. New York: Cambridge University Press.

People's Union Our Ukraine. 2006. Tymoshenko: Populism, Revisionism and Economic Illiteracy. *Our Ukraine Update* 2 (14). Retrieved from http://ourukraine.org/newsletter/eng/issue14/ (accessed February 28, 2006).

Pestoff, Victor A. 1998. *Beyond the Market and State: Social Enterprises and Civil Democracy in a Welfare Society.* Aldershot, England: Ashgate.

Petryna, Adriana. 2002. *Life Exposed: Biological Citizens after Chernobyl.* Princeton, N.J.: Princeton University Press.

Phillips, Sarah D. 2002. Half-Lives and Healthy Bodies: Discourses on "Contaminated" Foods and Healing in Post-Chernobyl Ukraine. *Food and Foodways* 10 (1–2): 27–53.

———. 2004. Chernobyl's Sixth Sense: The Symbolism of an Ever-Present Awareness. *Anthropology and Humanism* 29 (2): 159–185.

Poloziuk, Oleg. 2005. Problems of Socio-Legal Protection of Disabled Persons with Spinal Cord Injuries in Ukraine. Presented at the Sixth Congress of the International Association of Ukrainian Studies. Donets'k, Ukraine, June 29–July 1, 2005.

Popson, Nancy E., and Kimberly Righter. 2000. Politics and Gender in Ukraine: The Next Generation of Women Politicians? Presented at the Fifth Annual World Convention of the Association for the Study of Nationalities, New York City, April 13–15, 2000.

Popson, Nancy E., and Blair A. Ruble. 2000. Kyiv's Nontraditional Immigrants. *Post-Soviet Geography and Economics* 41 (5): 365–378.

Posadskaya, Anastasia, ed. 1994. *Women in Russia: New Era in Russian Feminism.* London: Verso.

Pry narodzhenni dytyny uriad vyplachuvatyme visim z polovynoiu tyciach hryven' zhyvymy hroshyma. 5tv.com.ua, April 10, 2005.

Rabinow, Paul. 1977. *Reflections on Fieldwork in Morocco.* Berkeley: University of California Press.

Radio-Era FM. 2006. Transcript of Interview with Volodymyr Semynozhenko and Mykhail Papiiev on Radio-Era FM, March 27, 2006. Retrieved from http://www.svidomo2006.org.ua/materials/964.html (accessed June 16, 2006).

Riabchuk, Mykola. 2002. Ukraine: One State, Two Countries? *Transit Online* 23. Retrieved from http://www.iwm.at/index.php?option=com_content&task=view&id=269&Itemid=447 (accessed April 1, 2003).

Richter, James. 2002. Evaluating Western Assistance to Russian Women's Organizations. In *The Power and Limits of NGOs: A Critical Look at Building Democracy in Eastern Europe and Eurasia,* ed. S. E. Mendelson and J. K. Glenn, 54–90. New York: Columbia University Press.

Ries, Nancy. 1994. The Burden of Mythic Identity: Russian Women at Odds with Themselves. In *Feminist Nightmares: Women at Odds: Feminism and the Problem of Sisterhood,* ed. S. O. Weisser and J. Fleischner, 242–268. New York: New York University Press.

———. 1997. *Russian Talk: Culture and Conversation during Perestroika.* Ithaca, N.Y.: Cornell University Press.

———. 2002. "Honest Bandits" and "Warped People": Russian Narratives about Money, Corruption, and Moral Decay. In *Ethnography in Unstable Places: Everyday Lives in Contexts of Dramatic Political Change,* ed. C. J. Greenhouse, E. Mertz, and K. B. Warren, 276–315. Durham, N.C.: Duke University Press.

Rivkin-Fish, Michele. 2000. Health Development Meets the End of State Socialism: Visions of Democratization, Women's Health, and Social Well-Being for Contemporary Russia. *Culture, Medicine and Psychiatry* 24 (1): 77–100.

———. 2004. Gender and Democracy: Strategies for Engagement and Dialogue on Women's Issues after Socialism in St. Petersburg. In *Post-Soviet Women Encountering Transition: Nation Building, Economic Survival, and Civic Activism*, ed. K. Kuehnast and C. Nechemias, 288–312. Washington, D.C.: Woodrow Wilson Center Press.

———. 2005. *Women's Health in Post-Soviet Russia: The Politics of Intervention*. Bloomington: Indiana University Press.

Romaniuk, Tamara. 1998. Zhinka na rynku pratsi: Problemy hendernoyi dyskryminatsiyi. In *Rivnist': Problemy hendernoyi dyskrymynatsiyi, materialy Vseukrayins'koho seminaru "Mekhanizm zabezpechennia rivnopravnosti zhinok ta cholovikiv v Ukrayini"*, 44–55. Kyiv: Ministerstvo u spravakh sim'yi ta molodi Ukrayiny; Mizhnarodna orhanizatsiia "Zhinocha Hromada."

Rotkirch, Anna, and Anna Temkina. 1997. Soviet Gender Contracts and Their Shifts in Contemporary Russia. *Idantutkimus* 4:6–24.

Rubchak, Marian J. 1996. Christian Virgin or Pagan Goddess: Feminism versus the Eternally Feminine in Ukraine. In *Women in Russia and Ukraine*, ed. R. Marsh, 315–330. New York: Cambridge University Press.

———. 2001. In Search of a Model: Evolution of a Feminist Consciousness in Ukraine and Russia. *European Journal of Women's Studies* 8 (2): 149–160.

———. 2005. Yulia Tymoshenko: Goddess of the Orange Revolution. Retrieved from http://eng.maidanua.org/node/111 (accessed January 25, 2005).

Ruble, Blair A. 2003. Kyiv's Troeshchyna: An Emerging International Migrant Neighborhood. *Nationalities Papers* 31 (2): 139–155.

———. 2005. *Creating Diversity Capital: Transnational Migrants in Montreal, Washington, and Kyiv*. Washington, D.C.: Woodrow Wilson Center Press; Baltimore, Md.: Johns Hopkins University Press.

Sachs, Wolfgang. 1999. Introduction. In *The Development Dictionary: A Guide to Knowledge as Power*, ed. W. Sachs, 1–5. Johannesburg: Witwatersrand University Press.

Sampson, Steven. 1996. The Social Life of Projects: Importing Civil Society to Albania. In *Civil Society: Challenging Western Models*, ed. C. Hann and E. Dunn, 121–142. London: Routledge.

———. 2002. Beyond Transition: Rethinking Elite Configurations in the Balkans. In *Postsocialism*, ed. C. Hann, 297–316. London: Routledge.

Sayenko, Yury et al. 1995. *Status of Women in Ukraine: National Report for the Fourth World Conference on the Women's Status*. Kyiv: UN Mission in Ukraine; Organizing Committee under the Cabinet of Ministers of Ukraine on Preparation to the Fourth World Conference Devoted to the Issue of Women's Status.

Scott, Hilda. 1974. *Does Socialism Liberate Women?* Boston: Beacon.

Shlapentokh, Vladimir. 1989. *Public and Private Life of the Soviet People: Changing Values in Post-Stalin Russia*. New York: Oxford University Press.

Silverman, Carol. 2000. Researcher, Advocate, Friend: An American Fieldworker among Balkan Roma, 1980–1996. In *Fieldwork Dilemmas: Anthropologists in Postsocialist States*, ed. H. G. DeSoto and N. Dudwick, 195–217. Madison: University of Wisconsin Press.

Singer, Merrill. 1994a. AIDS and the Health Crisis of the U.S. Urban Poor: The Perspective of Critical Medical Anthropology. *Social Science and Medicine* 39 (7): 931–948.

———. 1994b. Community-Centered Praxis: Toward an Alternative Non-dominative Applied Anthropology. *Human Organization* 53 (4): 336–344.

Sknar, Oksana. 2001. Zhinka v politytsi: Gendernyi aspekt. In *Gender i kul'tura,* ed. V. Aheieva and S. Oksamytna, 202–208. Kyiv: Fakt.

Skurativs'kyi, Vasyl'. 1988. *Berehynia.* Kyiv: Radians'kyi pys'mennyk.

Smoliar, Liudmyla. 2000a. Zhinochyi rukh Ukrayiny iak chynnyk hendernoyi rivnovahy ta hendernoyi demokratiyi v Ukrayins'komu sotsiumi. *Perekhrestia* 3 (8): 20–25.

———. 2000b. Zhinochyi rukh Ukrayiny iak chynnyk hendernoyi rivnovahy ta hendernoyi demokratiyi v Ukrayins'komu sotsiumi (prodovzhenie). *Perekhrestia* 4 (9): 15–20.

———. 2000c. Zhinochyi rukh Ukrayiny iak chynnyk hendernoyi rivnovahy ta hendernoyi demokratiyi v Ukrayins'komu sotsiumi (prodovzhenie II). *Perekhrestia* 5 (10): 8–12.

Sperling, Valerie. 1999. *Organizing Women in Contemporary Russia: Engendering Transition.* Cambridge: Cambridge University Press.

Sperling, Valerie, Myra Marx Ferree, and Barbara Risman. 2001. Constructing Global Feminism: Transnational Advocacy Networks and Women's Activism. *Signs* 26 (4): 1155–1186.

Stark, David. 1994. Recombinant Property in East European Capitalism. *Cornell Working Papers on Transitions from State Socialism,* 94–95.

Stark, David, and Laszlo Bruzst. 1998. *Postsocialist Pathways: Transforming Politics and Property in East Central Europe.* Cambridge, Mass.: Cambridge University Press.

Steshenko, Valentyna, ed. 1997. *The Health of Women and Children in Ukraine.* Kyiv: United Nations Development Programme Office in Ukraine.

Stites, Richard. 1978. *The Women's Liberation Movement in Russia: Feminism, Nihilism, and Bolshevism 1860–1930.* Princeton, N.J.: Princeton University Press.

Subtelny, Orest. 1994. *Ukraine: A History.* Toronto: University of Toronto Press.

Suslova, Olena. 1997. Introduction. In *Zhinoche liderstvo: Teoriia. Pidruchnyk dlia treneriv,* 3. Kyiv: NIS-US Women's Consortium.

Suslova, Olena, and Nataliia Karbovs'ka. 2002. "Zhinoche krylo" hromads'kykh orhanizatsii: Zaluchennia koshtiv dlia pidtrymky zhinochykh initsiatyv. *Perekhrestia* 6 (17): 14–15.

Sydorenko, Oleksander. 2001. Women's Organizations of Ukraine: Development Tendencies. In *Ukrainian Women's Non-Profit Organizations Directory,* ed. O. Sydorenko, 53–60. Kyiv: Innovation and Development Centre.

Tohidi, Nayereh. 2004. Women, Building Civil Society, and Democratization in Post-Soviet Azerbaijan. In *Post-Soviet Women Encountering Transition: Nation Building, Economic Survival, and Civic Activism,* ed. K. Kuehnast and C. Nechemias, 149–171. Washington, D.C.: Woodrow Wilson Center Press.

Truman, Harry S. 1949. Inaugural Address, January 20, 1949. Retrieved from http://www.yale.edu/lawweb/avalon/presiden/inaug/truman.htm (accessed July 11, 2006).

United Nations Development Programme. 2001. Human Development Report 2001. Retrieved from http://hdr.undp.org/reports/ (accessed March 9, 2006).

———. 2002. Human Development Report 2002. Retrieved from http://hdr.undp.org/reports/ (accessed March 9, 2006).

———. 2003. Human Development Report 2003. Retrieved from http://hdr.undp.org/reports/ (accessed March 9, 2006).

———. 2004. Human Development Report 2004. Retrieved from http://hdr.undp.org/reports/ (accessed March 9, 2006).

———. 2005. Human Development Report 2005. Retrieved from http://hdr.undp.org/reports/ (accessed March 9, 2006).

United States Department of State. 2005. Department of State Fact Sheet on U.S. Assistance to Ukraine for Fiscal Year 2005 (dated July 25, 2005). Retrieved from http://www.state.gov/p/eur/rls/fs/50839.htm (accessed June 4, 2006).

Uvin, Peter. 2000. From Local Organizations to Global Governance: The Role of NGOs in International Relations. In *Global Institutions and Local Empowerment: Competing Theoretical Perspectives,* ed. K. Stiles, 9–29. New York: St. Martin's.

Verdery, Katherine. 1996. *What Was Socialism, and What Comes Next?* Princeton, N.J.: Princeton University Press.

Verkhovna Rada of Ukraine. 2006. Summary of Plenary Session of the Verkhovna Rada of Ukraine, February 8, 2006. Retrieved from http://portal.rada.gov.ua/control/uk/publish/article/news_left?art_id=67813&cat_id=33449 (accessed June 7, 2006).

Volkov, Vadim. 2002. *Violent Entrepreneurs: The Use of Force in the Making of Russian Capitalism.* Ithaca, N.Y.: Cornell University Press.

Walsh, Martha. 1998. Mind the Gap: Where Feminist Theory Failed to Meet Development Practice—A Missed Opportunity in Bosnia and Herzegovina. *European Journal of Women's Studies* 5 (3–4): 329–343.

Wanner, Catherine. 1998. *Burden of Dreams: History and Identity in Post-Soviet Ukraine.* University Park: Pennsylvania State University Press.

Wanner, Catherine, and Nora Dudwick. 2003. "Children Have Become a Luxury": Everyday Dilemmas of Poverty in Ukraine. In *When Things Fall Apart: Qualitative Studies of Poverty in the Former Soviet Union,* ed. N. Dudwick, E. Gomart, A. Marc, and K. Kuehnast, 263–299. Washington, D.C.: World Bank.

Waters, Elizabeth. 1993. Finding a Voice: The Emergence of a Women's Movement. In *Gender Politics and Post-Communism: Reflections from Eastern Europe and the Former Soviet Union,* ed. N. Funk and M. Mueller, 287–302. New York: Routledge.

Watson, Peggy. 1997. (Anti)Feminism after Communism. In *Who's Afraid of Feminism? Seeing through the Backlash,* ed. A. Oakley and J. Mitchell, 144–161. London: Penguin.

Wedel, Janine. 1998. *Collision and Collusion: The Strange Case of Western Aid to Eastern Europe 1989–1998.* New York: St. Martin's.

Whitefield, Stephen. 2003. The Political Economy of Welfare Reform and Poverty Alleviation in Ukraine. In *Society in Transition: Social Change in Ukraine in Western Perspectives,* ed. W. W. Isajiw, 401–425. Toronto: Canadian Scholars' Press.

Whitten, Dorothea S. 1996. License to Practice? A View from the Rain Forest. *Anthropological Quarterly* 69 (3): 115–119.

Wilson, Andrew. 2000. *The Ukrainians: Unexpected Nation.* New Haven: Yale University Press.

———. 2005a. The Orange Revolution, One Year On. *The Moscow Times.Com.* Retrieved from http://www.themoscowtimes.com/stories/2005/11/23/006.html (accessed July 12, 2006).

———. 2005b. *Ukraine's Orange Revolution.* New Haven: Yale University Press.

Wolchik, Sharon L., and Alfred G. Meyer, eds. 1985. *Women, State, and Party in Eastern Europe.* Durham, N.C.: Duke University Press.

Wolchik, Sharon L., and Volodymyr Zviglianich, eds. 2000. *Ukraine: The Search for a National Identity.* Lanham, Md.: Rowman and Littlefield.

Wolcott, Harry. 1995. *The Art of Fieldwork.* Walnut Creek, Calif.: AltaMira.

Wolczuk, Kataryna. 2000. History, Europe and the "National Idea": The "Official" Narrative of National Identity in Ukraine. *Nationalities Papers* 28 (4): 671–694.

Wood, Elizabeth. 1997. *The Baba and the Comrade: Gender and Politics in Revolutionary Russia.* Bloomington: Indiana University Press.

Yurchak, Alexei. 2006. *Everything Was Forever, Until It Was No More: The Last Soviet Generation.* Princeton, N.J.: Princeton University Press.

Yushchenko, Viktor. 2005. Presidential address to the nation for International Women's Day. Retrieved from http://www.nbuv.gov.ua/fpu/2005/zp20050305.htm (accessed March 8, 2005).

Zarplata s nachala goda vyrosla na 30%. 2001. *Vechernie vesti* 128 (624): 2.

Zhurzhenko, Tatiana. 1998. Ukrainian Women in the Transitional Economy. *Labour Focus on Eastern Europe* 60. Retrieved from http://labourfocus.gn.apc.org/Zhurzhenko.html (accessed May 22, 2004).

———. 1999. Gender and Identity Formation in Post-Socialist Ukraine: The Case of Women in the Shuttle Business. In *Feminist Fields: Ethnographic Insights,* ed. R. Bridgman, S. Cole and H. Howard-Bobiwash, 243–263. Peterborough, Ontario: Broadview.

———. 2001a. (Anti)national Feminisms, Post-Soviet Gender Studies: Women's Voices of Transition and Nation-Building in Ukraine. *Osterreichische Osthefte* 43 (4): 503–523.

———. 2001b. Free Market Ideology and New Women's Identities in Post-Socialist Ukraine. *European Journal of Women's Studies* 8 (1): 29–49.

———. 2001c. *Sotsial'noe vosproizvodstvo i gendernaia politika v Ukraine.* Kharkov: Folio.

———. 2004. Strong Women, Weak State: Family Politics and Nation Building in Post-Soviet Ukraine. In *Post-Soviet Women Encountering Transition: Nation Building, Economic Survival, and Civic Activism,* ed. K. Kuehnast and C. Nechemias, 23–43. Washington, D.C: Woodrow Wilson Press.

Index

women, 54, 90, 164–65; and social enterprise, 81, 90; and training sessions, 92

entitlements: criticism of entitlement groups, 18, 114–15; ethos of, 15, 19, 115, 153; and marginalization, 157; and "Soviet" association, 18, 28

entrepreneurship: constraints on, 86; and democratization, 152; difficulties associated with, 162–63; distributorships, 49; emphasis on, 159; reluctance of women, 47–48; social entrepreneurship, 82–83, 87, 91, 162, 163; speculating activities, 48–49; support for, 74

equality, 8, 10, 46, 91, 143

Equus, 17

ethical issues in anthropological research, xi–xiii

ethnicities, 38, 39–40

ethnography, 20, 140, 160

eugenicism, 16

Eurasia Foundation, 66, 91

Euro-elites, 139–40, 158

Eurointegration, 43

"European Choice" program, 43

European Union, 40

families, 73, 96, 145. *See also* large families; mothers and motherhood

federalization of Ukraine, 41

feminism: and donor organizations, 92; "feminism-by-design," 79; "foundation feminism," 79; and gender roles, 150; hybrid feminists, 80; and maternalist character of women's NGOs, 80, 163; perceptions of, 78, 96

fertility rate, 16, 167n3

fieldwork, 22–23

Fifth Session of the UN General Assembly in Vienna, 58

Fighting Poverty initiative, 14

Fisher, William, 66–67, 85

folk culture icons, 41

For Life: allowances provided by, 134; and bureaucracy, 129–33; and civil society, 159–60; and class issues, 110; and death of Sofiia, 155–56; meeting of, 154–55; membership participation, 134, 161, 171n33; My Years, My Wealth holiday, 28, 127, 129; objectives of, 17, 22, 25–26, 28–29; office of, 26, 28, 136; support for, 158; and treatment of the elderly, 126–27, 129; and UN grant, 28, 132

Fourth World Conference on Women in Beijing, 58

Fowler, Alan, 82–83

Freedom House, 66

free market, 85

Fund for the Social Protection of Invalids, 88

Gal, Susan, 160

Galicia, 36, 40

gender and gender roles: and Consortium seminars, 149–50; cultural attitudes toward, 75, 96; and family responsibilities, 73, 96; and NGO sector, 3, 9, 163–64; romanticization of, 51; and social enterprise, 89–90; and Soviet ideology, 45–46, 176n25; and wage disparities, 48, 118, 144

gender theory, 96–97

genealogical research, 112

geography of Ukraine, 36, 39–40

Ghodsee, Kristen, 88, 162

glasnost, 38

globalization, influence of, 8, 19

Gongadze, Hryhorii, 38

Gorbachev, Mikhail, 6, 26, 38, 50, 73

Grant, Bruce, 41

grant-eaters (*hrantoyidy*), 70, 141

Gray, Mel, 82, 90

Guide to Foreign Funding Sources Available for Ukrainian Non-Profits (Innovation and Development Centre), 66

Gurt ("Cluster") Resource Center, 70

Haney, Lynne, 17, 119, 121, 167n4

Hann, Chris, 68

Hapsburg region, 40

health care insurance, 115

Healy, Karen, 82, 90

Hemment, Julie, 139, 140

Herzfeld, Michael, 129

history of activism, 71–78

Hope: Ivana's work in, 6, 141, 147, 148, 152; objectives of, 1, 75

housing, 15, 32, 171n2

Hrycak, Alexandra: on donor organizations, 80; on families, 16; on program implementation, 163–64; on roles of women in Soviet era, 73; on training efficacy, 79; on women's groups, 66

Hungary, 121, 167n4

Iaroslavsky, 98

identities, personal, 46, 102, 135

identity, national, 40–43

immigrants, 40

income: of activists, 109; and class differentiation, 111; gender disparity in, 48, 118, 144; increases in, 44; and needs-based assistance, 119; of NGO professionals, 139;

pensions: and employment status, 7, 122; and For Life organization, 129; pension insurance, 115; and reforms, 12, 13–14, 115–19, 179n17; under Soviet system, 118, 126; worker/pensioner ratio, 116; and Yushchenko administration, 12, 13

People's Democratic Party, 59

"People's Friendship" monument, 32

People's Opposition Bloc, 58

perceptions of NGOs, 70

perestroika, 26

Permanent Commission on the Status of Women, Family, Motherhood, and Childhood, 58

personalization, 8, 13

personal responsibility, 119

Pinchuk, Viktor, 58

pioneer girl's salute (statue), *101*

Podil district, 31

Poland, 164

political wives, 51–52, 74

politics: gender quotas in, 164–65; and history of Ukraine, 36–39; and marginalization of women, 50–59; and Soiuz Ukrainok, 74; women in, 10, 54, 56–58, 59, 78, 90, 164–65 (*see also* Tymoshenko, Yuliia). *See also* Parliament

Popular Movement for Restructuring in Ukraine (Rukh), 38, 50, 74

population: birth rates, 39, 72; childbirth incentives, 15–16, 170n25; demographic crisis, 16, 39–40, 121, 179n19; life expectancies, 130, 179n20; map, *37*

populism, 11

Pora, 66

Poroshenko, Petro, 122

Posadskaya, Anastasia, 51

poverty and the impoverished: and "basic needs" movement, 68; and changes in state policy, 14; and economic crisis of 1990s, 34–35; and gender differences, 168n11; increases in, 35; informants' accounts of, 35–36, 108–110; and large families, 16, 122; panhandlers and beggars, 31–32; perceptions and treatment of, 123

pregnancy, 46

Presidential Committee on the Status of Women and Children, 58

privatization: and inequalities, 136, 158; political emphasis on, 13; reactions to, 86; and women in NGO leadership, 102

problematic families (*neblahopoluchni*), 15, 16

professionalization of NGO work, 70–71, 138–39

Progressive Socialist Party, 56, 58

Project on Improvement of the System of Social Assistance, 13, 15

Prokhorenko, Natalya, 87

property ownership, 152

prostitution, 48

protests. *See* Orange Revolution

Provision on the individual program of rehabilitation and adaptation of the invalid (IPRI), 12

public transportation, 34, 169n17

public wages, 12, 44

Putin, Vladimir, 39

regions of Ukraine, 40–41

relational self-understanding, 94, 102

Renaissance Foundation, 70

reproductive role of women, 46

residential areas, 32–33

retirees and retirement: age of, 117, 171n33; early retirement, 15; empowerment of, 162; and pensions, 122, 126, 129; and productive/nonproductive citizenry, 111; and social insurance, 115. *See also* elderly; For Life

Riabchuk, Mykola, 43

Ries, Nancy, 78, 124

risk taking, 83

Rivkin-Fish, Michele, 156–57, 163

Romashka, 17

Rubchak, Marian, 50, 51, 52

Rukh (Popular Movement for Restructuring in Ukraine), 38, 50, 74

rural culture, 51

Russia, 43, 78, 139, 140, 156

Russian ethnicity, 40, 43

Russification of Ukraine, 36

Saakashvili, Mikheil, 56

Sachs, Wolfgang, 68

"saints' lives" speech genre, 124

Sampson, Steven, 139–40, 141

Sapeliak, Oksana, 73

self-determination, 82

self-employment, 48–49

self-esteem, 148

self-reliance: activists' emphasis on, 24–25, 134, 160; and foreign donor organizations, 102; and reforms, 13; and social enterprise, 83, 88; state emphasis on, 159; and training sessions, 91, 92, 94

Serhiy, 84, 86–87

shuttle trading and traders, 49

Sknar, Oksana, 54

Skurativs'kyi, Vasyl', 50–51
social capital, 111, 112–14, 142, 153
social enterprise, 81–91, 102, 104, 162
social entrepreneurship, 82–83, 87, 91, 162, 163
social insurance (*zakhyst*), 13, 115–19
socialist collapse in Ukraine, 3, 6
social networks, 22, 113–14, 142, 157. *See also* civil society
social welfare system, 11–17; benefits offered, 11; and differentiation, 8; and economic reforms, 7, 11; and economic slowdowns, 44; and end of state socialism, x; and increases in social spending, 12–13, 17, 159; passive and active approaches to, 13; and political debates, 44; and productive/nonproductive citizenry, 111, 135; public opinion on, 118–19; and reforms, 11–12, 17, 45, 102, 111, 160; responsibility for, 78; under Soviet system, 11, 14, 35; utilization of, 11; withdrawal of services, 9, 13, 14, 126; and Yushchenko administration, 12–13, 17
social worth, 120, 123–26, 127
Society of Ukrainian Businesswomen, 73
Sofiia: background of, 24; on Civil Parliament, 59; and class differentiation, 111; as Communist Party member, 100; and contributions of members, 134, 161; death of, 155–56, 157; in defense of the elderly, 25–26, 28–29, 126–29, 154–55, 157 (*see also* For Life); interviews with, 23; social and cultural capital of, 114; on Soviet system, 133–34; and state support, 111
Sofiia Square, 30–31
Soiuz Ukrainok (Ukrainian Women's Association), 71, 72, 73–74, 80
Soldiers' Mothers, 74–75, 80, 163
Solidarity of Women of Ukraine, 58
Sonia, 93
Soros Foundation, 66, 147
Southern Ukraine, 41
Soviet Union: attitudes toward Soviet system, 133–34, 160; and *blat* connections, 112–13; and business, 86; and civil society, 68–69; and community activism, 72–73; and contemporary Kyiv, 41; cultural legacy of, 92, 98–100, 102; discrimination under, 121–22; and emancipation of women, 45–46, 143, 144; employment under, 35, 45–46, 47; and entitlement culture, 18; and families, 145; and gender roles, 45–46; and glasnost, 38; and identity of Ukraine, 43; ideology of, 98–99, 100, 143, 144, 145; and large families, 7, 14, 121–22, 167n3; and "level of culture,"

111; and mothers, 46, 72–73, 121; and national identity of Ukraine, 40; and pensions, 118, 126; relationship with Ukraine, 36, 38; and Russification, 36, 38; and social enterprise, 83–84; and wage disparities, 144; welfare system of, 11–17, 35, 45–46, 114; and women politicians, 57
speculating, 48–49
Sperling, Valerie, 81
Spilka Zhinok Ukrainy (Confederation of Women of Ukraine), 73, 74
Stalin, Joseph, 72, 144, 170n30
state, responsibilities of, 7, 139, 158, 160, 162
Stites, Richard, 72
Subtelny, Orest, 36
suffering, 123–24
Sumy Center for Women's Studies, 78
Supreme Soviet of Ukraine, 57
Suprun, Liudmyla, 58, 59
sustainability, 83
Svetlana: on author, 76; background of, 4–6, 124–25; and class differentiation, 111; criticisms of, 115; employment status, 122, 125, 161; and empowerment, 162; and family background, 112; interviews with, 23, 136–37; marginalization of, 153; maternalist orientation of, 93; on need for Our House, 157; and needs assessments, 134–35, 161; poverty of, 35–36, 109, 123–26; social and cultural capital of, 114; social network of, 22; on Soviet system, 134; and state support, 111, 119–23; work at Our House, ix, 124, 157; work history of, 35, 122, 123
Sviatoshyn, 32
Svitanok, 17, 22
symbols of Ukraine, 41

targeted assistance ("active" social welfare), 13, 14, 15, 159
taxes, 86
Technical Aid to the Commonwealth of Independent States (TACIS), 66, 78
Temkina, Anna, 46
trade, 36, 49
trade unions, 100
training opportunities: and donor organizations, 69; effects of, 96, 141, 149; and gender-roles topic, 149–50; and Ivana, 1, 141, 142, 148, 149, 151; leadership skills training, 79, 91–95, 98, 103, 142, 148; limitations of, 102, 103, 162; and Maryna, 64; and Sofiia, 132; and Soviet ideology, 98; training positions, 77, 92. *See also* leadership

Zhenotdel (Women's Section of the Communist Party), 72

Zhensovet (Women's Soviet), 72–73

Zhinocha Hromada (Women's Community), 72, 74, 80

Zhinochi rady (Women's Councils), 73

Zhurzhenko, Tatiana: on entrepreneurship, 47; on neofamilism, 16; on shuttle trading, 49; on social welfare reform, 14; on transition economies, 10

Zhytomyr, 84

Zoia: and family background, 112; interviews with, 20, 21; poetry of, 103, 107; on self-reliance, 160; on Soviet system, 160; on state of mothers in Ukraine, 44; work at Lotus, 158

NEW ANTHROPOLOGIES OF EUROPE

FOUNDING EDITORS

Daphne Berdahl, Matti Bunzl, and Michael Herzfeld

PUBLICATIONS

SARAH D. PHILLIPS is Assistant Professor of Anthropology at
Indiana University, Bloomington.

Printed and bound by CPI Group (UK) Ltd, Croydon, CR0 4YY

13/04/2025

14656546-0004